Rabindranath Tagore

RABINDRANATH TAGORE

Series Editor
Dr. M.H. Syed

Editor
Anil Kathuria **Bharat Singh**

hbpl

Himalaya Books Pvt. Ltd.

'Ramdoot', Dr. Bhalerao Marg, Girgaon, Mumbai - 400 004
Tel : (022) 23863863. Fax : (022) 23877178
Email : himpub@vsnl.com

Edition : 2013

Published by : **H.B.P.L.**
"Pooja Apartments", 4-B, Murari Lal Street, Ansari Road,
Darya Ganj, New Delhi-110 002
Phones : 23270392, 23278631 Reliance : 30180392 to 396
Fax : 011-23256286 Email : hphdel@vsnl.com

Sole Distributers : HIMALAYA PUBLISHING HOUSE PVT. LTD.

Branch Offices

Mumbai : "Ramdoot", Dr. Bhalerao Marg, Girgaon, Mumbai-400 004.
Phones : 23860170/23863863 Fax : 022-23877178
Email : himpub@vsnl.com
Website : www.himpub.com

Nagpur : Kundanlal Chandak Industrial Estate, Ghat Road, **Nagpur - 440 018.**
Phone: 2738731, 3296733 Telefax : 0712-2721215

Bengaluru : No. 16/1 (Old 12/1), 1st Floor, Next to Hotel Highlands,
Madhava Nagar, Race Course Road, **Bengaluru - 560 001.**
Phone : 22281541, 22385461, Telefax: 080-22286611

Hyderabad : No. 3-4-184, Lingampally, Besides Raghavendra Swamy Matham,
Kachiguda, **Hyderabad - 500 027.** Phone: 040-27560041, 27550139,
Mobile:- 09848130433 Telefax: 040-27560041

Chennai : No. 85/50, Bazullah Road, T. Nagar, **Chennai - 600 017.**
Phone: 044-28344020, 32463737, 42124860

Pune : No. 527, "Laksha" Apartment, First Floor, Mehunpura, Shaniwarpeth,
(Near Prabhat Theatre), **Pune - 411 030.**
Phone: 020-24496323/24496333/32326733

Lucknow : House No. 731, Sehkhupura Colony, Near B.D. Convent School,
Lucknow - 226 024. Mobile : 09307501549

Ahmedabad : No. 114, "SHAIL", 1st Floor, Opp. Madhu Sudan House, C.G.Road,
Navrang Pura, **Ahmedabad – 380 009.**
Phone: 079-26560126, Mobiles: 09327324149, 09314679413

Ernakulam : No. 39/104 A, Lakshmi Apartment, Karikkamuri Cross Rd.,
Ernakulam, **Cochin – 682011**, Kerala.
Phone: 0484-2378012, 2378016, Mob.: 09344199799

Bhubaneswar : 5 Station Square, **Bhubaneswar (Orissa) - 751 001.**
Mobile: 9861046007, E-mail:- orissa@himpub.com

Indore : Kesardeep Avenue Extension, 73, Narayan Bagh.Flat No. 302,
IIIrd Floor, Near Humpty Dumpty School, Narayan Bagh,
Indore (M.P.) 452 007 Mobile: 09301386468

Kolkata : 108/4, Beliaghata, Main Road, Near ID Hospital, Opp. SBI Bank
Kolkata - 700 010.
Mobile: 09910440956, E-mail:- nkmitra@himpub.com

Guwahati : House No. 15, Behind Prajjyotish College, Near Sharma
Printing Press, P.O. Bharalumukh, Guwahati - 781009 (Assam)
Mobile: 07439040301; 07439040302

Printed by : Printed at : Sri Prints & Sales, Delhi Ph. : 23262724

Preface

Biography, is now a form of literature, very much in vogue. In fact, biography is a description or account of someone's life and the times, which is usually published in the form of a book. A biography is more than a mention of personal facts (life, education, work, relationships and death), it also portrays the subject's experience of events. Technically speaking, a work is biographical, if it covers, all of a person's life. Biography writing has a long history. A biography is real. Ancient Greeks developed the biographical tradition, which we have inherited, although until the 5th century AD, when the word 'biographia' first appeared, in Damascius' "Life of Isodorus," biographical pieces were called simply "lives". It is quite likely that the Greeks were drawing on a pre-existing eastern tradition. Certainly Herodotus' "Histories" contains more detailed biographical information on Persian kings and subjects. The earliest surviving pieces, which we would identify as biographical are Isocrates' "Life of Evagoras" and Xenophon's "Life of Agesilaos," both from the fifth century BC. "Parallel Lives" by Plutarch, a Greek writing under the Roman empire, is a series of short biographies of eminent men.

The Golden Age of English biography emerged in late eighteenth century, the century in which the terms "biography" and "autobiography" entered English lexicon. The classic works of the period were Samuel Johnson's "Critical Lives of the Poets" and James Boswell's "Massive Life of Johnson". Generally American biography followed English model. By World War I, cheap hardcover reprints had become popular. The decade of the

1920s witnessed a biographical 'boom'. Later, biographical writings developed a lot and today biographies are written and compiled in the finest form of the genre. In India too, biography, as a form of literature has been evolved, cultivated and polished over the years. Here is an effort to promote this tradition further.

This series of biographies of great men, great women and celebrities in all walks of life is an adventurous academic endeavour, in its own right. A team of researchers and compilers has worked for a good period of time to accomplish the project. For this purpose, hundreds of books by eminent authors and editors have been consulted and referred to. We have benefited from various works, liberally, in order to illustrate and enrich this effort of ours. Present book is devoted to the great personality of Rabindranath Tagore.

Rabindranath Tagore (7 May 1861 – 7 August 1941), sobriquet Gurudev, was a great Bengali polymath. He was a popular poet, novelist, musician, and playwright, who reshaped Bengali literature and music in the late 19th and early 20th centuries. As author of *Gitanjali* and its "profoundly sensitive, fresh and beautiful verse", and as the first Asian to win the Nobel Prize in Literature, Tagore was perhaps the most widely regarded Indian literary figure of all times. He was a mesmerising representative of the Indian culture whose influence and popularity internationally, perhaps could only be compared to that of Gandhiji, whom Tagore named 'Mahatma' out of his deep admiration for him. Tagore modernised Bengali art by spurning rigid classical forms. His novels, stories, songs, dance-dramas, and essays spoke to political and personal topics. *Gitanjali* (*Song Offerings*), *Gora* (*Fair-Faced*), and *Ghare-Baire* (*The Home and the World*) are his best-known works, and his verse, short stories, and novels were acclaimed for their lyricism, colloquialism, naturalism and contemplation.

This is a compact and comprehensive account of the above mentioned great life, which is bound to attract the attention of scholars, researchers, students and the general readers alike. Let's hope this humble effort would receive a warm welcome and due applause.

— Editors

Contents

1

An Illustrious Life

The great Indian poet, Rabindranath Tagore (7 May 1861 - 7 August 1941), sobriquet Gurudev, was a Bengali polymath. As a poet, novelist, musician, and playwright, he reshaped Bengali literature and music in the late-19th and early-20th centuries. As author of Gitanjali and its "profoundly sensitive, fresh and beautiful verse", in 1913 being the first non-European to win the Nobel Prize in Literature, Tagore was perhaps the most important literary figure of Bengali literature. He was a mesmerising representative of the Indian culture whose influence and popularity internationally perhaps could only be compared to that of Gandhi, whom Tagore named 'Mahatma' out of his deep admiration for him.

A Pirali Brahmin from Kolkata, Tagore was already writing poems at age eight. At age sixteen, he published his first substantial poetry under the pseudonym Bhanushingho (Sun Lion) and wrote his first short stories and dramas in 1877. Tagore denounced the British Raj and supported independence. His efforts endure in his vast canon and in the institution he founded, Vishva Bharati University.

Tagore modernised Bengali art by spurning rigid classical forms. His novels, stories, songs, dance-dramas, and essays spoke to political and personal topics. *Gitanjali* (Song Offerings), *Gora*

(Fair-Faced), and *Ghare-Baire* (The Home and the World) are his best-known works, and his verse, short stories, and novels were acclaimed for their lyricism, colloquialism, naturalism, and contemplation. Tagore was perhaps the only litterateur who penned anthems of two countries: Bangladesh and India: Amar Shonar Bangla and Jana Gana Mana.

Family Background and Early Influences

Rabindranath Tagore was born on 7 May 1861. At some time towards the end of the seventeenth century, his forefathers had migrated from their native lands to Govindpur, one of the three villages which later came to constitute Calcutta. In the course of time, the family came to acquire property and considerable business interests through the pursuit of commercial and banking activities. They had particularly benefited from the growing power of the British East India Company. Rabindranath's grandfather, Dwarkanath Tagore, lived lavishly and broke the Hindu religious ban of those times by travelling to Europe, just like his contemporary, Rammohan Roy, the nineteenth century social and religious reformer.

Roy started a religious reform movement in 1828 that came to be known as the Brahma Samaj Movement. Rabindranath's grandfather supported Roy in his attempts at reforming Hindu society. Dwarkanath's son, Devendranath Tagore, also became a staunch supporter of the Brahma Samaj Movement. In order to encourage its spread, in 1863 he established a meditation centre and guest house on some land about 100 miles from Calcutta at a place called 'Shantiniketan', the Abode of Peace.

Although deeply steeped in Hindu and Islamic traditions, Tagore's family contributed large sums of money for the introduction of Western education, including colleges for the study of science and medicine. This peculiar situation explains the combination of tradition and experiment that came to characterise Rabindranath Tagore's attitude to life.

Rabindranath's father was one of the leading figures of the newly awakened phase of Bengali society. He had been educated at one stage in Rammohan Roy's Anglo-Hindu school and had been greatly influenced by Roy's character, ideals and religious devotion. Debendranath Tagore was well versed in European philosophy and, though deeply religious, did not accept all aspects of Hinduism. He was to have a profound influence on his son's mental and practical attitudes.

Rabindranath was the fourteenth child of his parents. His brothers and sisters were poets, musicians, playwrights and novelists and the Tagore home was thus filled with musical, literary and dramatic pursuits. The family was also involved with diverse activities at the national level.

Important changes were taking place in Bengal at the time Rabindranath was born. Ishwar Chandra Vidyasagar had been attempting to reform the position of women in society. Schools using English as the language of teaching were being established, alongside the traditional Sanskrit schools. Vidyasagar had established Bengali-medium schools at different places in Bengal with little or limited government support. He had also established a centre to train teachers for these schools. Rabindranath attended this school and, as he says himself, owed his love of Bengali language and literature to it. He was also sent to a number of English-speaking schools, but he did not like their teaching style and had no wish to be taught in a foreign language.

He gradually withdrew from formal schooling when he was around 14 years old. The remainder of his education was carried out at home through his own personal efforts and with the help of tutors in various subjects. He also had lessons from professionals in wrestling, music and drawing. The manner of his early schooling was to leave a deep impression on him.

When Rabindranath was 12, his father took him to Shantiniketan, the meditation centre established in 1863. During their brief stay there, Devendranath gave his son lessons in Sanskrit, astronomy and the scriptures that formed the basis of his reformed religion. After these lessons were over, Rabindranath was free to roam among the fields and forests. This routine continued when father and son journeyed on and stayed at Dalhousie in the Himalayan foothills. After lessons in Sanskrit, English literature and religion, the would-be poet explored the mountains and forests. Life in close proximity to nature was unknown to him in the urban surroundings of Calcutta.

The close and affectionate contact between teacher and pupil that he felt when his father taught him was also completely absent in Calcutta. It was this childhood experience of the willing pupil enthusiastically following lessons given by his father in the manner of a noble teacher among agreeable surroundings that guided Rabindranath in establishing a school at Shantiniketan in 1901.

In 1878, when he was 17, he was sent to London by his father to qualify for the Indian Civil Service or as a lawyer. He took his matriculation examination and then joined University College, London. He came to like his lessons in English literature, and became exposed to British social life and Western music, both of which he enjoyed. But he returned home suddenly after some eighteen months without completing his education. However, he did gain the impression that human nature was perhaps the same everywhere.

Back in India he continued with his personal education and his creative writing and music. His *Sandhya Sangeet* (Evening Songs), a volume of Bengali verse, came out in 1882. It was at about this time that he had a kind of mystical experience that led him to appreciate the unity of all that exists and himself as an integral part of it. In the same year, he wrote his famous poem *Nirjharer Swapna Bhanga* (The Awakening of the Fountain). He became aware of his unusual talent as a poet. Between 1884 and 1890 various volumes of his poems appeared, together with a profuse output of prose articles, criticism, plays and novels.

Tagore married when he was 23. At this stage, beyond his literary pursuits, he had begun sharing his father's religious responsibilities. In 1890 he made a second trip to the United Kingdom, but came back after a month to look after the family estates.

This responsibility opened up new vistas of inspiration for him. Whereas his previous literary work had been primarily based on imagination, he now came to acquire a direct and intimate experience of the wretched life led by the poor Bengali peasants. This new experience led to the composition of *Galpaguccha* (A Bunch of Stories) (1900), and the many letters he wrote to his niece, subsequently published as *Chhinnapatra* (Torn Letters) and *Chhinnapatravali* (A Collection of Torn Letters), considered to be landmarks in the writing of Bengali prose and in describing the countryside of Bengal.

Tagore was overwhelmed by the economic, social and political misery in which the peasants lived. He gave a description of them at a later date:

> Our so-called responsible classes live in comfort because the common man has not yet understood his situation. That is why the landlord beats him. The money-lender holds him in his clutches; the foreman abuses him; the policeman fleeces him; the priest exploits him; and the magistrate picks his pocket.

These conditions, he thought, cannot be changed by appealing to the religious sentiments of the landlord, policeman or money-lender. In human society, necessity is a greater force than charity. The first requirement therefore is that people should discover the bond that holds them together as a society. If there is one path likely to achieve this, it is education. Tagore realised from his own experience of the farmers' attitudes and their social behaviour that strength can be generated only in a self-reliant village society developing its own locus of power and its own momentum of growth. He turned again and again in various contexts to this theme of local self-reliance, local initiatives, local leadership and local self-government centring on cooperative ways of life. This could be the basis for reorganising India's fragmented rural society, and could serve as an instrument of welfare. Tagore realised that education and village councils or panchayats were the only available instruments of economic and social change, and that the villagers should obtain various forms of expert help from outside to accomplish this change. As he says: 'Poverty springs from disunity and wealth from cooperation. From all points of view this is the fundamental truth of human civilization.'

As a young landlord managing his family's rural estates, Tagore came to realise the possibilities of introducing education and cooperation to transform rural life. Thus, he began to turn his thoughts towards the problems of education. He spoke publicly on 'The Vicissitudes of Education' in which he made a strong plea for the use of the mother-tongue. His first experiments in teaching also date from this period. He started his own school in Seliadah, the headquarters of his estate, to which he sent his own children to be taught by teachers in various subjects, including an

Englishman to teach them the English language. He also started organising cooperatives, schools and hospitals in the villages of his estates and tried to introduce improved farming methods. All these efforts for rural reconstruction went on while he pursued his creative writing. Tagore called this the period of his Sadhana-preparation, reflection, austerity and self-education for an active social life. He lived either at Seliadah or on his houseboat on the river Padma, visiting villages, talking to people and listening to their problems. Tagore's later educational experiments arose from this experience.

In 1901 he left Seliadah where he had undertaken these experiments and moved to Shantiniketan where, with his father's consent, he started a boarding school. The Brahamacharyashram (or Ashram) School was inaugurated on 22 December 1901 with only a few pupils, his son being one of them, and with an equal number of teachers. It was to be run on the pattern of teachers and pupils living together amidst natural surroundings and willingly accepting an austere standard of living, often working with their own hands. Of the five teachers, three were Christians-two of whom were Catholics and the third was his son's English teacher from Seliadah. The orthodox Hindus were offended by this situation and he did not get any assistance from them. No fees were accepted from students, all expenses being borne by Tagore himself. In the course of time, this Ashram School expanded as the poet's reputation grew.

Life at Shantiniketan left its impression on the poet's literary work. He wrote about India's past and present, and stories of noble self-sacrifice. He published more realistic novels such as *Choker Bali* (Eyesore) (1901), *Naukadubi* (The Wreck) (1903) and *Gora* (1910). He was trying to discover the eternal India that succeeds in achieving unity amidst a bewildering diversity of races, cultures and religions.

In 1912 Tagore left for the United Kingdom once again. Some of his poems and writings had already been translated into English and had attracted the attention of the well-known English painter Sir William Rothenstein and the poet W. B. Yeats. He made such an impression on the British writers and intellectuals that he was at once accepted as a great poet and intellectual. He was awarded the Nobel Prize for Literature in November 1913 and came back to India after visiting the United States of America, delivering there his '*Sadhana*' lectures (The Realisation of Life, 1913). In 1916 Tagore went abroad again to Japan and then to the United States of America delivering lectures, published later in two volumes as Nationalism (1917) and Personality (1917).

This international experience gave him a new idea, that he must bring his country into contact with the world at large. He felt that overemphasis on narrow nationalism led men and countries into paths of conflict. There should be an institution that emphasised the unity of the world's cultures and streams of knowledge. He considered Shantiniketan to be that institution. He was thus already contemplating the foundation of Vishva Bharati, an international centre of culture and humanistic studies.

The foundation stone of Vishva Bharati was laid on 24 December 1918. A separate institution called Shantiniketan was established in 1921.

Early Life (1861-1901)

The youngest of the surviving children, Tagore was born in the Jorasanko mansion in Kolkata of parents Debendranath Tagore (1817-1905) and Sarada Devi (1830-75). Tagore family patriarchs were the Brahmo founding fathers of the Adi Dharm faith. He was mostly raised by servants, as his mother had died in his early childhood; his father travelled extensively. Tagore largely declined classroom schooling, preferring to roam the mansion or nearby idylls: Bolpur, Panihati, and others. Upon his upanayan initiation at age eleven, Tagore left Kolkata on 14 February 1873 to tour India with his father for several months. They visited his father's Shantiniketan estate and stopped in Amritsar before reaching the Himalayan hill station of Dalhousie. There, young "Rabi" read biographies and was home-educated in history, astronomy, modern science, and Sanskrit, and examined the poetry of Kalidasa. He completed major works in 1877, one a long poem of the Maithili style pioneered by Vidyapati. Published pseudonymously, experts accepted them as the lost works of Bhanusimha, a newly discovered 17th-century Vaisnava poet. He wrote "Bhikharini" (1877; "The Beggar Woman" — the Bengali language's first short story) and

Sandhya Sangeet (1882)-including the famous poem "Nirjharer Swapnabhanga" (The Rousing of the Waterfall).

A prospective barrister, Tagore enrolled at a public school in Brighton, East Sussex, England in 1878. He read law at University College London, but left school to explore Shakespeare and more: Religio Medici, Coriolanus, and Antony and Cleopatra; he returned degreeless to Bengal in 1880. On 9 December 1883 he married Mrinalini Devi (born Bhabatarini, 1873-1900); they had five children, two of whom died before reaching adulthood. In 1890, Tagore began managing his family's vast estates in Shilaidaha, a region now in Bangladesh; he was joined by his wife and children in 1898. In 1890, Tagore released his Manasi poems, among his best-known work. As "Zamindar Babu", Tagore crisscrossed the holdings while living out of the family's luxurious barge, the Padma, to collect (mostly token) rents and bless villagers, who held feasts in his honour. These years 1891-95: Tagore's Sadhana period, after one of Tagore's magazines-were his most fecund. During this period, more than half the stories of the three-volume and eighty-four-story Galpaguchchha were written. With irony and gravity, they depicted a wide range of Bengali lifestyles, particularly village life.

Shantiniketan (1901-32)

In 1901, Tagore left Shilaidaha and moved to Shantiniketan to found an ashram which grew to include a marble-floored prayer hall (The Mandir), an experimental school, groves of trees, gardens, and a library. There, Tagore's wife and two of his children died. His father died on 19 January 1905. He received monthly payments as part of his inheritance and additional income from the Maharaja of Tripura, sales of his family's jewellery, his seaside bungalow in Puri, and mediocre royalties (Rs. 2,000) from his works. By now, his work was gaining him a large following among Bengali and foreign readers alike, and he published such works as Naivedya (1901) and Kheya (1906) while translating his poems into free verse. On 14 November 1913, Tagore learned that he had won the 1913 Nobel Prize in Literature, becoming the first Asian Nobel laureate. The Swedish Academy appreciated the idealistic and — for Western readers — accessible nature of a small body of his translated material, including the 1912 Gitanjali: Song Offerings. In 1915, Tagore was knighted by the British Crown. He later returned his knighthood in protest of the massacre of unarmed Indians in 1919 at Jalianwala Bagh.

In 1921, Tagore and agricultural economist Leonard Elmhirst set up the Institute for Rural Reconstruction, later renamed *Shantiniketan* (Abode of Peace) in Surul, a village near the ashram at Shantiniketan. Through it, Tagore bypassed Gandhi's symbolic Swaraj protests, which he despised. He sought aid from donors, officials, and scholars worldwide to "free village[s] from the shackles of helplessness and ignorance" by "vitalising knowledge". In the early-1930s, he targeted India's "abnormal caste consciousness" and untouchability. Lecturing against these, he penned untouchable heroes for his poems and dramas and campaigned — successfully —to open Guruvayoor Temple to Dalits.

Twilight Years (1932-41)

To the end, Tagore scrutinised orthodoxy. He upbraided Gandhi for declaring that a massive 15 January 1934 earthquake in Bihar — leaving thousands dead — was divine retribution brought on by the oppression of Dalits. He mourned the endemic poverty of Kolkata and the accelerating socioeconomic decline of Bengal, which he detailed in an unrhymed hundred-line poem whose technique of searing double-vision would foreshadow Satyajit Ray's film Apur Sansar. Fifteen new volumes of Tagore writings appeared, among them the prose-poems works Punashcha (1932), Shes Saptak (1935), and Patraput (1936).

Experimentation continued: he developed prose-songs and dance-dramas, including Chitrangada (1914), Shyama (1939), and Chandalika (1938), and wrote the novels Dui Bon (1933), Malancha (1934), and Char Adhyay (1934). Tagore took an interest in science in his last years, writing Vishva Parichay (a collection of essays) in 1937. His exploration of biology, physics, and astronomy impacted his poetry, which often contained extensive naturalism that underscored his respect for scientific laws. He also wove the process of science, including narratives of scientists, into many stories contained in such volumes as Se (1937), Tin Sangi (1940), and Galpasalpa (1941).

Tagore's last four years were marked by chronic pain and two long periods of illness. These began when Tagore lost consciousness in late-1937; he remained comatose and near death for an extended period. This was followed three years later, in late-1940, by a similar spell, from which he never recovered. The poetry Tagore wrote in these years is among his finest, and is distinctive for its preoccupation with death. After extended suffering, Tagore died on 7 August 1941 (22 Shravan 1348) in an upstairs room of the Jorasanko mansion in which he was raised; his death anniversary is mourned across the Bengali-speaking world.

Travels

Between 1878 and 1932, Tagore visited more than thirty countries on five continents; many of these trips were crucial in familiarising non-Indian audiences with his works and spreading his political ideas. In 1912, he took a sheaf of his translated works to England, where they impressed missionary and Gandhi protege Charles F. Andrews, Anglo-Irish poet William Butler Yeats, Ezra Pound, Robert Bridges, Ernest Rhys, Thomas Sturge Moore, and others. Indeed, Yeats wrote the preface to the English translation of Gitanjali, while Andrews joined Tagore at Shantiniketan.

On 10 November 1912, Tagore began touring the United States and the United Kingdom, staying in Butterton, Staffordshire with Andrews's clergymen friends. From 3 May 1916 until April 1917, Tagore went on lecturing circuits in Japan and the United States and denounced nationalism. His essay "Nationalism in India" was scorned and praised, this latter by pacifists, including Romain Rolland.

Shortly after returning to India, the 63-year-old Tagore accepted the Peruvian government's invitation to visit. He then travelled to Mexico. Each government pledged US $100,000 to the school at Shantiniketan (Vishva Bharati) in commemoration of his visits. A week after his 6 November 1924 arrival in Buenos Aires, Argentina, an ill Tagore moved into the Villa Miralrio at the behest of Victoria Ocampo. He left for India in January 1925. On 30 May 1926, Tagore reached Naples, Italy; he met Benito Mussolini in Rome the next day. A warm rapport ended when Tagore criticised Mussolini on 20 July 1926.

On 14 July 1927, Tagore and two companions began a four-month tour of South East Asia, visiting Bali, Java, Kuala Lumpur, Malacca, Penang, Siam, and Singapore. Tagore's travelogues from the tour were collected into the work "Jatri". In early-1930 he left Bengal for a nearly year-long tour of Europe and the United States. Once he returned to the UK, while his paintings were being exhibited in Paris and London, he stayed at a Friends settlement in Birmingham. There he wrote his Oxford Hibbert Lectures and spoke at London's annual Quaker gathering.

There (addressing relations between the British and Indians, a topic he would grapple with over the next two years), Tagore spoke of a "dark chasm of aloofness". He visited Agha Khan III, stayed at Dartington Háll, and toured Denmark, Switzerland, and Germany from June to mid-September 1930, then the Soviet Union. Lastly, in April 1932, Tagore-who was acquainted with the legends and works of the Persian mystic Hafez-was hosted by Reza Shah Pahlavi of Iran. Such extensive travels allowed Tagore to interact with many notable contemporaries, including Henri Bergson, Albert Einstein, Robert Frost, Thomas Mann, George Bernard Shaw, H. G. Wells and Romain Rolland. Tagore's last travels abroad, including visits to Persia and Iraq (in 1932) and Ceylon (in 1933), only sharpened his opinions regarding human divisions and nationalism.

Works

Though known mostly for his poetry, Tagore also wrote novels, essays, short stories, travelogues, dramas, and thousands of songs. Of Tagore's prose, his short stories are perhaps most highly regarded; indeed, he is credited with originating the Bengali-language version of the genre. His works are frequently noted for their rhythmic, optimistic, and lyrical nature. Such stories mostly borrow from deceptively simple subject matter: common people.

Novels and Non-fiction

Tagore wrote eight novels and four novellas, among them Chaturanga, Shesher Kobita, Char Odhay, and Noukadubi. *Ghare Baire* (The Home and the World) — through the lens of the idealistic zamindar protagonist Nikhil-excoriates rising Indian nationalism, terrorism, and religious zeal in the Swadeshi Movement; a frank expression of Tagore's conflicted sentiments, it emerged out of a 1914 bout of depression. The novel ends in Hindu-Muslim violence and Nikhil's (likely mortal) wounding. Gora raises controversial questions regarding the Indian identity. As with Ghore Baire, matters of self-identity (jati), personal freedom, and religion are developed in the context of a family story and love triangle.

In *Jogajog* (Relationships), the heroine Kumudini-bound by the ideals of Siva-Sati, exemplified by Dakshayani-is torn between her pity for the sinking fortunes of her progressive and compassionate elder brother and his foil: her exploitative, rakish, and patriarchical husband. In it, Tagore demonstrates his feminist leanings, using pathos to depict the plight and ultimate demise of Bengali women trapped by pregnancy, duty, and family honour; simultaneously, he treats the decline of Bengal's landed oligarchy.

Others were uplifting: *Shesher Kobita* (translated twice as Last Poem and Farewell Song) is his most lyrical novel, with poems and rhythmic passages written by the main character, a poet. It also contains elements of satire and post-modernism; stock characters gleefully attack the reputation of an old, outmoded, oppressively renowned poet who, incidentally, goes by the name of Rabindranath Tagore. Though his novels remain among the least-appreciated of his works, they have been given renewed attention via film adaptations by Satyajit Ray and others: Chokher Bali and Ghare Baire are exemplary. Their soundtracks often feature *rabindrasangeet*. Tagore wrote many non-fiction books, writing on topics ranging from Indian history to linguistics. Aside from autobiographical works, his travelogues, essays, and lectures were compiled into several volumes, including *Europe Jatrir Patro* (Letters from Europe) and *Manusher Dhormo* (The Religion of Man).

Short Stories

The "Sadhana" period, 1891-95, was among Tagore's most fecund, yielding more than half the stories contained in the three-volume Galpaguchchha, itself a group of eighty-four stories. They reflect upon Tagore's surroundings, on modern and fashionable ideas, and on mind puzzles. Tagore associated his earliest stories, such as those of the "Sadhana" period, with an exuberance of vitality and spontaneity; these traits were cultivated by zamindar Tagore's life in villages such as Patisar, Shajadpur, and Shilaida. Seeing the common and the poor, he examined their lives with a depth and feeling singular in Indian literature up to that point.

In "The Fruitseller from Kabul", Tagore speaks in first person as a town-dweller and novelist who chances upon the Afghani seller. He channels the longing of those trapped in mundane, hardscrabble Indian urban life, giving play to dreams of a different existence in the distant and wild mountains: "There were autumn mornings, the time of year when Kings of old went forth to conquest; and I, never stirring from my little corner in Kolkata, would let my mind wander over the whole world. At the very name of another country, my heart would go out to it ... I would fall to weaving a network of dreams: the mountains, the glens, the forest .... ". Many of the other Galpaguchchha stories were written in Tagore's Sabuj Patra period (1914-17; also named for one of Tagore's magazines).

Tagore's *Golpoguchchho* (Bunch of Stories) remains among Bengali literature's most popular fictional works, providing subject matter for many successful films and theatrical plays. Satyajit Ray's film Charulata was based upon Tagore's controversial novella, *Nastanirh* (The Broken Nest). In *Atithi* (also made into a film), the young Brahmin boy Tarapada shares a boat ride with a village zamindar. The boy reveals that he has run away from home, only to wander around ever since. Taking pity, the zamindar adopts him and ultimately arranges his marriage to the zamindar's own daughter. However, the night before the wedding, Tarapada runs off-again. *Strir Patra* (The Letter from the Wife) is among Bengali literature's earliest depictions of the bold emancipation of women. The heroine Mrinal, the wife of a typical patriarchical Bengali middle class man, writes a letter while she is ravelling (which constitutes the whole story). It details the pettiness of her life and struggles; she finally declares that she will not return to her husband's home with the statement Amio bachbo. Ei bachlum: "And I shall live. Here, I live".

Haimanti assails Hindu marriage and the dismal lifelessness of married Bengali women, hypocrisies plaguing the Indian middle classes, and how Haimanti, a sensitive young woman, must-due to her sensitiveness and free spirit-sacrifice her life. In the last passage, Tagore directly attacks the Hindu custom of glorifying Sita's attempted self-immolation as a means of appeasing her husband Rama's doubts. Musalmani Didi examines Hindu-Muslim tensions and, in many ways, embodies the essence of Tagore's humanism. Darpaharan exhibits Tagore's self-consciousness, describing a fey young man harbouring literary ambitions. Though he loves his wife, he wishes to stifle her own literary career, deeming it unfeminine. Tagore himself, in his youth, seems to have harboured similar ideas about women. Darpaharan depicts the final humbling of the man as he acknowledges his wife's talents. As do many other Tagore stories, Jibito o Mrito equips Bengalis with a ubiquitous epigram: *Kadombini moriya proman korilo she more nai* — "Kadombini died, thereby proving that she hadn't".

Poetry

Tagore's poetry-which varied in style from classical formalism to the comic, visionary, and ecstatic-proceeds from a lineage established by 15th- and 16th-century Vaishnava poets. Tagore was awed by the mysticism of the rishi-authors who-including Vyasa-wrote the Upanishads, the Bhakti-Sufi mystic Kabir, and Ramprasad Sen. Yet Tagore's poetry became most innovative and mature after his exposure to rural Bengal's folk music, which included Baul ballads-especially those of bard Lalon. These-rediscovered and popularised by Tagore-resemble 19th-century Kartabhaja hymns that emphasise inward divinity and rebellion against religious and social orthodoxy. During his Shilaidaha years, his poems took on a lyrical quality, speaking via the *maner manus* (the Bauls' "man within the heart") or meditating upon the *jivan devata* (living God within). This figure thus sought connection with divinity through appeal to nature and the emotional interplay of human drama. Tagore used such techniques in his Bhanusimha poems (which chronicle the romance between Radha and Krishna), which he repeatedly revised over the course of seventy years.

Tagore responded to the mostly crude emergence of modernism and realism in Bengali literature by writing experimental works in the 1930s. Examples works include Africa and Camalia, which are among the better known of his latter poems. He occasionally wrote poems using *Shadhu Bhasha* (a

Sanskritised dialect of Bengali); later, he began using *Cholti Bhasha* (a more popular dialect). Other notable works include Manasi, *Sonar Tori* (Golden Boat), *Balaka* (Wild Geese-the title being a metaphor for migrating souls), and Purobi. Sonar Tori's most famous poem-dealing with the ephemeral nature of life and achievement-goes by the same name; hauntingly it ends: "*Shunno nodir tire rohinu pori/Jaha chhilo loe gelo shonar tori*" — "all I had achieved was carried off on the golden boat-only I was left behind."). Internationally, Gitanjali is Tagore's best-known collection, winning him his Nobel Prize. Song VII of Gitanjali:

> Free-verse translation by Tagore (Gitanjali, verse VII):
>
> "My song has put off her adornments. She has no pride of dress and decoration. Ornaments would mar our union; they would come between thee and me; their jingling would drown thy whispers."
>
> "My poet's vanity dies in shame before thy sight. O master poet, I have sat down at thy feet. Only let me make my life simple and straight, like a flute of reed for thee to fill with music."

Tagore's poetry has been set to music by various composers, among them classical composer Arthur Shepherd's triptych for soprano and string quartet, as well as composer Garry Schyman's "Praan", an adaptation of Tagore's poem "Stream of Life" from Gitanjali. The latter was composed and recorded with vocals by Palbasha Siddique to accompany Internet celebrity Matt Harding's 2008 viral video. In 1917 his words were translated adeptly and set to music by Richard Hageman (an Anglo-Dutch composer) to produce what is regarded as one of the finest art songs in the English language: Do not go my love (Ed. Schirmer NY 1917).

Theatre

At age sixteen, Tagore led his brother Jyotirindranath's adaptation of Moliere's Le Bourgeois Gentilhomme. At age twenty, he wrote his first drama — opera-Valmiki Pratibha (The Genius of Valmiki) — which describes how the bandit Valmiki reforms his ethos, is blessed by Saraswati, and composes the Ramayana. Through it, Tagore vigorously explores a wide range of dramatic styles and emotions, including usage of revamped kirtans and adaptation of traditional English and Irish folk melodies as drinking songs. Another notable play, *Dak Ghar* (The Post Office), describes how a child-striving to escape his stuffy confines-ultimately "fall[s] asleep" (which suggests his physical death). A story with worldwide appeal (it received rave reviews in Europe), Dak Ghar dealt with death as, in Tagore's words, "spiritual freedom" from "the world of hoarded wealth and certified creeds". During World War II, Polish doctor and educator Janusz Korczak selected "The Post Office" as the play the orphans in his care in the Warsaw Ghetto would perform. This occurred on 18 July 1942, less than three weeks before they were to be deported to the Treblinka extermination camp. According to his main English-language biographer, Betty Jean Lifton, in her book The King of Children, Dr. Korszak thought a great deal about whether one should be able to determine when and how to die. He may have been trying to find a way for the children in his orphanage to accept death.

His other works-emphasising fusion of lyrical flow and emotional rhythm tightly focused on a core idea-were unlike previous Bengali dramas. His works sought to articulate, in Tagore's words, "the play of feeling and not of action". In 1890 he wrote *Visarjan* (Sacrifice), regarded as his finest drama. The Bengali-language originals included intricate subplots and extended monologues. Later, his dramas probed more philosophical and allegorical themes; these included Dak Ghar.

Another is Tagore's *Chandalika* (Untouchable Girl), which was modelled on an ancient Buddhist legend describing how Ananda-the Gautama Buddha's disciple-asks water of an *Adivasi* (untouchable) girl. Lastly, among his most famous dramas is *Raktakaravi* (Red Oleanders), which tells of a kleptocratic King who enriches himself by forcing his subjects to mine. The heroine, Nandini, eventually rallies the common people to destroy these symbols of subjugation. Tagore's other plays include Chitrangada, Raja, and Mayar Khela. Dance dramas based on Tagore's plays are commonly referred to as *rabindra nritya natyas.*

Music and Art

Tagore composed roughly 2,230 songs and was a prolific painter. His songs comprise *rabindrasangeet* (Tagore Song), an integral part of Bengali culture. Tagore's music is inseparable from his literature, most of which-poems or parts of novels, stories, or plays alike-became lyrics for his songs. Influenced by the thumri style of Hindustani music, they ran the entire gamut of human emotion, ranging from his early dirge-like Brahmo devotional hymns to quasi-erotic compositions. They emulated the tonal colour of classical ragas to varying extents. Though at times his songs mimicked a given raga's melody and rhythm faithfully, he also blended elements of different ragas to create innovative works.

For Bengalis, their appeal, stemming from the combination of emotive strength and beauty described as surpassing even Tagore's poetry, was such that the Modern Review observed that "there is in Bengal no cultured home where Rabindranath's songs are not sung or at least attempted to be sung ... Even illiterate villagers sing his songs".

Arthur Strangways of The Observer introduced non-Bengalis to rabindrasangeet in The Music of Hindustan, calling it a "vehicle of a personality ... [that] go behind this or that system of music to that beauty of sound which all systems put out their hands to seize." Among them are Bangladesh's national anthem Amar Shonar Bangla and India's national anthem Jana Gana Mana, making Tagore unique in having scored two national anthems. He influenced the styles of such musicians as sitar maestro Vilayat Khan, and the sarodiyas Buddhadev Dasgupta and Amjad Ali Khan.

At age sixty, Tagore took up drawing and painting; successful exhibitions of his many works-which made a debut appearance in Paris upon encouragement by artists he met in the south of France-were held throughout Europe. Tagore-who likely exhibited protanopia (colour blindness), or partial lack of (red-green, in Tagore's case) colour discernment-painted in a style haracterised by peculiarities in aesthetics and colouring schemes. Tagore emulated numerous styles, including craftwork from northern New Ireland, Haida carvings from the west coast of Canada (British Columbia), and woodcuts by Max Pechstein. Tagore also had an artist's eye for his own handwriting, embellishing the scribbles, crossouts, and word layouts in his manuscripts with simple artistic leitmotifs, including simple rhythmic designs.

Political Views

Tagore's political thought was complex. He opposed imperialism and supported Indian nationalists. His views have their first poetic release in Manast, mostly composed in his twenties. Evidence produced during the Hindu-German Conspiracy trial and later accounts affirm his awareness of the Ghadarite conspiracy, and stated that he sought the support of Japanese Prime Minister Terauchi Masatake and former Premier Okuma Shigenobu. Yet he lampooned the Swadeshi Movement, denouncing it in "The Cult of the Charka", an acrid 1925 essay. He emphasised self-help and intellectual uplift of the masses as an alternative, stating that British imperialism was a "political symptom of our social disease", urging Indians to accept that "there can be no question of blind revolution, but of steady and purposeful education".

Such views enraged many. He narrowly escaped assassination by Indian expatriates during his stay in a San Francisco hotel in late-1916. The plot failed only because the would-be assassins fell into argument. Yet Tagore wrote songs lionising the Indian Non-cooperation Movement and renounced his knighthood in protest against the 1919 Jalianwala Bagh Massacre. Two of Tagore's more politically charged compositions, "*Chitto Jetha Bhayshunyo*" (Where the Mind is Without Fear) and "*Ekla Chalo Re*" (*If They Answer Not to Thy Call, Walk Alone*), gained mass appeal, with the latter favoured by Gandhi. Despite his tumultuous relations with Gandhi, Tagore was key in resolving a Gandhi-Ambedkar dispute involving separate electorates for untouchables, ending Gandhi's fast "unto death".

Tagore lampooned rote schooling: in "The Parrot's Training", a bird is caged and force-fed pages torn from books until it dies. These views led Tagore, while visiting Santa Barbara on 11 October 1917, to conceive of a new type of university, desiring to "make Shantiniketan the connecting thread between India and the world [and] a world centre for the study of humanity somewhere beyond the limits of nation and geography." The school, which he named Vishva Bharati had its foundation stone laid on 22 December 1918; it was later inaugurated on 22 December 1921. Here, Tagore implemented a brahmacharya pedagogical structure employing gurus to provide individualised guidance for pupils. Tagore worked hard to fundraise for and staff the school, even contributing all of his Nobel Prize monies. Tagore's duties as steward and mentor at Shantiniketan kept him busy; he taught classes in mornings and wrote the students' textbooks in afternoons and evenings. Tagore also fundraised extensively for the school in Europe and the US between 1919 and 1921.

The Impact

Tagore's relevance can be gauged by festivals honouring him: Kabipranam, Tagore's birth anniversary; the annual Tagore Festival held in Urbana, Illinois, in the United States; Rabindra Path Parikrama walking pilgrimages from Kolkata to Shantiniketan; ceremonial recitals of Tagore's poetry held on important anniversaries; and others. This legacy is most palpable in Bengali culture, ranging from language and arts to history and politics. Nobel laureate Amartya Sen saw Tagore as a "towering figure", being a "deeply relevant and many-sided contemporary thinker". Tagore's Bengali-language writings-the 1939 Rabindra Rachanavali-is also canonised as one of Bengal's greatest cultural treasures. Tagore himself was proclaimed "the greatest poet India has produced".

Tagore was famed throughout much of Europe, North America, and East Asia. He co-founded Dartington Hall School, a progressive coeducational institution; in Japan, he influenced such figures as Nobel laureate Yasunari Kawabata. Tagore's works were widely translated into English, Dutch, German, Spanish, and other European languages by Czech indologist Vincenc Lesny, French Nobel laureate Andre Gide, Russian poet Anna Akhmatova, former Turkish Prime Minister Bulent Ecevit, and others. In the United States, Tagore's lecturing circuits, particularly those in 1916-17, were widely attended and acclaimed. Yet, several controversies involving Tagore resulted in a decline in his popularity in Japan and North America after the late-1920s, concluding with his "near total eclipse" outside of Bengal.

Via translations, Tagore influenced Spanish literature: Chileans Pablo Neruda and Gabriela Mistral, Mexican writer Octavio Paz, and Spaniards Jose Ortega y Gasset, Zenobia Camprubí, and Juan

Ramon Jimenez. Between 1914 and 1922, the Jimenez-Camprubí spouses translated twenty-two of Tagore's books from English into Spanish and extensively revised and adapted such works as Tagore's The Crescent Moon. In this time, Jimenez developed "naked poetry" (Spanish: "poesia desnuda"), a landmark innovation. Ortega y Gasset wrote that "Tagore's wide appeal [may stem from the fact that] he speaks of longings for perfection that we all have ... Tagore awakens a dormant sense of childish wonder, and he saturates the air with all kinds of enchanting promises for the reader, who ... pays little attention to the deeper import of Oriental mysticism". Tagore's works circulated in free editions around 1920 alongside those of Dante Alighieri, Miguel de Cervantes, Johann Wolfgang von Goethe, Plato, and Leo Tolstoy.

Tagore was deemed overrated by some Westerners. Graham Greene doubted that "anyone but Mr. Yeats can still take his poems very seriously." Modern remnants of a past Latin American reverence of Tagore were discovered, for example, by an astonished Salman Rushdie during a trip to Nicaragua.

2

India of Tagore's Vision

Voice of Bengal

Rabindranath Tagore, who died in 1941 at the age of eighty, is a towering figure in the millennium-old literature of Bengal. Anyone who becomes familiar with this large and flourishing tradition will be impressed by the power of Tagore's presence in Bangladesh and in India. His poetry as well as his novels, short stories, and essays are very widely read, and the songs he composed reverberate around the eastern part of India and throughout Bangladesh.

In contrast, in the rest of the world, especially in Europe and America, the excitement that Tagore's writings created in the early years of the twentieth century has largely vanished. The enthusiasm with which his work was once greeted was quite remarkable. Gitanjali, a selection of his poetry for which he was awarded the Nobel Prize in Literature in 1913, was published in English translation in London in March of that year, and had been reprinted ten times by November, when the award was announced. But he is not much read now in the West, and already by 1937, Graham Greene was able to say: "As for Rabindranath Tagore, I cannot believe that anyone but Mr. Yeats can still take his poems very seriously."

The Mystic

The contrast between Tagore's commanding presence in Bengali literature and culture, and his near-total eclipse in the rest of the world, is perhaps less interesting than the distinction between the view of Tagore as a deeply relevant and many-sided contemporary thinker in Bangladesh and India, and his image in the West as a repetitive and remote spiritualist. Graham Greene had, in fact, gone on to explain that he associated Tagore "with what Chesterton calls 'the bright pebbly eyes' of the Theosophists." Certainly, an air of mysticism played some part in the "selling" of Rabindranath Tagore to the West by Yeats, Ezra Pound, and his other early champions. Even Anna Akhmatova, one of Tagore's few later admirers (who translated his poems into Russian in the mid-1960s), talks of "that mighty flow of poetry which takes its strength from Hinduism as from the Ganges, and is called Rabindranath Tagore."

Confluence of Cultures

Rabindranath did come from a Hindu family-one of the landed gentry who owned estates mostly in what is now Bangladesh. But whatever wisdom there might be in Akhmatova's invoking of Hinduism and the Ganges, it did not prevent the largely Muslim citizens of Bangladesh from having a deep sense of identity with Tagore and his ideas. Nor did it stop the newly independent Bangladesh from choosing one of Tagore's songs-the "Amar Sonar Bangla" which means "my golden Bengal" — as its national anthem. This must be very confusing to those who see the contemporary world as a "clash of civilizations" — with "the Muslim civilization," "the Hindu civilization," and "the Western civilization," each forcefully confronting the others. They would also be confused by Rabindranath Tagore's own description of his Bengali family as the product of "a confluence of three cultures: Hindu, Mohammedan, and British".

Rabindranath's grandfather, Dwarkanath, was well known for his command of Arabic and Persian, and Rabindranath grew up in a family atmosphere in which a deep knowledge of Sanskrit and ancient Hindu texts was combined with an understanding of Islamic traditions as well as Persian literature. It is not so much that Rabindranath tried to produce — or had an interest in producing — a "synthesis" of the different religions (as the great Mughal Emperor Akbar tried hard to achieve) as that his outlook was persistently non-sectarian, and his writings-some two hundred books-show the influence of different parts of the Indian cultural background as well as of the rest of the world.

Abode of Peace

Most of his work was written at Shantiniketan (Abode of Peace), the small town that grew around the school he founded in Bengal in 1901, and he not only conceived there an imaginative and innovative system of education, but through his writings and his influence on students and teachers, he was able to use the school as a base from which he could take a major part in India's social, political, and cultural movements.

The profoundly original writer, whose elegant prose and magical poetry Bengali readers know well, is not the sermonising spiritual guru admired — and then rejected — in London. Tagore was not only an immensely versatile poet; he was also a great short story writer, novelist, playwright, essayist, and composer of songs, as well as a talented painter whose pictures, with their mixture of representation and abstraction, are only now beginning to receive the acclaim that they have long deserved. His essays, moreover, ranged over literature, politics, culture, social change, religious beliefs, philosophical analysis, international relations, and much else. The coincidence of the fiftieth anniversary of Indian independence with the publication of a selection of Tagore's letters by Cambridge University Press, brought Tagore's ideas and reflections to the fore, which makes it important to examine what kind of leadership in thought and understanding he provided in the Indian subcontinent in the first half of this century.

Gandhi and Tagore

Since Rabindranath Tagore and Mahatma Gandhi were two leading Indian thinkers in the twentieth century, many commentators have tried to compare their ideas. On learning of Rabindranath's death, Jawaharlal Nehru, then incarcerated in a British jail in India, wrote in his prison diary for August 7, 1941:

> "Gandhi and Tagore. Two types entirely different from each other, and yet both of them typical of India, both in the long line of India's great men ... It is not so much because of any single virtue but because of the tout ensemble, that I felt that among the world's great men today Gandhi and Tagore were supreme as human beings. What good fortune for me to have come into close contact with them."

Romain Rolland was fascinated by the contrast between them, and when he completed his book on Gandhi, he wrote to an Indian academic, in March 1923: "I have finished my Gandhi, in which I pay tribute to your two great river-like souls, overflowing with divine spirit, Tagore and Gandhi." The following month, he recorded in his diary an account of some of the differences between Gandhi and Tagore written by Reverend C. F. Andrews, the English clergyman and public activist who was a close friend of both men (and whose important role in Gandhi's life in South Africa as well as India is well portrayed in Richard Attenborough's film Gandhi [1982]). Andrews described to Rolland a discussion between Tagore and Gandhi, at which he was present, on subjects that divided them:

> "The first subject of discussion was idols; Gandhi defended them, believing the masses incapable of raising themselves immediately to abstract ideas. Tagore cannot bear to see the people eternally treated as a child. Gandhi quoted the great things achieved in Europe by the flag as an idol; Tagore found it easy to object, but Gandhi held his ground, contrasting European flags bearing eagles, etc., with his own, on which he has put a spinning wheel. The second point of discussion was nationalism, which Gandhi defended. He said that one must go through nationalism to reach internationalism, in the same way that one must go through war to reach peace."

Tagore greatly admired Gandhi but he had many disagreements with him on a variety of subjects, including nationalism, patriotism, the importance of cultural exchange, the role of rationality and of science, and the nature of economic and social development. These differences, I shall argue, have a clear and consistent pattern, with Tagore pressing for more room for reasoning, and for a less traditionalist view, a greater interest in the rest of the world, and more respect for science and for objectivity generally.

Rabindranath knew that he could not have given India the political leadership that Gandhi provided, and he was never stingy in his praise for what Gandhi did for the nation (it was, in fact, Tagore who popularised the term "Mahatma" — great soul — as a description of Gandhi). And yet each remained deeply critical of many things that the other stood for. That Mahatma Gandhi has received incomparably more attention outside India and also within much of India itself makes it important to understand "Tagore's side" of the Gandhi-Tagore debates.

In his prison diary, Nehru wrote: "Perhaps it is as well that [Tagore] died now and did not see the many horrors that are likely to descend in increasing measure on the world and on India. He had seen enough and he was infinitely sad and unhappy." Towards the end of his life, Tagore was indeed becoming discouraged about the state of India, especially as its normal burden of problems, such as hunger and poverty, was being supplemented by politically organised incitement to "communal" violence between Hindus and Muslims. This conflict would lead in 1947, six years after Tagore's death, to the widespread killing that took place during partition; but there was much gore already during his declining days. In December 1939, he wrote to his friend Leonard Elmhirst, the English philanthropist and social reformer who had worked closely with him on rural reconstruction in India (and who had gone on to found the Dartington Hall Trust in England and a progressive school at Dartington that explicitly invoked Rabindranath's educational ideals):

> "It does not need a defeatist to feel deeply anxious about the future of millions who, with all their innate culture and their peaceful traditions are being simultaneously subjected to hunger, disease, exploitations foreign and indigenous, and the seething discontents of communalism."

How would Tagore have viewed the India of today? Would he see progress there, or wasted opportunity, perhaps even a betrayal of its promise and conviction? And, on a wider subject, how would he react to the spread of cultural separatism in the contemporary world?

East and West

Given the vast range of his creative achievements, perhaps the most astonishing aspect of the image of Tagore in the West is its narrowness; he is recurrently viewed as "the great mystic from the East," an image with a putative message for the West, which some would welcome, others dislike, and still others find deeply boring. To a great extent this Tagore was the West's own creation, part of its tradition of message-seeking from the East, particularly from India, which — as Hegel put it — had "existed for millennia in the imagination of the Europeans."

Friedrich Schlegel, Schelling, Herder, and Schopenhauer were only a few of the thinkers who followed the same pattern. They theorised, at first, that India was the source of superior wisdom. Schopenhauer at one stage even argued that the New Testament "must somehow be of Indian origin: this is attested by its completely Indian ethics, which transforms morals into asceticism, its pessimism, and its avatar," in "the person of Christ." But then they rejected their own theories with great vehemence, sometimes blaming India for not living up to their unfounded expectations.

We can imagine that Rabindranath's physical appearance-handsome, bearded, dressed in non-Western clothes-may, to some extent, have encouraged his being seen as a carrier of exotic wisdom. Yasunari Kawabata, the first Japanese Nobel Laureate in Literature, treasured memories from his middle-school days of "this sage-like poet":

> His white hair flowed softly down both sides of his forehead; the tufts of hair under the temples also were long like two beards, and linking up with the hair on his cheeks, continued into his beard, so that he gave an impression, to the boy I was then, of some ancient Oriental wizard.

That appearance would have been well-suited to the selling of Tagore in the West as a quintessentially mystical poet, and it could have made it somewhat easier to pigeonhole him. Commenting on Rabindranath's appearance, Frances Cornford told William Rothenstein, "I can now imagine a powerful and gentle Christ, which I never could before." Beatrice Webb, who did not like Tagore and resented what she took to be his "quite obvious dislike of all that the Webbs stand for" (there is, in fact, little evidence that Tagore had given much thought to this subject), said that he was "beautiful to look at" and that "his speech has the perfect intonation and slow chant-like moderation of the dramatic saint." Ezra Pound and W. B. Yeats, among others, first led the chorus of adoration in the Western appreciation of Tagore, and then soon moved to neglect and even shrill criticism.

The contrast between Yeats's praise of his work in 1912 ("These lyrics...display in their thought a world I have dreamed of all my life long," "the work of a supreme culture") and his denunciation in 1935 (Damn Tagore) arose partly from the inability of Tagore's many-sided writings to fit into the narrow box in which Yeats wanted to place and keep him. Certainly, Tagore did write a huge amount, and published ceaselessly, even in English (sometimes in indifferent English translation), but Yeats was also bothered, it is clear, by the difficulty of fitting Tagore's later writings into the image Yeats had presented to the West. Tagore, he had said, was the product of "a whole people, a whole civilization, immeasurably strange to us," and yet "we have met our own image,...or heard, perhaps for the first time in literature, our voice as in a dream."

Yeats did not totally reject his early admiration (as Ezra Pound and several others did), and he included some of Tagore's early poems in The Oxford Book of Modern Verse, which he edited in 1936. Yeats also had some favourable things to say about Tagore's prose writings. His censure of Tagore's later poems was reinforced by his dislike of Tagore's own English translations of his work ("Tagore does not know English, no Indian knows English," Yeats explained), unlike the English version of Gitanjali which Yeats had himself helped to prepare. Poetry is, of course, notoriously difficult to translate, and anyone who knows Tagore's poems in their original Bengali cannot feel satisfied with any of the translations (made with or without Yeats's help). Even the translations of his prose works suffer, to some extent, from distortion. E. M. Forster noted, in a review of a translation of one of Tagore's great Bengali novels, The Home and the World, in 1919: "The theme is so beautiful," but the charms have "vanished in translation," or perhaps "in an experiment that has not quite come off."

Tagore himself played a somewhat bemused part in the boom and bust of his English reputation. He accepted the extravagant praise with much surprise as well as pleasure, and then received denunciations with even greater surprise, and barely concealed pain. Tagore was sensitive to criticism, and was hurt by even the most far-fetched accusations, such as the charge that he was getting credit for the work of Yeats, who had "rewritten" Gitanjali. (This charge was made by a correspondent for The Times, Sir Valentine Chirol, whom E. M. Forster once described as "an old Anglo-Indian reactionary hack.") From time to time Tagore also protested the crudity of some of his overexcited advocates. He wrote to C. F. Andrews in 1920: "These people...are like drunkards who are afraid of their lucid intervals."

God and Others

Yeats was not wrong to see a large religious element in Tagore's writings. He certainly had interesting and arresting things to say about life and death. Susan Owen, the mother of Wilfred Owen, wrote to Rabindranath in 1920, describing her last conversations with her son before he left for the war which would take his life. Wilfred said goodbye with "those wonderful words of yours-beginning at 'When I go from hence, let this be my parting word.'" When Wilfred's pocket notebook was returned to his mother, she found "these words written in his dear writing with your name beneath."

The idea of a direct, joyful, and totally fearless relationship with God can be found in many of Tagore's religious writings, including the poems of Gitanjali. From India's diverse religious traditions he drew many ideas, both from ancient texts and from popular poetry. But "the bright pebbly eyes of the Theosophists" do not stare out of his verses. Despite the archaic language of the original translation of Gitanjali, which did not, I believe, help to preserve the simplicity of the original, its elementary humanity comes through more clearly than any complex and intense spirituality:

> Leave this chanting and singing and telling of beads! Whom dost thou worship in this lonely dark corner of a temple with doors all shut?
>
> Open thine eyes and see thy God is not before thee!
>
> He is there where the tiller is tilling the hard ground and where the pathmaker is breaking stones.
>
> He is with them in sun and in shower, and his garment is covered with dust.

An ambiguity about religious experience is central to many of Tagore's devotional poems, and makes them appeal to readers irrespective of their beliefs; but excessively detailed interpretation can ruinously strip away that ambiguity. This applies particularly to his many poems which combine images of human love and those of pious devotion. Tagore writes:

> I have no sleep tonight. Ever and again I open my door and look out on the darkness, my friend!
>
> I can see nothing before me. I wonder where lies thy path!
>
> By what dim shore of the ink-black river, by what far edge of the frowning forest, through what mazy depth of gloom, art thou threading thy course to come to see me, my friend?

I suppose it could be helpful to be told, as Yeats hastens to explain, that "the servant or the bride awaiting the master's homecoming in the empty house" is "among the images of the heart turning to God." But in Yeats's considerate attempt to make sure that the reader does not miss the "main point," something of the enigmatic beauty of the Bengali poem is lost — even what had survived the antiquated language of the English translation.

Tagore certainly had strongly held religious beliefs (of an unusually non-denominational kind), but he was interested in a great many other things as well and had many different things to say about them.

Some of the ideas he tried to present were directly political, and they figure rather prominently in his letters and lectures. He had practical, plainly expressed views about nationalism, war and peace, cross-cultural education, freedom of the mind, the importance of rational criticism, the need for openness, and so on. His admirers in the West, however, were tuned to the more otherworldly themes which had been emphasised by his first Western patrons. People came to his public lectures in Europe and America, expecting ruminations on grand, transcendental themes; when they heard instead his views on the way public leaders should behave, there was some resentment, particularly (as E. P. Thompson reports) when he delivered political criticism "at $700 a scold."

Reasoning in Freedom

For Tagore it was of the highest importance that people be able to live, and reason, in freedom. His attitudes towards politics and culture, nationalism and internationalism, tradition and modernity, can all be seen in the light of this belief. Nothing, perhaps, expresses his values as clearly as a poem in Gitanjali:

> Where the mind is without fear
> and the head is held high;
> Where knowledge is free;
> Where the world has not been
> broken up into fragments
> by narrow domestic walls; ...
> Where the clear stream of reason
> has not lost its way into the
> dreary desert sand of dead habit; ...
> Into that heaven of freedom,
> my Father, let my country awake.

Rabindranath's qualified support for nationalist movements — and his opposition to the unfreedom of alien rule — came from this commitment. So did his reservations about patriotism, which, he argued, can limit both the freedom to engage ideas from outside "narrow domestic walls" and the freedom also to support the causes of people in other countries. Rabindranath's passion for freedom underlies his firm opposition to unreasoned traditionalism, which makes one a prisoner of the past (lost, as he put it, in "the dreary desert sand of dead habit").

Tagore illustrates the tyranny of the past in his amusing yet deeply serious parable "*Kartar Bhoot*" (The Ghost of the Leader). As the respected leader of an imaginary land is about to die, his panic-stricken followers request him to stay on after his death to instruct them on what to do. He consents. But his followers find their lives are full of rituals and constraints on everyday behaviour and are not responsive to the world around them. Ultimately, they request the ghost of the leader to relieve them of his domination, when he informs them that he exists only in their minds.

Tagore's deep aversion to any commitment to the past that could not be modified by contemporary reason extended even to the alleged virtue of invariably keeping past promises. On one occasion when Mahatma Gandhi visited Tagore's school at Shantiniketan, a young woman got him to sign her autograph book. Gandhi wrote: "Never make a promise in haste. Having once made it fulfil it at the cost of your life." When he saw this entry, Tagore became agitated. He wrote in the same book a short poem in Bengali to the effect that no one can be made "a prisoner forever with a chain of clay." He went on to conclude in English, possibly so that Gandhi could read it too, "Fling away your promise if it is found to be wrong."

Tagore had the greatest admiration for Mahatma Gandhi as a person and as a political leader, but he was also highly skeptical of Gandhi's form of nationalism and his conservative instincts regarding the country's past traditions. He never criticised Gandhi personally. In the 1938 essay, "Gandhi the Man," he wrote:

> Great as he is as a politician, as an organiser, as a leader of men, as a moral reformer, he is greater than

> all these as a man, because none of these aspects and activities limits his humanity. They are rather inspired and sustained by it.

And yet there is a deep division between the two men. Tagore was explicit about his disagreement:

> We who often glorify our tendency to ignore reason, installing in its place blind faith, valuing it as spiritual, are ever paying for its cost with the obscuration of our mind and destiny. I blamed Mahatmaji for exploiting this irrational force of credulity in our people, which might have had a quick result [in creating] a superstructure, while sapping the. Thus, began my estimate of Mahatmaji, as the guide of our nation, and it is fortunate for me that it did not end there.

But while it "did not end there," that difference of vision was a powerful divider. Tagore, for example, remained unconvinced of the merit of Gandhi's forceful advocacy that everyone should spin at home with the "charka," the primitive spinning wheel. For Gandhi this practice was an important part of India's self-realisation. "The spinning-wheel gradually became," as his biographer B. R. Nanda writes, "the centre of rural uplift in the Gandhian scheme of Indian economics." Tagore found the alleged economic rationale for this scheme quite unrealistic.

As Romain Rolland noted, Rabindranath "never tires of criticising the charka." In this economic judgement, Tagore was probably right. Except for the rather small specialised market for high-quality spun cloth, it is hard to make economic sense of hand-spinning, even with wheels less primitive than Gandhi's charka. Hand-spinning as a widespread activity can survive only with the help of heavy government subsidies. However, Gandhi's advocacy of the charka was not based only on economics. He wanted everyone to spin for "thirty minutes every day as a sacrifice," seeing this as a way for people who are better off to identify themselves with the less fortunate. He was impatient with Tagore's refusal to grasp this point:

> The poet lives for the morrow, and would have us do likewise.... "Why should I, who have no need to work

> for food, spin?" may be the question asked. Because I am eating what does not belong to me. I am living on the spoliation of my countrymen. Trace the source of every coin that finds its way into your pocket, and you will realise the truth of what I write. Every one must spin. Let Tagore spin like the others. Let him burn his foreign clothes; that is the duty today. God will take care of the morrow.

If Tagore had missed something in Gandhi's argument, so did Gandhi miss the point of Tagore's main criticism. It was not only that the charka made little economic sense, but also, Tagore thought, that it was not the way to make people reflect on anything: "The charka does not require anyone to think; one simply turns the wheel of the antiquated invention endlessly, using the minimum of judgement and stamina."

Celibacy and Personal Life

Tagore and Gandhi's attitudes towards personal life were also quite different. Gandhi was keen on the virtues of celibacy, theorised about it, and, after some years of conjugal life, made a private commitment — publicly announced — to refrain from sleeping with his wife. Rabindranath's own attitude on this subject was very different, but he was gentle about their disagreements:

> [Gandhiji] condemns sexual life as inconsistent with the moral progress of man, and has a horror of sex as great as that of the author of The Kreutzer Sonata, but, unlike Tolstoy, he betrays no abhorrence of the sex that tempts his kind. In fact, his tenderness for women is one of the noblest and most consistent traits of his character, and he counts among the women of his country some of his best and truest comrades in the great movement he is leading.

Tagore's personal life was, in many ways, an unhappy one. He married in 1883, lost his wife in 1902, and never remarried. He sought close companionship, which he did not always get (perhaps even during his married life-he wrote to his wife, Mrinalini: "If you and I could be comrades in all our work and in all our thoughts it would be splendid, but we cannot attain all that we desire"). He maintained a warm friendship with, and a strong Platonic attachment to, the literature-loving wife, Kadambari, of his elder brother, Jyotirindranath. He dedicated some poems to her before his marriage, and several books afterwards, some after her death (she committed suicide, for reasons that are not fully understood, at the age of twenty-five, four months after Rabindranath's wedding).

Much later in life, during his tour of Argentina in 1924-25, Rabindranath came to know the talented and beautiful Victoria Ocampo, who later became the publisher of the literary magazine Sur. They became close friends, but it appears that Rabindranath deflected the possibility of a passionate relationship into a confined intellectual one. His friend Leonard Elmhirst, who accompanied Rabindranath on his Argentine tour, wrote:

> Besides having a keen intellectual understanding of his books, she was in love with him — but instead of being content to build a friendship on the basis of intellect, she was in a hurry to establish that kind of proprietary right over him which he absolutely would not brook.

Ocampo and Elmhirst, while remaining friendly, were both quite rude in what they wrote about each other. Ocampo's book on Tagore (of which a Bengali translation was made from the Spanish by the distinguished poet and critic Shankha Ghosh) is primarily concerned with Tagore's writings but also discusses the pleasures and difficulties of their relationship, giving quite a different account from Elmhirst's, and never suggesting any sort of proprietary intentions.

Victoria Ocampo, however, makes it clear that she very much wanted to get physically closer to Rabindranath: "Little by little he [Tagore] partially tamed the young animal, by turns wild and docile, who did not sleep, dog-like, on the floor outside his door, simply because it was not done." Rabindranath, too, was clearly very much attracted to her. He called her "Vijaya" (the Sanskrit equivalent of Victoria), dedicated a book of poems to her, Purabi-an "evening melody," and expressed great admiration for her mind (like a star that was distant"). In a letter to her he wrote, as if to explain his own reticence:

> When we were together, we mostly played with words and tried to laugh away our best opportunities to see each other clearly ... Whenever there is the least sign of the nest becoming a jealous rival of the sky [,] my mind, like a migrant bird, tries to take ... flight to a distant shore.

Five years later, during Tagore's European tour in 1930, he sent her a cable: "Will you not come and see me." She did. But their relationship did not seem to go much beyond conversation, and their somewhat ambiguous correspondence continued over the years. Written in 1940, a year before his death at eighty, one of the poems in *Sesh Lekha* (Last Writings), seems to be about her: "How I wish I could once again find my way to that foreign land where waits for me the message of love!...

Her language I knew not, but what her eyes said will forever remain eloquent in its anguish." However indecisive, or confused, or awkward Rabindranath may have been, he certainly did not share Mahatma Gandhi's censorious views of sex. In fact, when it came to social policy, he advocated contraception and family planning while Gandhi preferred abstinence.

Science and the People

Gandhi and Tagore severely clashed over their totally different attitudes towards science. In January 1934, Bihar was struck by a devastating earthquake, which killed thousands of people. Gandhi, who was then deeply involved in the fight against untouchability (the barbaric system inherited from India's divisive past, in which "lowly people" were kept at a physical distance), extracted a positive lesson from the tragic event. "A man like me," Gandhi argued, "cannot but believe this earthquake is a divine chastisement sent by God for our sins" — in particular the sins of untouchability. "For me there is a vital connection between the Bihar calamity and the untouchability campaign."

Tagore, who equally abhorred untouchability and had joined Gandhi in the movements against it, protested against this interpretation of an event that had caused suffering and death to so many innocent people, including children and babies. He also hated the epistemology implicit in seeing an earthquake as caused by ethical failure. "It is," he wrote, "all the more unfortunate because this kind of unscientific view of [natural] phenomena is too readily accepted by a large section of our countrymen."

The two remained deeply divided over their attitudes towards science. However, while Tagore believed that modern science was essential to the understanding of physical phenomena, his views on epistemology were interestingly heterodox. He did not take the simple "realist" position often associated with modern science. The report of his conversation with Einstein, published in The New York Times in 1930, shows how insistent Tagore was on interpreting truth through observation and reflective concepts. To assert that something is true or untrue in the absence of anyone to observe or perceive its truth, or to form a conception of what it is, appeared to Tagore to be deeply questionable. When Einstein remarked, "If there were no human beings any more, the Apollo Belvedere no longer would be beautiful?" Tagore simply replied, "No." Going further-and into much more interesting territory — Einstein said, "I agree with regard to this conception of beauty, but not with regard to truth." Tagore's response was: "Why not? Truth is realised through men."

Tagore's epistemology, which he never pursued systematically, would seem to be searching for a line of reasoning that would later be elegantly developed by Hilary Putnam, who has argued: "Truth depends on conceptual schemes and it is nonetheless 'real truth.'" Tagore himself said little to explain his convictions, but it is important to take account of his heterodoxy, not only because his speculations were invariably interesting, but also because they illustrate how his support for any position, including his strong interest in science, was accompanied by critical scrutiny.

Nationalism and Colonialism

Tagore was predictably hostile to communal sectarianism (such as a Hindu orthodoxy that was antagonistic to Islamic,

ing a particularly active part in contemporary ed to assert India's right to be independent without portance of what India could learn — freely and om abroad.

aid that a rejection of the West in favour of an ian tradition was not only limiting in itself; it could hostility to other influences from abroad, including which came to parts of India by the fourth century; h came through Jewish immigration shortly after rusalem, as did Zoroastrianism through Parsi ater on (mainly in the eighth century), and, of course- portantly-Islam, which has had a very strong presence e the tenth century.

criticism of patriotism is a persistent theme in his early as 1908, he put his position succinctly in a letter the criticism of Abala Bose, the wife of a great Indian gadish Chandra Bose: "Patriotism cannot be our final elter; my refuge is humanity. I will not buy glass for diamonds, and I will never allow patriotism to triumph nity as long as I live." His novel *Ghare Baire* (The Home Vorld) has much to say about this theme.

novel, Nikhil, who is keen on social reform, including liberation, but cool towards nationalism, gradually loses n of his spirited wife, Bimala, because of his failure to siastic about anti-British agitations, which she sees as a patriotic commitment. Bimala becomes fascinated with nationalist friend Sandip, who speaks brilliantly and acts triotic militancy, and she falls in love with him. Nikhil to change his views: "I am willing to serve my country; worship I reserve for Right which is far greater than my . To worship my country as a god is to bring a curse upon it."

the story unfolds, Sandip becomes angry with some of his ymen for their failure to join the struggle as readily as he they should (Some Muhammadan traders are still obdurate). ranges to deal with the recalcitrants by burning their meagre ng stocks and physically attacking them. Bimala has to owledge the connection between Sandip's rousing nationalistic

Christian, or Sikh perspectives). But even nationalism seemed to him to be suspect. Isaiah Berlin summarises well Tagore's complex position on Indian nationalism:

> Tagore stood fast on the narrow causeway, and did not betray his vision of the difficult truth. He condemned romantic over attachment to the past, what he called the tying of India to the past "like a sacrificial goat tethered to a post," and he accused men who displayed it — they seemed to him reactionary — of not knowing what true political freedom was, pointing out that it is from English thinkers and English books that the very notion of political liberty was derived. But against cosmopolitanism he maintained that the English stood on their own feet, and so must Indians. In 1917 he once more denounced the danger of 'leaving everything to the unalterable will of the Master,' be he brahmin or Englishman.

The duality Berlin points to is well reflected also in Tagore's attitude towards cultural diversity. He wanted Indians to learn what is going on elsewhere, how others lived, what they valued, and so on, while remaining interested and involved in their own culture and heritage. Indeed, in his educational writings the need for synthesis is strongly stressed. It can also be found in his advice to Indian students abroad. In 1907 he wrote to his son-in-law Nagendranath Gangulee, who had gone to America to study agriculture:

> To get on familiar terms with the local people is a part of your education. To know only agriculture is not enough; you must know America too. Of course if, in the process of knowing America, one begins to lose one's identity and falls into the trap of becoming an Americanised person contemptuous of everything Indian, it is preferable to stay in a locked room.

Tagore was strongly involved in protest against the Raj on a number of occasions, most notably in the movement to resist the 1905 British proposal to split in two the province of Bengal, a plan that was eventually withdrawn following popular resistance. He was forthright in denouncing the brutality of British rule in India, never more so than after the Amritsar massacre of April 13, 1919, when 379 unarmed people at a peaceful meeting were gunned down by the army, and two thousand more were wounded. Between April 23 and 26, Rabindranath wrote five agitated letters to C. F. Andrews, who himself was extremely disturbed, especially after he was told by a British civil servant in India that thanks to this show of strength, the "moral prestige" of the Raj had "never been higher."

A month after the massacre, Tagore wrote to the Viceroy of India, asking to be relieved of the knighthood he had accepted four years earlier:

> The disproportionate severity of the punishments inflicted upon the unfortunate people and the methods of carrying them out, we are convinced, are without parallel in the history of civilized governments, barring some conspicuous exceptions, recent and remote. Considering that such treatment has been meted out to a population, disarmed and resourceless, by a power which has the most terribly efficient organisation for destruction of human lives, we must strongly assert that it can claim no political expediency, far less moral justification.... The universal agony of indignation roused in the hearts of our people has been ignored by our rulers - possibly congratulating themselves for imparting what they imagine as salutary lessons.... I for my part want to stand, shorn of all special distinctions, by the side of those of my countrymen who for their so-called insignificance are liable to suffer a degradation not fit for human beings.

Both Gandhi and Nehru expressed their appreciation of the important part Tagore took in the national struggle. It is fitting that after independence, India chose a song of Tagore ("*Jana Gana Mana Adhinayaka*," which can be roughly translated as "the leader of people's minds") as its national anthem. Since Bangladesh would later choose another song of Tagore (*Amar Sonar Bangla*) as its national anthem, he may be the only one ever to have authored the national anthems of two different countries.

sentiments and his sectarian — and ultimately violent — actions. The dramatic events that follow (Nikhil attempts to help the victims, risking his life) include the end of Bimala's political romance.

This is a difficult subject, and Satyajit Ray's beautiful film of The Home and the World brilliantly brings out the novel's tensions, along with the human affections and disaffections of the story. Not surprisingly, the story has had many detractors, not just among dedicated nationalists in India. Georg Lukacs found Tagore's novel to be "a petit bourgeois yarn of the shoddiest kind," "at the intellectual service of the British police," and "a contemptible caricature of Gandhi." It would, of course, be absurd to think of Sandip as Gandhi, but the novel gives a "strong and gentle" warning, as Bertolt Brecht noted in his diary, of the corruptibility of nationalism, since it is not even-handed. Hatred of one group can lead to hatred of others, no matter how far such feeling may be from the minds of large-hearted nationalist leaders like Mahatma Gandhi.

Admiration and Criticism of Japan

Tagore's reaction to nationalism in Japan is particularly telling. As in the case of India, he saw the need to build the self-confidence of a defeated and humiliated people, of people left behind by developments elsewhere, as was the case in Japan before its emergence during the nineteenth century. At the beginning of one of his lectures in Japan in 1916 (Nationalism in Japan), he observed that "the worst form of bondage is the bondage of dejection, which keeps men hopelessly chained in loss of faith in themselves."

Tagore shared the admiration for Japan widespread in Asia for demonstrating the ability of an Asian nation to rival the West in industrial development and economic progress. He noted with great satisfaction that Japan had "in giant strides left centuries of inaction behind, overtaking the present time in its foremost achievement." For other nations outside the West, he said, Japan "has broken the spell under which we lay in torpor for ages, taking it to be the normal condition of certain races living in certain geographical limits."

But then Tagore went on to criticise the rise of a strong nationalism in Japan, and its emergence as an imperialist nation. Tagore's outspoken criticisms did not please Japanese audiences and, as E. P. Thompson wrote, "the welcome given to him on his first arrival soon cooled." Twenty-two years later, in 1937, during the Japanese war on China, Tagore received a letter from Rash Behari Bose, an anti-British Indian revolutionary then living in Japan, who sought Tagore's approval for his efforts there on behalf of Indian independence, in which he had the support of the Japanese government. Tagore replied:

> Your cable has caused me many restless hours, for it hurts me very much to have to ignore your appeal. I wish you had asked for my cooperation in a cause against which my spirit did not protest. I know, in making this appeal, you counted on my great regard for the Japanese for I, along with the rest of Asia, did once admire and look up to Japan and did once fondly hope that in Japan Asia had at last discovered its challenge to the West, that Japan's new strength would be consecrated in safeguarding the culture of the East against alien interests. But Japan has not taken long to betray that rising hope and repudiate all that seemed significant in her wonderful, and, to us symbolic, awakening, and has now become itself a worse menace to the defenceless peoples of the East.

How to view Japan's position in the Second World War was a divisive issue in India. After the war, when Japanese political leaders were tried for war crimes, the sole dissenting voice among the judges came from the Indian judge, Radhabinod Pal, a distinguished jurist. Pal dissented on various grounds, among them that no fair trial was possible in view of the asymmetry of power between the victor and the defeated. Ambivalent feelings in India towards the Japanese military aggression, given the unacceptable nature of British imperialism, possibly had a part in predisposing Pal to consider a perspective different from that of the other judges.

More tellingly, Subhash Chandra Bose (no relation of Rash Behari Bose), a leading nationalist, made his way to Japan during the war via Italy and Germany after escaping from a British prison; he helped the Japanese to form units of Indian soldiers, who had earlier surrendered to the advancing Japanese army, to fight on the Japanese side as the "Indian National Army." Rabindranath had formerly entertained great admiration for Subhash Bose as a dedicated non-sectarian fighter for Indian independence. But their ways would have parted when Bose's political activities took this turn, although Tagore was dead by the time Bose reached Japan.

Tagore saw Japanese militarism as illustrating the way nationalism can mislead even a nation of great achievement and promise. In 1938 Yone Noguchi, the distinguished poet and friend of Tagore (as well as of Yeats and Pound), wrote to Tagore, pleading with him to change his mind about Japan. Rabindranath's reply, written on September 12, 1938, was altogether uncompromising:

> It seems to me that it is futile for either of us to try to convince the other, since your faith in the infallible right of Japan to bully other Asiatic nations into line with your Government's policy is not shared by me.... Believe me, it is sorrow and shame, not anger, that prompt me to write to you. I suffer intensely not only because the reports of Chinese suffering batter against my heart, but because I can no longer point out with pride the example of a great Japan.

He would have been much happier with the postwar emergence of Japan as a peaceful power. Then, too, since he was not free of egotism, he would also have been pleased by the attention paid to his ideas by the novelist Yasunari Kawabata and others.

International Concerns

Tagore was not invariably well-informed about international politics. He allowed himself to be entertained by Mussolini in a short visit to Italy in May-June 1926, a visit arranged by Carlo Formichi, professor of Sanskrit at the University of Rome. When he asked to meet Benedetto Croce, Formichi said, "Impossible! Impossible!" Mussolini told him that Croce was "not in Rome." When Tagore said he would go "wherever he is," Mussolini assured him that Croce's whereabouts were unknown.

Such incidents, as well as warnings from Romain Rolland and other friends, should have ended Tagore's flirtation with Mussolini more quickly than it did. But only after he received graphic accounts of the brutality of Italian fascism from two exiles, Gaetano Salvemini and Gaetano Salvadori, and learned more of what was happening in Italy, did he publicly denounce the regime, publishing a letter to the Manchester Guardian in August. The next month, Popolo d'Italia, the magazine edited by Benito Mussolini's brother, replied: "Who cares? Italy laughs at Tagore and those who brought this unctuous and insupportable fellow in our midst."

With his high expectations of Britain, Tagore continued to be surprised by what he took to be a lack of official sympathy for international victims of aggression. He returned to this theme in the lecture he gave on his last birthday, in 1941:

> While Japan was quietly devouring North China, her act of wanton aggression was ignored as a minor incident by the veterans of British diplomacy. We have also witnessed from this distance how actively the British statesmen acquiesced in the destruction of the Spanish Republic.

But distinguishing between the British government and the British people, Rabindranath went on to note "with admiration how a band of valiant Englishmen laid down their lives for Spain."

Tagore's view of the Soviet Union has been a subject of much discussion. He was widely read in Russia. In 1917 several Russian translations of Gitanjali (one edited by Ivan Bunin, later the first Russian Nobel Laureate in Literature) were available, and by the late-1920s many of the English versions of his work had been rendered into Russian by several distinguished translators. Russian versions of his work continued to appear: Boris Pasternak translated him in the 1950s and 1960s.

When Tagore visited Russia in 1930, he was much impressed by its development efforts and by what he saw as a real commitment to eliminate poverty and economic inequality. But what impressed him most was the expansion of basic education across the old Russian Empire. In Letters from Russia, written in Bengali and published in 1931, he unfavourably compares the acceptance of widespread illiteracy in India by the British administration with Russian efforts to expand education:

> In stepping on the soil of Russia, the first thing that caught my eye was that in education, at any rate, the peasant and the working classes have made such enormous progress in these few years that nothing comparable has happened even to our highest classes in the course of the last hundred and fifty years.... The people here are not at all afraid of giving complete education even to Turcomans of distant Asia; on the contrary, they are utterly in earnest about it.

When parts of the book were translated into English in 1934, the under-secretary for India stated in Parliament that it was "calculated by distortion of the facts to bring the British Administration in India into contempt and disrepute," and the book was then promptly banned. The English version would not be published until after independence.

Views on Education

As one of the earliest educators to think in terms of the global village, Rabindranath Tagore's educational model has a unique sensitivity and aptness for education within multi-racial, multi-lingual and multi-cultural situations, amidst conditions of acknowledged economic discrepancy and political imbalance.

Rabindranath Tagore, Asia's first Nobel Laureate, was born into a prominent Calcutta family known for its socio-religious and cultural innovations during the 19th Bengal Renaissance. The profound social and cultural involvement of his family would later play a strong role in the formulation of Rabindranath's educational priorities. His grandfather Dwarkanath was involved in supporting medical facilities, educational institutions and the arts, and he fought for religious and social reform and the establishment of a free press.

His father was also a leader in social and religious reform, who encouraged a multi-cultural exchange in the family mansion Jorasanko. Within the joint family, Rabindranath's thirteen brothers and sisters were mathematicians, journalists, novelists, musicians, artists. His cousins, who shared the family mansion, were leaders in theatre, science and a new art movement.

The tremendous excitement and cultural richness of his extended family permitted young Rabindranath to absorb and learn subconsciously at his own pace, giving him a dynamic open model of education, which he later tried to recreate in his school at Shantiniketan. Not surprisingly, he found his outside formal schooling to be inferior and boring and, after a brief exposure to several schools, he refused to attend school. The only degrees he ever received were honorary ones bestowed late in life.

His experiences at Jorasanko provided him with a lifelong conviction concerning the importance of freedom in education. He also realised in a profound manner the importance of the arts for developing empathy and sensitivity, and the necessity for an intimate relationship with one's cultural and natural environment. In participating in the cosmopolitan activities of the family, he came to reject narrowness in general, and in particular, any form of narrowness that separated human being from human being. He saw education as a vehicle for appreciating the richest aspects of other cultures, while maintaining one's own cultural specificity. As he wrote:

> I was brought up in an atmosphere of aspiration, aspiration for the expansion of the human spirit. We in our home sought freedom of power in our language, freedom of imagination in our literature, freedom of soul in our religious creeds and that of mind in our social environment. Such an opportunity has given me confidence in the power of education which is one with life and only which can give us real freedom, the highest that is claimed for man, his freedom of moral communion in the human world.... I try to assert in my words and works that education has its only meaning and object in freedom-freedom from ignorance about the laws of the universe, and freedom from passion and prejudice in our communication with the human world. In my institution I have attempted to create an atmosphere of naturalness in

> our relationship with strangers, and the spirit of hospitality which is the first virtue in men that made civilization possible.
>
> I invited thinkers and scholars from foreign lands to let our boys know how easy it is to realise our common fellowship, when we deal with those who are great, and that it is the puny who with their petty vanities set up barriers between man and man.

As well as growing up in a household that was the meeting place for leading artists and intellectuals from India and the West, Rabindranath had a further experience which was unusual for someone of his upbringing. In the 1890s, he was put in charge of the family's rural properties in East Bengal. His first experiments in adult education were carried out there as he gradually became aware of the acute material and cultural poverty that permeated the villages, as well as the great divide between the uneducated rural areas and the city elites.

His experiences made him determined to do something about rural uplift, and later at Shantiniketan, students and teachers were involved with literacy training and social work and the promotion of cooperative schemes. As an alternative to the existing forms of education, he started a small school at Shantiniketan in 1901 that developed into a university and rural reconstruction centre, where he tried to develop an alternative model of education that stemmed from his own learning experiences.

Rabindranath composed his first poem at age eight, and by the end of his life, had written over twenty-five volumes of poetry, fifteen plays, ninety short stories, eleven novels, thirteen volumes of essays, initiated and edited various journals, prepared Bengali textbooks, kept up a correspondence involving thousands of letters, composed over two thousand songs; and — after the age of seventy — created more than two thousand pictures and sketches.

He dedicated forty years of his life to his educational institution at Shantiniketan, West Bengal. Rabindranath's school contained a children's school as well as a university known as Vishva Bharati and a rural education Centre known as Shantiniketan.

Key Ideas

Rabindranath did not write a central educational treatise, and his ideas must be gleaned through his various writings and educational experiments at Shantiniketan In general, he envisioned an education that was deeply rooted in one's immediate surroundings but connected to the cultures of the wider world, predicated upon pleasurable learning and individualised to the personality of the child.

He felt that a curriculum should revolve organically around nature with classes held in the open air under the trees to provide for a spontaneous appreciation of the fluidity of the plant and animal kingdoms, and seasonal changes. Children sat on hand-woven mats beneath the trees, which they were allowed to climb and run beneath between classes. Nature walks and excursions were a part of the curriculum and students were encouraged to follow the life cycles of insects, birds and plants. Class schedules were made flexible to allow for shifts in the weather or special attention to natural phenomena, and seasonal festivals were created for the children by Tagore. In an essay entitled "A Poet's School," he emphasises the importance of an empathetic sense of interconnectedness with the surrounding world:

> We have come to this world to accept it, not merely to know it. We may become powerful by knowledge, but we attain fullness by sympathy. The highest education is that which does not merely give us information but makes our life in harmony with all existence. But we find that this education of sympathy is not only systematically ignored in schools, but it is severely repressed. From our very childhood habits are formed and knowledge is imparted in such a manner that our life is weaned away from nature and our mind and the world are set in opposition from the beginning of our days. Thus, the greatest of educations for which we came prepared is neglected, and we are made to lose our world to find a bagful of information instead. We rob the child of his earth to teach him geography, of language to teach him

> grammar. His hunger is for the Epic, but he is supplied with chronicles of facts and dates...Child-nature protests against such calamity with all its power of suffering, subdued at last into silence by punishment.

In Tagore's philosophy of education, the aesthetic development of the senses was as important as the intellectual — if not more so — and music, literature, art, dance and drama were given great prominence in the daily life of the school. This was particularly so after the first decade of the school. Drawing on his home life at Jorasanko, Rabindranath tried to create an atmosphere in which the arts would become instinctive. One of the first areas to be emphasised was music. Rabindranath writes that in his adolescence, a 'cascade of musical emotion' gushed forth day after day at Jorasanko. 'We felt we would try to test everything,' he writes, 'and no achievement seemed impossible...We wrote, we sang, we acted, we poured ourselves out on every side.'

In keeping with his theory of subconscious learning, Rabindranath never talked or wrote down to the students, but rather involved them with whatever he was writing or composing. The students were allowed access to the room where he read his new writings to teachers and critics, and they were encouraged to read out their own writings in special literary evenings. In teaching also he believed in presenting difficult levels of literature, which the students might not fully grasp, but which would stimulate them. The writing and publishing of periodicals had always been an important aspect of Jorasanko life, and students at Shantiniketan were encouraged to create their own publications and put out several illustrated magazines. The children were encouraged to follow their ideas in painting and drawing and to draw inspiration from the many visiting artists and writers.

Most of Rabindranath's dramas were written at Shantiniketan and the students took part in both the performing and production sides. He writes how well the students were able to enter into the spirit of the dramas and perform their roles, which required subtle understanding and sympathy without special training.

As Rabindranath began conceiving of Vishva Bharati as a national centre for the arts, he encouraged artists such as Nandalal Bose to take up residence at Shantiniketan and to devote themselves full-time to promoting a national form of art. Without music and the fine arts, he wrote, a nation lacks its highest means of national self-expression and the people remain inarticulate. Tagore was one of the first to support and bring together different forms of Indian dance. He helped revive folk dances and introduced dance forms from other parts of India, such as Manipuri, Kathak and Kathakali. He also supported modern dance and was one of the first to the talents of Uday Sankar, who was invited to perform at Shantiniketan.

The meeting-ground of cultures, as Rabindranath envisioned it at Vishva Bharati, should be a learning centre where conflicting interests are minimised, where individuals work together in a common pursuit of truth and realise 'that artists in all parts of the world have created forms of beauty, scientists discovered secrets of the universe, philosophers solved the problems of existence, saints made the truth of the spiritual world organic in their own lives, not merely for some particular race to which they belonged, but for all mankind.'

To encourage mutuality, Rabindranath invited artists and scholars from other parts of India and the world to live together at Shantiniketan on a daily basis to share their cultures with Vishva Bharati. The Constitution designated Vishva Bharati as an Indian, Eastern and Global cultural centre whose goals were:

- To study the mind of Man in its realisation of different aspects of truth from diverse points of view.
- To bring into more intimate relation with one another through patient study and research, the different cultures of the East on the basis of their underlying unity.
- To approach the West from the standpoint of such a unity of the life and thought of Asia.
- To seek to realise in a common fellowship of study the meeting of East and West and thus ultimately to strengthen the fundamental conditions of world peace through the free communication of ideas between the two hemispheres.
- And with such Ideals in view to provide at Shantiniketan a centre of culture where research into the study of the religion, literature, history, science and art of Hindu,

> Buddhist, Jain, Zoroastrian, Islamic, Sikh, Christian and other civilizations may be pursued along with the culture of the West, with that simplicity of externals which is necessary for true spiritual realisation, in amity, good-fellowship and cooperation between the thinkers and scholars of both Eastern and Western countries, free from all antagonisms of race, nationality, creed or caste and in the name of the One Supreme Being who is Shantam, Shivam, Advaitam.

In terms of curriculum, he advocated a different emphasis in teaching. Rather than studying national cultures for the wars won and cultural dominance imposed, he advocated a teaching system that analysed history and culture for the progress that had been made in breaking down social and religious barriers. Such an approach emphasised the innovations that had been made in integrating individuals of diverse backgrounds into a larger framework, and in devising the economic policies which emphasised social justice and narrowed the gap between rich and poor. Art would be studied for its role in furthering the aesthetic imagination and expressing universal themes.

It should be noted that Rabindranath in his own person was a living icon of the type of mutuality and creative exchange that he advocated. His vision of culture was not a static one, but one that advocated new cultural fusions, and he fought for a world where multiple voices were encouraged to interact with one another and to reconcile differences within an overriding commitment to peace and mutual interconnectedness. His generous personality and his striving to break down barriers of all sorts gives us a model for the way multiculturalism can exist within a single human personality, and the type of individual which the educational process should be aspiring towards.

Tagore's educational efforts were ground-breaking in many areas. He was one of the first in India to argue for a humane educational system that was in touch with the environment and aimed at overall development of the personality. Shantiniketan became a model for vernacular instruction and the development of Bengali textbooks; as well, it offered one of the earliest coeducational programmes in South Asia. The establishment of

Vishva Bharati and Shantiniketan led to pioneering efforts in many directions, including models for distinctively Indian higher education and mass education, as well as pan-Asian and global cultural exchange.

One characteristic that sets Rabindranath's educational theory apart is his approach to education as a poet. At Shantiniketan, he stated, his goal was to create a poem 'in a medium other than words.' It was this poetic vision that enabled him to fashion a scheme of education which was all inclusive, and to devise a unique programme for education in nature and creative self-expression in a learning climate congenial to global cultural exchange.

Education and Freedom

The British Indian administrators were not, however, alone in trying to suppress Tagore's reflections on Russia. They were joined by Soviet officials. In an interview with Izvestia in 1930, Tagore sharply criticised the lack of freedom that he observed in Russia:

> I must ask you: Are you doing your ideal a service by arousing in the minds of those under your training anger, class-hatred, and revengefulness against those whom you consider to be your enemies?... Freedom of mind is needed for the reception of truth; terror hopelessly kills it..... For the sake of humanity I hope you may never create a vicious force of violence, which will go on weaving an interminable chain of violence and cruelty.... You have tried to destroy many of the other evils of [the czarist] period. Why not try to destroy this one also?

The interview was not published in Izvestia until 1988-nearly sixty years later. Tagore's reaction to the Russia of 1930 arose from two of his strongest commitments: his uncompromising belief in the importance of "freedom of mind" (the source of his criticism of the Soviet Union), and his conviction that the expansion of basic education is central to social progress (the source of his praise, particularly in contrast to British-run India). He identified the lack of basic education as the fundamental cause of many of India's social and economic afflictions:

> In my view the imposing tower of misery which today rests on the heart of India has its sole foundation in the absence of education. Caste divisions, religious conflicts, aversion to work, precarious economic conditions — all centre on this single factor.

It was on education (and on the reflection, dialogue, and communication that are associated with it), rather than on, say, spinning "as a sacrifice" (the charka does not require anyone to think), that the future of India would depend.

Tagore was concerned not only that there be wider opportunities for education across the country (especially in rural areas where schools were few), but also that the schools themselves be more lively and enjoyable. He himself had dropped out of school early, largely out of boredom, and had never bothered to earn a diploma.

He wrote extensively on how schools should be made more attractive to boys and girls and thus more productive. His own co-educational school at Shantiniketan had many progressive features. The emphasis here was on self-motivation rather than on discipline, and on fostering intellectual curiosity rather than competitive excellence.

Much of Rabindranath's life was spent in developing the school at Shantiniketan. The school never had much money, since the fees were very low. His lecture honoraria, "$700 a scold," went to support it, as well as most of his Nobel Prize money. The school received no support from the government, but did get help from private citizens-even Mahatma Gandhi raised money for it.

The dispute with Mahatma Gandhi on the Bihar earthquake touched on a subject that was very important to Tagore: the need for education in science as well as in literature and the humanities. At Shantiniketan, there were strong "local" elements in its emphasis on Indian traditions, including the classics, and in the use of Bengali rather than English as the language of instruction. At the same time there were courses on a great variety of cultures, and study programmes devoted to China, Japan, and the Middle East. Many foreigners came to Shantiniketan to study or teach, and the fusion of studies seemed to work.

Shantiniketan was unusual in many different ways, such as the oddity that classes, excepting those requiring a laboratory, were held outdoors (whenever the weather permitted). No matter what we thought of Rabindranath's belief that one gains from being in a natural setting while learning (some of us argued about this theory), we typically found the experience of outdoor schooling extremely attractive and pleasant.

Academically, our school was not particularly exacting (often we did not have any examinations at all), and it could not, by the usual academic standards, compete with some of the better schools in Calcutta. But there was something remarkable about the ease with which class discussions could move from Indian traditional literature to contemporary as well as classical Western thought, and then to the culture of China or Japan or elsewhere. The school's celebration of variety was also in sharp contrast with the cultural conservatism and separatism that has tended to grip India from time to time.

The cultural give and take of Tagore's vision of the contemporary world has close parallels with the vision of Satyajit Ray, also an alumnus of Shantiniketan who made several films based on Tagore's stories. Ray's words about Shantiniketan in 1991 would have greatly pleased Rabindranath:

> I consider the three years I spent in Shantiniketan as the most fruitful of my life.... Shantiniketan opened my eyes for the first time to the splendours of Indian and Far Eastern art. Until then I was completely under the sway of Western art, music and literature. Shantiniketan made me the combined product of East and West that I am.

Summary

Rabindranath Tagore, by his efforts and achievements, is part of a global network of pioneering educators, such as Rousseau, Pestalozzi, Froebel, Montessori and Dewey — and in the contemporary context, Malcolm Knowles — who have striven to create non-authoritarian learning systems appropriate to their respective surroundings. In a poem that expresses Tagore's goals for international education, he writes:

Where the mind is without fear and the head is held high,

Where knowledge is free;

Where the world has not been broken up into fragments by narrow domestic walls;

Where words come out from the depth of truth;

Where tireless striving stretches its arms towards perfection;

Where the clear stream of reason has not lost its way into the dreary desert sand of dead habit;

Where the mind is led forward by thee into ever-widening thought and action — into that heaven of freedom,

My Father,

Let my country awake.

India After Fifty Years of Independence

At the fiftieth anniversary of Indian independence, the reckoning of what India had or had not achieved in half a century was a subject of considerable interest: "What has been the story of those first fifty years?" (as Shashi Tharoor asked in his balanced, informative, and highly readable account of India: From Midnight to the Millennium). If Tagore were to see the India of today, more than half a century after independence, nothing perhaps would shock him so much as the continued illiteracy of the masses. He would see this as a total betrayal of what the nationalist leaders had promised during the struggle for independence-a promise that had figured even in Nehru's rousing speech on the eve of independence in August 1947 (on India's "tryst with destiny").

In view of his interest in childhood education, Tagore would not be consoled by the extraordinary expansion of university education, in which India sends to its universities six times as many people per unit of population as does China. Rather, he would be stunned that, in contrast to East and South East Asia, including China, half the adult population and two thirds of Indian women remain unable to read or write. Statistically reliable surveys indicate that even in the late-1980s, nearly half of the rural girls between the ages of twelve and fourteen did not attend any school for a single day of their lives.

This state of affairs is the result of the continuation of British imperial neglect of mass education, which has been reinforced by India's traditional elitism, as well as upper-class-dominated contemporary politics (except in parts of India such as Kerala, where anti-upper-caste movements have tended to concentrate on education as a great leveller). Tagore would see illiteracy and the neglect of education not only as the main source of India's continued social backwardness, but also as a great constraint that restricts the possibility and reach of economic development in India (as his writings on rural development forcefully make clear). Tagore would also have strongly felt the need for a greater commitment-and a greater sense of urgency-in removing endemic poverty.

At the same time, Tagore would undoubtedly find some satisfaction in the survival of democracy in India, in its relatively free press, and in general from the "freedom of mind" that post-independence Indian politics has, on the whole, managed to maintain. He would also be pleased by the fact noted by the historian E. P. Thompson (whose father Edward Thompson had written one of the first major biographies of Tagore:-

> All the convergent influences of the world run through this society: Hindu, Moslem, Christian, secular; Stalinist, liberal, Maoist, democratic socialist, Gandhian. There is not a thought that is being thought in the West or East that is not active in some Indian mind.

Tagore would have been happy also to see that the one governmental attempt to dispense generally with basic liberties and political and civil rights in India, in the 1970s, when Prime Minister Indira Gandhi (ironically, herself a former student at Shantiniketan) declared an "emergency," was overwhelmingly rejected by the Indian voters, leading to the precipitate fall of her government.

Rabindranath would also see that the changes in policy that have eliminated famine since independence had much to do with the freedom to be heard in a democratic India. In Tagore's play *Raja O Rani* (The King and the Queen), the sympathetic Queen eventually rebels against the callousness of state policy towards the hungry. She begins by enquiring about the ugly sounds outside the palace, only to be told that the noise is coming from "the coarse, clamorous crowd who howl unashamedly for food and disturb the sweet peace of the palace." The Viceregal office in India could have taken a similarly callous view of Indian famines, right up to the easily preventable Bengal famine of 1943, just before independence, which killed between two and three million people. But a government in a multi-party democracy, with elections and free newspapers, cannot any longer dismiss the noise from "the coarse, clamorous crowd."

Unlike Gandhi, Rabindranath would not resent the development of modern industries in India, or the acceleration of technical progress, since he did not want India to be shackled to the turning of "the wheel of an antiquated invention." Tagore was concerned that people not be dominated by machines, but he was not opposed to making good use of modern technology. "The mastery over the machine," he wrote in Crisis in Civilization, "by which the British have consolidated their sovereignty over their vast Empire, has been kept a sealed book, to which due access has been denied to this helpless country." Rabindranath had a deep interest in the environment — he was particularly concerned about deforestation and initiated a "festival of tree-planting" (*vriksha ropana*) as early as 1928. He would want increased private and government commitments to environmentalism; but he would not derive from this position a general case against modern industry and technology.

On Cultural Separation

Rabindranath would be shocked by the growth of cultural separatism in India, as elsewhere. The "openness" that he valued so much is certainly under great strain right now — in many countries. Religious fundamentalism still has a relatively small following in India; but various factions seem to be doing their best to increase their numbers. Certainly religious sectarianism has had much success in some parts of India (particularly in the west and the north). Tagore would see the expansion of religious sectarianism as being closely associated with an artificially separatist view of culture.

He would have strongly resisted defining India in specifically Hindu terms, rather than as a "confluence" of many cultures. Even after the partition of 1947, India is still the third- largest Muslim country in the world, with more Muslims than in Bangladesh, and nearly as many as in Pakistan. Only Indonesia has substantially more followers of Islam. Indeed, by pointing to the immense heterogeneousness of India's cultural background and its richly diverse history, Tagore had argued that the "idea of India" itself militated against a culturally separatist view "against the intense consciousness of the separateness of one's own people from others."

Tagore would also oppose the cultural nationalism that has recently been gaining some ground in India, along with an exaggerated fear of the influence of the West. He was uncompromising in his belief that human beings could absorb quite different cultures in constructive ways:

> Whatever we understand and enjoy in human products instantly becomes ours, wherever they might have their origin. I am proud of my humanity when I can acknowledge the poets and artists of other countries as my own. Let me feel with unalloyed gladness that all the great glories of man are mine. Therefore, it hurts me deeply when the cry of rejection rings loud against the West in my country with the clamour that Western education can only injure us.

In this context, it is important to emphasise that Rabindranath was not short of pride in India's own heritage, and often spoke about it. He lectured at Oxford, with evident satisfaction, on the importance of India's religious ideas-quoting both from ancient texts and from popular poetry (such as the verses of the sixteenth-century Muslim poet Kabir). In 1940, when he was given an honorary doctorate by Oxford University, in a ceremony arranged at his own educational establishment in Shantiniketan ("In Gangem Defluit Isis," Oxford helpfully explained), to the predictable "volley of Latin" Tagore responded "by a volley of Sanskrit," as Marjorie Sykes, a Quaker friend of Rabindranath, reports. Her cheerful summary of the match, "India held its own," was not out of line with Tagore's pride in Indian culture. His welcoming attitude to

Western civilization was reinforced by this confidence: he did not see India's culture as fragile and in need of "protection" from Western influence.

In India, he wrote, "circumstances almost compel us to learn English, and this lucky accident has given us the opportunity of access into the richest of all poetical literatures of the world." There seems to us much force in Rabindranath's argument for clearly distinguishing between the injustice of a serious asymmetry of power (colonialism being a prime example of this) and the importance nevertheless of appraising Western culture in an open-minded way, in colonial and post-colonial territories, in order to see what uses could be made of it.

Rabindranath insisted on open debate on every issue, and distrusted conclusions based on a mechanical formula, no matter how attractive that formula might seem in isolation (such as "This was forced on us by our colonial masters - we must reject it," "This is our tradition-we must follow it," "We have promised to do this-we must fulfil that promise," and so on). The question he persistently asks is whether we have reason enough to want what is being proposed, taking everything into account. Important as history is, reasoning has to go beyond the past. It is in the sovereignty of reasoning-fearless reasoning in freedom-that we can find Rabindranath Tagore's lasting voice.

3

Tagore's Nationalism

General Aspects

In a poem entitled, "The Sunset of the Century," written on the last day of the nineteenth century, India's messianic poet and Asia's first Nobel Laureate, Rabindranath Tagore (1861-1941), launched a fierce diatribe on nationalism. In a mood of outrage and disenchantment, tempered with intermittent hope, he wrote:

> The last sun of the century sets amidst the blood-red clouds of the West and the whirlwind of hatred.
>
> The naked passion of the self-love of Nations, in its drunken delirium of greed, is dancing to the clash of steel and howling verses of vengeance.
>
> The hungry self of the Nation shall burst in a violence of fury from its shameless feeding.
>
> For it has made the world its food.
>
> And licking it, crunching it and swallowing it in big morsels,
>
> It swells and swells

> Till in the midst of its unholy feast descends the sudden
> shaft of heaven piercing its heart of grossness.

This anti-nationalitarian sentiment-that nationalism is a source of war and carnage; death, destruction and divisiveness, rather than international solidarity, that induces a larger and more expansive vision of the world — remains at the heart of Tagore's imagination in most of his writings: his letters, essays, lectures, poems, plays and fiction. He was always opposed to the nationalism of Realpolitik and hyper-nationalism that breathed meaning into Thucydides's ancient maxim that "large nations do what they wish, while small nations accept what they must" and that in which, as Radhakrishnan said, "self-interest is the end; brute force, the means; conscience is taboo". Radical nationalism that acted as opiate of the people, making them irrational and fanatical, blind to the senses of truth and justice, and willing to both kill and die for it, perpetuating a logic of "lunacy" and war, instead of a cycle of freedom and peace, was an anathema to Tagore. He spurned it as "a cruel epidemic of evil . . . sweeping over the human world of the present age and eating into its moral fibre"; a terrible absurdity that is seeking to engulf humanity in a suicidal conflagration.

Tagore was a believer in an interactive, dialogic world, given to a deep sense of sympathy, generosity and mutuality, and in which nations would not be parochial, xenophobic and centripetal, or guided by mere selfishness and self-aggrandisement, but poised towards a morally and politically enlightened community of nations through the espousal of a centrifugal outlook, multilateral imagination, principal of universality and reciprocal recognitions. In this sense Tagore stands a precursor to many of the modern critics and philosophers of post/trans-nationalism and globalism such as Frantz Fanon, Edward Said and Noam Chomsky.

Much like Chomsky, Tagore believed, to put it in Chomsky's words, that "'another world is possible' [by] seeking to create constructive alternatives of thought, actions and institutions," and by bringing "a measure of peace and justice and hope to the world". Tagore imagined of a commonwealth of nations in which no nation (or race) would deprive another "of its rightful place in the world festival" and every nation would "keep alight its own lamp of mind as its part of the illumination of the world".

Tagore was an avid advocate of inter-civilizational alliance; his vision was given to a symbiosis of the East and West. He was no doubt furious with the British cruelty and oppression in India during the colonial period, and felt that the West was often immersed in commercialism, "moral cannibalism", "political expediency", militarism and "war-madness", and was unduly full of contempt for the East; yet he never gave up hope for a possible union of the East and West, in which the East and the West would meet as equal partners in a creative engagement; "I believe in the true meeting of the East and the West", he affirmed in a letter to Charles Andrews. In a letter to Foss Westcott, Tagore further wrote, "Believe me, nothing would give me greater happiness than to see the people of the West and the East march in a common crusade against all that robs the human spirit of its significance". Moreover, he took exception to Kipling's remark that the East and the West were too divergent and "'Never the twain shall meet" by affirming, much like in Emerson's spirit in his essay "Compensation," that the realisation of a unitary and stable world was contingent upon the meeting of these two opposing halves, which compensated one another:

> Earnestly I ask the poet of the western world to realise and sing . . . with all the great power of music which he has, that the East and West are ever in search of each other, and that they must meet not merely in the fullness of physical strength, but in fullness of truth; that the right hand, which wields the sword, has the need of the left, which holds the shield of safety.

Tagore's indictment of nationalism elicited furious criticisms from many of his contemporaries, especially in the West, with the Marxist critic, Georg Lukacs, and the English writer, D. H. Lawrence, leading the pack, making the duo strange bedfellows in their Tagore hatred. Lukacs, who found both Tagore and Gandhi counter-revolutionary, took the opportunity to pounce on Tagore, after the publication of his anti-nationalist, anti-revolutionary novel, The Home and the World (1915). In the characteristic tone of one who saw a Cause greater than a living, breathing human being, and to whom the abstract was more sanctified than the palpable, Lukacs condemned Tagore as "a wholly insignificant figure. . . [Who] survives by sticking scraps of the Upanishads and the Bhagvad Gita into his works amid the sluggish flow of his tediousness". Lawrence, on the other hand, felt outraged by what he called the "wretched worship of-Tagore attitude" and admonished that Tagore was a "horribly decadent [figure] reverting to all forms of barbarism in all sorts of ugly ways." Lawrence further said, creating the same us/them, West/East hierarchical binary, which Tagore had found disagreeable in Kipling's imagination, "our European civilization stands [far higher] than the East, India, or Persia ever dreamed of".

Lawrence's arrogance and contempt in the above statement only ratified Tagore's claim that the chasm between the East and the West was created by the West's unwarranted contempt for the East, which in return generated hatred in the East against the West. His response to such contempt was, "The blindness of contempt is more hopeless than the blindness of ignorance; for contempt kills the light which ignorance merely leaves unignited". Tagore urged the West to overcome its "logic of egoism", ignoble triumphalism, "forcible parasitism" and intentional ignorance, and seek to understand the East in a true spirit of creativity, fellowship and welfare of humanity. He reminded that the British belligerency and its singular passion for power and wealth during the colonial period turned the world into a cauldron of animosities; the way to conquer the world, Tagore said, was not war but active sympathy. In his novel The Home and the World, his protagonist, Nikhil, bursts out against the British atrocities in India as well as the atrocities perpetrated by the Indian nationalist terrorists:

> It was Buddha who conquered the world, not Alexander-this is untrue when stated in dry prose-oh when shall we be able to sing it? When shall all these most intimate truths of the universe overflow the pages of printed books and leap out in a sacred stream like the Ganges from the Gangotri?

However, in spite of the derogatory remarks made by Lukacs and Lawrence, and the attempts to dismiss him as a sentimental alarmist by others, Tagore's assertive denunciation of the Nation proved prophetic with the outbreak of two world wars, costing millions of lives; UK's war in Kenya in the 1950s, to quell the rebels against its colonial rule, costing 150,000 lives; the genocide in Bangladesh by the Pakistani junta in 1970, claiming a toll of three million lives (to name only a few of the gigantic evils perpetrated in the name of the familiar devil, radical nationalism, in the twentieth century), but most importantly, the nuclear arms race that pushed the world to the brink of destruction in the 1960s. The Cuban missile crisis was the most dangerous moment in human history, Chomsky reminds us.

In October 1962, during the height of the crisis, he explains, it was one Soviet submarine officer named Vasili Arkhipov who saved the world by blocking "an order to fire nuclear armed torpedoes on October 27. . . when the submarines were under attack by US destroyers". Thus, ironically, this world of pomp and finery, wealth and power, at its height of crisis, was left to the wisdom of one person; and had Arkhipov been as "insane" as some of the other nationalist chauvinists, the world would have almost surely been extinct now through a major nuclear warfare — if not the world, the Northern Hemisphere.

After humanity was plentifully gorged with the blood of some 50 million people, killed in violent circumstances in the twentieth century, mostly in wars that invoked the nation in one form or another, many had thought that peace and sanity would return to the world, especially since the Cold War was over. But that was not to be. As the world had barely crossed the portal of a new millennium, and stepped into the twenty-first century, it found itself again battered in torrents of blood and locked in a devil dance of destruction.

The "*jihadists*" (by which we refer not only to the radical Islamists but also the ferocious jingoists, who seem equally enthusiastic in violence and to kill innocent civilians with utter abandon like the "terrorists") have struck again and the world has suffered colossal disasters. The horrendous events of 9-11 which caused "the most devastating instant human toll on record, outside of war"; America's military response to 9 11, defying world opinion, with massive coordinated bombings in Afghanistan, which turned "major urban concentrations [in the country] into 'ghost towns'" —

a campaign, in which, the veteran Spanish journalist Miguel Angel Aguilar says, "we were trying to kill mosquitoes with bombs. Innocents were killed and democracy suffered and we are no safer"; America's "pre-emptive/preventive" war in Iraq, which Paul O'Neill painfully explains to Ron Suskind, America started hatching at the very first meeting of the current American President with the National Security Council, on "January 30, ten days after his inauguration" such destructive events, which have changed the world, leaving humanity peering into the abyss of the future, have all been undertaken in the name of national safety and national security, whether it is the pan-Islamic religious nationalism of the militants or secular nationalism of the West.

However, we are not done yet, security of the homeland has not been achieved, as President Bush has thoughtfully declared, "There is no telling how many wars it will take to secure freedom in the homeland". Perhaps respite will come only when the "pious warlords" after all their calculated savagery and sacrifices to the "dark gods of war" will have successfully realised Bertrand Russell's sombre prediction about world peace:

> After ages during which the earth produced harmless trilobites and butterflies, evolution progressed to the point at which it has generated Neroes, Genghis Khans, and Hitlers. This, however, I believe is a passing nightmare; in time the earth will become again incapable of supporting life, and peace will return.

Vision for Nationalism

Benedict Anderson defines the nation as "imagined community" but acknowledges that it is "notoriously difficult to define, let alone to analyse" "Nation, nationality, nationalism". Hugh Seton-Watson maintains, "no 'scientific definition' of the nation can be devised". Ernst Gellner observes that nationalism is an 'invention,' 'fabrication': "Nationalism is not the awakening of nations to self-consciousness: it invents nations where they do not exist". Despite its "mythical" quality, and the difficulties involved in defining it, the phenomenon still enjoys profound political and emotional legitimacy in modern society. Bill Ashcroft et al. affirm that in spite of "all its contentiousness, and the difficulty of theorising it adequately, [nation/nationalism] remains the most implacably powerful force in twentieth century politics".

Nationalism as a political expression, with people sharing a common geographical boundary and some unifying cultural/ political signifier is relatively new, although cultural nationalism has prevailed since the beginning of society. Anderson suggests that the nation as a political institution is the product of European Enlightenment and Industrial Revolution. He argues that the rise of nationalism in Western Europe was made possible by the decline, if not the death, of religious modes of thought, in the wake of the rationalist secularism of the Enlightenment, or the Age of Reason.

The guiding principles of this intellectual movement were the glorification of reason and faith in human dignity, both of which were sufficient to break down the old belief systems that gave centrality to the church and a theocentric worldview. Thus, a more pragmatic and worldly socio political system of nationalism emerged to suit the post-religious, secular world. Anderson explains, "What then was required was a secular transformation of fatality into continuity, contingency into meaning . . . few things were (are) better suited to this end than an idea of nation".

Ernest Gellner, on the other hand, attributes the emergence of nationalism to the rise of industrial-capitalism in the eighteenth and nineteenth centuries. The epochal shift of human society from pre-industrial to industrial economies, he argues, set up the conditions required for the creation of larger social units and economies that would be culturally "homogenous" and cooperative as workforce, thus paving the way for the formation of the more complex and intricate social organisation of the nation-state. Effectively, the expansion of the workforce and the market made the earlier pre industrial, tribal societies and their structures both inadequate and obsolete.

Timothy Brennan examines the role of literature, especially the novel, in the formation of national consciousness during its early period: "the end of the eighteenth and the beginning of the nineteenth centuries". He maintains:

> It was the novel that historically accompanied the rise of nations by objectifying the 'one, yet many' of

> national life, and by mimicking the structures of the nation. . . . But it did more than that. Its manner of presentation allowed people to imagine the special community that the nation was.

Despite literature's such active complicity in the formation of the institution and the global acceptance of nationalism as the only legitimate form of political organisation, India's myriad-minded poet, Rabindranath Tagore — whom Bertrand Russell considered "worthy of the highest honour", and Ezra Pound deemed "greater than any of us" as a poet — shared not an iota of positive sentiment towards the ideology. His foremost objection came from its very nature and purpose as an institution. The very fact that it is a social institution, a mechanical organisation, modelled on certain utilitarian objectives in mind, made it unpalatable to Tagore, who was a champion of creation over construction, imagination over reason and the natural over the artificial and the man-made: "Construction is for a purpose, it expresses our wants; but creation is for itself, it expresses our very beings".

Tagore took the view that since nationalism emerged in the post-religious laboratory of industrial-capitalism, it was only an "organisation of politics and commerce", that brings "harvests of wealth" or "carnivals of materialism", by spreading tentacles of greed, selfishness, power and prosperity, or churning up the baser instincts of mankind, and sacrificing in the process "the moral man, the complete man . . . to make room for the political and commercial man, the man of limited purpose".

Nationalism, according to Tagore, is not "a spontaneous self-expression of man as social being," where human relationships are naturally regulated, "so that men can develop ideals of life in cooperation with one another", but rather a political and commercial union of a group of people, in which they congregate to maximise their profit, progress and power; it is "the organised self-interest of a people, where it is least human and least spiritual". Tagore deemed nationalism a recurrent threat to humanity, because with its propensity for the material and the rational, it trampled over the human spirit and human emotion; it upset man's moral balance, "obscuring his human side under the shadow of soul-less organisation".

Thus, Tagore called into question both the constructed aspect of nationalism, which stifled the innate and instinctive qualities of the human individual, and its overemphasis on the commercial and political aspects, at the expense of man's moral and spiritual qualities. Both of these limitations reduced nationalism to an incomplete, monolithic and unipolar ideology — essentially inadequate for human beings given to an inherent multiplicity and seeming contraries, that needed to be unified and synthesised, through a process of soulful negotiation and striking of an axial line between opposites, to create the whole and wholesome person.

As seen previously, Tagore also found the fetish of nationalism a source of war, hatred and mutual suspicion between nations. In The Home and the World, Nikhil, Tagore's alter ego in the novel, who is patriotic but wouldn't place nation above truth and conscience says, "I am willing to serve my country; but my worship I reserve for Right which is far greater than country. To worship my country as a god is to bring curse upon it".

However, Nikhil's friend, Sandip, a charismatic but unconscionable nationalist, to whom any action in the name of the nation is right, no matter how far it may be from truth or justice, exclaims, "country's needs must be made into a god", and one must "set aside . . . conscience . . . by putting the country in its place". Tagore saw this radical view of Sandip, in which the nation is apotheosised and placed above truth and conscience, as a recipe for disaster. It breeds exclusivism and dogmatism through the Hegelian dichotomous logic of self's fundamental hostility towards the other; thus every nation becomes narcissistic and considers the presence of another a threat to itself; waging war against other nations for its self-fulfilment and self-aggrandisement becomes a justifiable and even "holy" act. Tagore explains:

> The Nation, with all its paraphernalia of power and prosperity, its flags and pious hymns, its blasphemous prayers in the churches, and the literary mock thunders of its patriotic bragging, cannot hide the fact that the Nation is the greatest evil for the Nation, that all its precautions are against it, and any new birth of its fellow in the world is always followed in its mind by the dread of a new peril.

Tagore argued that British colonialism found its justification in the ideology of nationalism, as the coloniser came to India and other rich pastures of the world to plunder and so further the prosperity of their own nation. They were never sincere in developing colonised countries/nations, as to convert their "hunting grounds" into "cultivated fields" would have been contrary to their national interest. Like predators (and nationalism, as we saw above, inherently cultivates a rapacious logic), they thrived by victimising and violating other nations, and never felt deterred in their heinous actions by the principles of love, sympathy or universal fellowship.

The logic is simple but cruel, and is sustained by a privileging norm, that in order to have rich and powerful nations, some nations ought to be left poor and pregnable: "Because this civilization is the civilization of power, therefore it is exclusive, it is naturally unwilling to open its sources of power to those whom it has selected for its purposes for exploitation". By its very nature as an organisation, Tagore argued, nationalism could ill afford any altruism in this regard.

One might think that Tagore's critique of nationalism is a little lofty and far-fetched "too pious" as Pound might have said; his arguments are layered in atavistic spiritualism and romantic idealism. However, much of what Tagore said is intellectually valid and some of it is borne out by contemporary post-colonial criticism. Critics concur that nation is a necessity, it has laboured on behalf of modernity, and it helps to bolster the present civilization; as a political organisation it befits the social and intellectual milieu of present-day society, but they hardly claim its moral authority or its beneficial role in the reinforcement of human virtue.

Critics also view the constructed aspect of nationalism as a weakness in the ideology. It is vulnerable to regressing into more natural social units of clan, tribe and race, or language and religious groups. Its very formative process introduces a self-deconstructing logic in it. The process of formation/invention further makes it a potent site of power discourse; although it is meant to stand for horizontal comradeship, exploitation and inequality remain a daily occurrence in its body, and the nation never speaks of the hopes and aspirations of its entire "imagined community." In conceiving its overarching ideologies it often places the dominant group at the centre, pushing the minority population to the periphery. Thus, instead of a fraternity, it creates a new hierarchy and hegemony within its structure, and exposes the fracture between its rhetoric and reality. Fanon expresses this misgiving, when he says, "National consciousness, instead of being the all-embracing crystallisation of the innermost hopes of the whole people [becomes] a crude and fragile travesty of what it might have been [when] the nation is passed over for the race, and the tribe is preferred to the state".

Several post-colonial critics agree with Tagore's view that nationalism begets a disquisition of intolerance and "othering." Ernest Gellner, Benedict Anderson and Tom Nairn have pointed out the irrationality, prejudice and hatred that nationalism generates, and Leela Gandhi speaks of its attendant racism and loathing, and the alacrity with which citizens are willing to both kill and die for the sake of the nation. I have also pointed out in the introduction of the essay how nationalism is often used as a pretext for terrorism, factional or state, and war.

Sometimes these wars, especially by the rich and powerful nations, are disguised with expressions of noble intent, such as "liberating the people from an evil dictator" and/or "introducing democracy." But such rhetoric is always disingenuous. In a letter to Yone Noguchi, a Japanese writer who had asked for Tagore's moral support for Japan's invasion of China in 1937, in the name of "saving China for Asia", Tagore roundly criticises Noguchi for his naive acceptance of the grotesque rhetoric meant to veil an adventure of greed:

> I was amused to read the recent statement of a Tokyo politician that the military alliance of Japan with Italy and Germany was made for 'highly spiritual and moral reasons' and 'had no materialistic considerations behind it.' Quite so. What is not so amusing is that writers and thinkers should echo such remarkable sentiments that translate military swagger into spiritual bravados.

Thomas Jefferson's observation on the world situation of his day sums up the hypocrisy behind such use of exalted language in war, most tellingly:

> We believe no more in Bonaparte's fighting for the liberties of the seas, than in Great Britain's fighting for the liberties of mankind. The object is the same, to draw to themselves the power, the wealth, and the resources of other nations.

Jefferson's point further helps bolster Tagore's claim that the discourse of nationalism overlaps with the discourse imperialism; the imperialist nations adopt the role of the Lacanian grand Other and seek to inscribe their authority unilaterally over the colonised nations; they are not impelled by the ideology of benevolence towards the colonised countries. Tagore describes them as aggressive people essentially driven by greed; who "go out of their way and spread their coat-tails in other peoples' thoroughfares, claiming indemnity when these are trodden upon".

According to Amy Cesaire, the imperial objective is to "thingify" the colonial subjects, and Fanon suggest that the colonisers are inherently bent upon not only plundering the wealth of the colonised nations but also to rob them of their culture: "By a kind of perverted logic, it turns the past of the oppressed people, and distorts, disfigures, and destroys it". A classic example of this later instance was the introduction of English language in India in 1835 with the view of anglicising a group of Indians who would serve the colonial cause.

Tagore and Indian Nationalism

Tagore was opposed to the idea of the nation; he was even more fiercely opposed to India joining the bandwagon of nationalism. This would compromise India's history and identity as a culture and bring it under the shadow of the West. He warned:

> We, in India, must make up our minds that we cannot borrow other people's history, and that if we stifle our own we are committing suicide. When you borrow things that do not belong to your life, they only serve

> to crush your life. . . . I believe that it does India no good to compete with Western civilization in its own field. . . . India is no beggar of the West.

Tagore was born in 1861, a period during which the nationalist movement in India against the British rule was crystallising and gaining momentum. In 1857, only four years before the poet was born, the first military uprising for self-rule broke out in India. In 1905, the Swadeshi Movement started on Tagore's doorstep, as a response to the British policy of partitioning Bengal. Although apolitical by temperament, Tagore at first was drawn to the movement and started giving lectures and writing patriotic songs with such fervour that Ezra Pound quipped, "Tagore has sung Bengal into a nation".

But soon after, Tagore saw the movement turning violent with the nationalists agitating against innocent civilians who were indifferent to their cause, and especially the Muslims who were in favour of the partition for practical as well as political reasons (the partition gave the Muslims of East Bengal a new capital in Dhaka). A champion of non-violence or Ahimsa, Tagore found it difficult to accept the insanity of the nationalists in their burning of all foreign goods as a mark of non-cooperation, although it was hurting the poor in Bengal who found homemade products more expensive than foreign goods. He was further disheartened to see that many of the impassioned youths turned to the cult of the bomb, hoping to liberate their motherland from the yoke of foreign tyranny by violence and terror. Thus, finally, Tagore withdrew from the movement, when a young Bengali radical, Khudiram Bose (widely regarded a hero in the annals of Bengal), hurled a bomb, killing two innocent British civilians, in 1908.

This sudden withdrawal of Tagore was seen as an act of betrayal by many of the nationalists, but nothing could alter his decision. He would not have anything to do with a movement that was hijacked by the Bengali Bhadroloks (elites) for their vested interest, and that saw the individual through the prism of a giant cause. Tagore's response to his critics was fictionally articulated in both The Home and the World and Four Chapters (both seen as Tagore's profound testament to non-violence). In both the novels, Tagore dramatises how exploitation, violence and killing become ritual acts when the individual sacrifices his/her self to an abstraction, and nationalism is put on a pedestal, sacrificing righteousness and conscience; how the nationalist movements in Bengal and later, during Gandhi's Satyagraha Movement, in India, often veered into terrorist movements because of the excessiveness of the nationalist leaders, and sometimes their tendency to abuse the movement for personal political gain, as, for example, do both Sandip and Indranath, respectively in The Home and the World and Four Chapters. Both Sandip and Indranath, begin as charismatic nationalist figures, but gradually become self-obsessed and vainglorious in their cause, losing sight of their dharma of dispassionate, disinterested action (as advised by Krishna to Arjuna in The Bhagavad Gita), and use violence as a fetish for personal gain; thus their early optimism is replaced later by a sense of *nada*.

Tagore and Gandhi were on friendly terms, and in many ways Tagore was a precursor of Gandhi; it was Tagore who gave the title "*Mahatma*" (the great soul) to Gandhi, and in return Gandhi dubbed Tagore "*Gurudev*" (the venerable teacher) and greeted him as "poet of the world." Romain Rolland once described a meeting between Tagore and Gandhi as one between "a philosopher and an apostle, a St. Paul and a Plato". Yet Tagore and Gandhi never saw eye to eye on the way towards India's future, as Tagore stubbornly refused to support Gandhi's nationalist movement against the British rule. Unlike Gandhi, Tagore believed that political freedom and attainment of a nationalist identity by driving the British out was not the right solution for India's problems; "I am not for thrusting off Western civilization and becoming segregated in our independence.

Let us have a deep association", he said in his characteristic hopefulness. In a letter to an American lawyer Myron H. Phelps, he rhetorically stated, "Must we not have that greater vision of humanity which will impel us to shake off the fetters that shackle our individual life before we begin to dream of national freedom?". Tagore took the view that what India needed was not a "blind revolution" or the "miracle of [political] freedom [built] upon the quicksand of social slavery", "but steady purposeful education", or an evolution from within; "what India most needed was constructive work coming from within herself," he argued in

"Nationalism in India". He believed that a "thought impetus" similar to the one experienced by Europe during the Renaissance that broke up "the feudal system and the tyrannical conventionalism of the Latin Church" was the right remedy for a country languishing on the "dry sand-bed of dead customs".

Tagore maintained that India's immediate problems were social and cultural and not political. India is the world in miniature, this is where the races and the religions have met; therefore she must constantly strive to resolve her "burden of heterogeneity," by evolving out of "these warring contradictions a great synthesis". First and foremost, India must address the caste issue. The caste system has become too rigid and taken a hypnotic hold on the mind of the people; what was once meant to introduce social order by accommodating the various racial groups in India, has now become a gigantic system of cold-blooded repression. India ought to come out of this social stagnation by educating the people out of their trance; only when the immovable walls of society were removed, or made flexible, will India regain her vitality and dynamism as a society and find true freedom. What is the purpose of political freedom when the elites in society are exploiting the lower classes, especially the untouchables so ruthlessly?

In his short story, "Purification," he exposes the absurdity of Gandhi's Satyagraha Movement and the hypocrisy of the Indian nationalists by showing how selfish and superficial the nationalists were in their quest for freedom; they were fervently opposed to the British oppression, but oppressed the poor as well as the untouchables themselves; they wanted dignity and respect but wouldn't allow the same to their less fortunate brethren.

Kalika, a young wife and a nationalist dogmatist, who badgers her husband, a moderate but sensitive person, for not being fervent enough, refuses to come to the aid of an old municipal sweeper, who is being assaulted by a group of orthodox Hindus for accidentally touching someone in the crowd, just because he is an untouchable. Such "mendicant politics" that fails to tear down the customary barriers between people, was of little worth to Tagore. His hope was that if India could establish equanimity between the various races and religious groups, through a basis of social cooperation and regeneration of the spirit, then she could hold herself as a model of unity for the rest of the world.

Tagore emphasises racial and religious unity persistently in his writings. In a beautiful hymn to India, entitled *Bharat Tirtha* (The Indian Pilgrimage), he urges all Indians to unite across race, class and religion, shedding their differences, to fulfil the noble destiny of their homeland, standing above the whirlwind of dusty politics:

> Come, O Aryans, come, non-Aryans, Hindus and Mussulmans-
>
> Come today, O Englishmen, come, Oh come, Christians!
>
> Come, O Brahmin, cleansing your mind
>
> Join hands with all-
>
> Come, O Downtrodden, let the burden
>
> Of every insult be forever dispelled.
>
> Make haste and come to Mother's coronation, the vessel auspicious
>
> Is yet to be filled
>
> With sacred water sanctified by the touch of all
>
> By the shore of the sea of Bharat's Great Humanity!

Tagore was of the view that such unity and plurality of consciousness could be achieved only through proper education of the people, eradication of poverty through modernisation and cultivation of freedom of thought and imagination; "Freedom of mind is needed for the reception of truth", he said. It was education, and not adulation for the *Charka* (the spinning wheel) that Gandhi suggested, which could liberate India from the tyranny of the past and the towering misery of unreasoned, unbridled orthodoxy. When Gandhi chastised Tagore for his disregard for the Charka as well as Swaraj saying, "Every one must spin. Let Tagore spin like the others. Let him burn his foreign clothes; that is his duty today. God will take care of the morrow", Tagore respectfully replied, "The charka does not require anyone to think; one simply turns the wheel of the antiquated invention endlessly, using the minimum of judgement and stamina".

To break the spell of stasis through intellectual/cultural revival and find freedom, India ought to keep itself open to the West and not become insular from the rest of the world through the appropriation of a provincial nationalism; "We of the Orient should learn from the Occident . . . to say that it is wrong to cooperate with the West is to encourage the worst form of provincialism and can produce nothing but intellectual indigence". The West could in fact help liberate India from its "mind-forg'd manacles" and lift the dead weight of tradition from its soul through a constructive engagement and inducement of energy, strength, elasticity, tolerance, resolve and courage among its people-qualities that the West possessed but India lacked. Tagore's vision of a free India-free from the fetters of materialism, nationalism as well as religious and racial orthodoxy-actively seeking a common destiny with the rest of mankind, constantly evolving towards a global society, is most ardently and expressly expressed in the following poem in Gitanjali, written in the form of a supplication:

> Where the mind is without fear and the head is held high;
>
> Where knowledge is free;
>
> Where the world has not been broken up into fragments by narrow domestic walls;
>
> Where words come from the depth of truth;
>
> Where tireless striving stretches its arms towards perfection;
>
> Where the clear stream of reason has not lost its way into the dreary desert sand of dead habit;
>
> Where the mind is led forward by thee into ever widening thought and action-
>
> Into that heaven of freedom, my Father, let my country awake.

Tagore could perhaps be faulted for impracticality; his vision for India was too sublime and unrealisable in an imperfect world. His wish that the West could help India in her mission was also impracticable, especially since he knew that the West came to the subcontinent, as he recounted in his essay "East and West," "not with the imagination and sympathy to create and unite, but with a shock of passion-passion for power and wealth". West had its own axe to grind; in spite of their "superior force of character", they were not interested in the "nest-building of truth" but in money, machine and matter. Yet his transcendent thought provides a testament to his noble and beautiful mind, and strikes a cord in the moral person in each of us.

Moreover, the on-going violence in the subcontinent vindicates his position. India has since been broken up into three countries: India, Pakistan and Bangladesh; ten million people were made homeless in the aftermath of the independence of India and Pakistan in 1947, one million of which also lost their lives in inter-religious riots; two major wars have been fought in the subcontinent, with border skirmishes and threats of further wars, including a nuclear war, casting a shadow of desperation on the people; several riots have also broken out between the Hindus and the Muslims, claiming thousands of lives. India still remains a poor country, with political corruption rife, and plights of the downtrodden a daily reality.

Tagore's prediction that joining the bandwagon of nationalism would make India a beggar of the West has also come true. Although India is a free country now (ironically broken up into three fragments), the appropriation of nationalist ideology has erased the sense of India's difference as a society, capable of standing on its own; forging of links with the West on unequal terms (since India has merely copied the Western thoughts and has nothing to offer of her own) has allowed neo-colonialist controls to operate over the country both explicitly and implicitly, spelling political and cultural doom for its people. Finally, India's assumption of a separate identity by driving the British out has also dealt a blow to the possible realisation of Tagore's vision for "one world," at least for the time being, since anti-colonial nationalism also carries the seeds of provincialism and cultural particularism.

Tagore's Vision of Non-national Neo-universalism

He was not only the first Asian to receive the Nobel Prize for Literature (in 1913) 'but also only the second writer in English to receive it'. Fondly dubbed 'Gurudev' (venerable teacher) by Mahatma Gandhi (whose title 'Mahatma,' or 'the great soul' was suitably given by Tagore) and 'eagle-sized lark' by Romain Rolland, his exquisite poetic power and gifted musical sensibility made him the author of the national anthems of three countries - Bangladesh, Sri Lanka and India - a feat still unmatched in history. He was knighted by King George V of England in 1915 (which he renounced in protest of the heinous massacre at Jalianwala Bagh, Amritsar in 1919) and awarded an honorary doctorate by Oxford in 1940, for which Oxford had to travel to the poet's doorstep because of his ill health.

When Tagore was alive, he played on the heartstrings of many with his wizard fingers and breathtaking creativity. On reading Tagore's Gitanjali, a volume of poetry that earned him the Nobel Prize for Literature, W. B. Yeats was so moved by the 'simplicity' and 'abundance' of his work that he instantaneously hailed Tagore as founder of a 'new Indian Renaissance,' and said in an extraordinary tribute to the poet:

> [The poems of] Rabindranath Tagore have stirred my blood as nothing has for years ... These lyrics ... display in their thought a world I have dreamed all my life ... Rabindranath Tagore ... is so abundant, so spontaneous, so daring in his passion, so full of surprise, because he is doing something which has never seemed strange, unnatural, or in need of defence. These verses will not die in little well-printed books upon ladies' tables ... or be carried about by students at the university to be laid aside when the work of life begins, but as the generations pass, travellers will hum them on the highway and men rowing upon rivers. Lovers, while they await one another, shall find, in murmuring them, this love of God a magic gulf wherein their own more bitter passion may bathe and renew its youth.

Tagore's reputation far exceeded the boundary of the literary-cultural world. He was in the company of the likes of Russell, Einstein, Mussolini and Gandhi, and they all held him in the highest esteem. Albert Schweitzer called him 'the Goethe of India' and Romain Rolland described a meeting between him and Gandhi as a 'meeting between... a St. Paul and a Plato'. So why has Tagore's reputation suffered since his death? Why is the poet who was considered a literary titan in his time, a supreme symbol of India's culture and spirit, now so widely neglected? Is it because of some change of taste in poetry? As Tagore has aptly said, 'poetry is... a matter of taste'. Or is it because Tagore was too provincial a poet to retain a universal appeal after his death?

Perhaps the reasons are not so much poetical but ideological and philosophical, for Tagore was a poet-philosopher and the world simply chose not to tread the path that he sought to pave. Tagore's vision of universal human unity, of 'living bonds in society'; of 'spontaneous expression of man as a social being'; of 'wholeness and wholesomeness of human ideals', proved too good for a world that believed in the 'bondage of the dust,' the tyranny of matter, machine and money, and in the fetish of nationalism. According to Tagore, such 'ideals' replace the true identity of the self with a blend of corporate identity, rooted not in truth, beauty, sympathy or moral welfare of mankind but in a 'spirit of conflict and conquest' and a whirlwind of greed, jealousy and suspicion, reducing mankind, Tagore poignantly suggests, to 'a pack of predatory creatures' or 'band of robbers'.

Critics are often apologetic when discussing Tagore, as though it is for some inherent weakness that he is neglected now; for instance, his lack of a proper understanding of the world, or his overly mystical tone, which suggests a blindness to the realities of life. But such apologies are unnecessary — and Tagore is never in 'need of defence,' as Yeats rightfully said — since he stood for the totality of life, for the physical as well as the spiritual; for the real and the ideal; and for the values of truth, compassion and justice that the world will reckon its own, as soon as it chooses to break the current hypnotic allure of money and materialism, and rise from the dungeon of illusion. We believe that, given the present crisis in the world, in which nations, fiercely locked in a devil-dance of destruction, are perpetuating cycles of retribution and retaliation, and hollow hysteria between fanatics of nation and fanatics of religion is taking its toll on innocent civilians everywhere, Tagore's alternative vision based on peace, harmony and the spiritual unity of humankind has become more relevant than ever. What the world needs at this juncture of widespread agitation and unrest is Tagore's healing message and the restoration of his blissful, paradisiacal imagination, imbued with teachings of simplicity, self-restraint and ahimsa, or non-violence. Remembering Tagore's advice in the 1915 lecture, "Nationalism in the West," which was delivered as the West was engrossed in the savage bloodbath of World War I, may help to instil some sense as our planet grapples afresh with the global ramifications of recent disastrous events that opened the doors to a new pandemonium:

> Be more good, more just, more true in your relation to man, control your greed, make your life wholesome in its simplicity and let your consciousness of the divine in humanity be more perfect in its expression.

Tagore's vision of human unity and equality, and his critique of modern civilization, with its twin principles of materialism and nationalism, is recurrent in all his works. His vision emerges most explicitly and powerfully, however, in several of his lectures and addresses, including "My Life," "My School," "My Religion," "Civilization and Progress," "Construction versus Creation," "Nationalism in India," "Nationalism in Japan," "Nationalism in the West," "International Relations," "The Voices of Humanity," and "The Realisation of the Infinite," as well as in his novels The Home and the World (*Ghare Baire*) and Four Chapters (*Char Adhyay*), the poems of Gitanjali and "The Sunset of the Century." In each of these works, Tagore most engagingly and energetically investigates what has gone wrong with the world and where the remedy lies.

Tagore was opposed to modern civilization for its lack of completeness; its fragmented and fragmenting nature; its undue bias towards the physical, the intellectual and the practical; its predilection for the material rather than the moral progress of humankind; and its celebration of bloodless policies and canned, constructed ideas, in lieu of a fearless striving for truth, creativity and imagination. Modern civilization, Tagore believed, is built on the law of necessity rather than the law of truth; the law of might instead of the law of right; and of self-interest and success, rather than perfection in humanity. In "Civilization and Progress," he explains:

> Civilization cannot merely be a growing totality of happenings that by chance have assumed a particular shape and tendency which we consider to be excellent. It must be the expression of some guiding moral force which we have evolved in our society for the object of attaining perfection ... A civilization remains healthy and strong as long as it contains in its centre some creative ideal that binds its members in a rhythm of relationship. It is a relationship which is beautiful and not merely utilitarian. When the creative ideal which is dharma gives place to some overmastering passion, then this civilization bursts into conflagration.

In other words, for its absence of a moral centre, this civilization is, to Tagore, a civilization of adhrama, in which, as he explains using a quote from the Upanishads, 'man prospers, gains what appears desirable, conquers enemies, but perishes at the root'. It both shoots out of and caters to the baser instincts of the individual and has nothing to do with that innate spiritual power that ennobles us and brings us together as one large family living in the reality and unity of one ineffable God. Thus, progress, as it is understood in the modern civilization, is nothing but a millstone on the human spirit, bringing with it dehumanisation, despiritualisation, deformity and doom.

Tagore was essentially a religious thinker and he always upheld the primacy of the soul. In "My Religion," he emphasised, 'Man's religion is his innermost truth.... One's religion is at the source of one's being'. However, he was not religious in the traditional sense and was least concerned with the practices of the communal religion he belonged to, i.e. Hinduism. Rather, he was influenced by the teachings of the Upanishads and, like the English Romantics and American Transcendentalists before him, came to believe in its pantheistic teachings. In this regard, his firsthand influence was his father, a leading member of a religious movement called the Brahmo Samaj who, Tagore explains, believed in 'a strict monotheism based upon the teachings of the Upanishads'.

The Upanishadic God is, paradoxically, both transcendent and immanent; both present and absent in His creation. He is a Personality who does not dissociate Himself fully from His creation but recurrently manifests Himself in all created objects, making this world a 'living expression of the spirit'. In Svetasatara Upanishad, for example, God is described thus: O Brahman Supreme! Formless art thou, and yet (Though the reason none knows) Thou bringest forth many forms; Thou bringest them forth, and then Withdrawest them to thyself. Fill us with thoughts of thee! Thou art the fire, Thou art the sun, Thou art the air, Thou art the moon, Thou art the starry firmament: Thou art the waters - thou, The creator of all. God is also present in every human heart: 'Self-luminous is Brahman, ever present in the hearts of all.... In him exists all that is'.

The Upanishadic faith in a living God, a 'deep abiding creative force' as Tagore describes it — a force that expresses itself in the living objects of the world, including human begins — runs through all of his works and forms the cornerstone of his visvovod, or vision of universal human unity. His argument is simple: since God dwells in every human heart, we are innately inseparable, and to realise God we must therefore overcome the visible differences between us as individuals and learn to treat one another — in spite of caste, creed and race — with love and utmost respect. In "My Life," Tagore explains:

> In the night we stumble over things and become acutely conscious of their individual separateness, but the day reveals the great unity which embraces them. And the man, whose inner vision is bathed in an illumination of his consciousness, at once realises the spiritual unity reigning supreme over all differences of race, and his mind no longer awkwardly stumbles over individual facts of separateness in the human world, accepting them as final; he realises that

> peace is in the inner harmony which dwells in truth, and in any outer adjustments; that beauty carries an eternal assurance of our spiritual relationship to reality, which waits for its perfection in the response of our love.

In "International Relations," a lecture delivered in Japan, in 1923, he further affirms that:

> The Kingdom of Heaven is here on this earth. It is there, where we realise our best relations with our fellow-beings, where there is no mutual suspicion and misunderstanding — there is the Kingdom of Heaven, in the spirit of comradeship and love.

Tagore's pantheistic and anthropocentric worldview is exquisitely dramatised, in the following poem, through a series of dialogues between God and His devotee, which he used as an epigraph to his essay "My Religion":

In the deep of the night, the man averse to worldly pleasures said:

'I shall leave home to seek my desired God.

Who is it that has kept me here, tied?'

God said, 'It is I,' but the man paid no heed.

Clasping the sleeping infant to her breast

the loving wife lay at one end of the bed in deep slumber.

The man said, 'what are you all — the trickery of illusion?'

'It is I,' said God. No one paid any heed.

Leaving his bed the man called 'Where are Thou, my Lord?'

God said, 'I am here!' Still His words were not heard.

The child cried out in his sleep hugging his mother;

God said, 'Turn back.' But His words were lost.

God heaved a sigh and said, 'Alas! Deserting me,

whither goes my devotee to find me?'

This view of a divine presence in the human individual, which forms the basis of universal unity, contains clear overtones of Emerson. Like Tagore, Emerson, as mentioned earlier, was also much influenced by the teachings of the Upanishads. In "The American Scholar," for example, Emerson comments:

> The old fable covers a doctrine ever new and sublime; that there is one Man, — present to all particular men only partially, or through one faculty; and that you must take the whole society to find the whole man. Man is not a farmer, or a professor, or an engineer, but he is all. Man is priest, and scholar, and statesman, and producer, and soldier ... man is one ... It is one soul which animates all men.

To both Emerson and Tagore, soul was at the centre as well as the circumference of life; soul, in their view, is what makes us wholesome and whole; and, as they saw it, the remedy to human deformity in modern society, in its carnival of materialism and perpetual pursuit of wealth, was, as Emerson put it, 'first, soul, and second soul, and evermore, soul'. To both, the doctrine of the soul was anything but outmoded or ancient. To Emerson it was 'ever new,' and so to Tagore, who announced affirmatively in "My Life," 'The impertinence of material things is extremely old. The revelation of spirit in man is truly modern: I am on its side, for I am modern'.

The Isha Upanishad says, 'To darkness are they doomed who worship only the body, and to greater darkness they who worship only the spirit'. In the Katha Upanishad it is stated, 'What is within us is also without. What is without is also within. He who sees difference between what is within and what is without goes evermore from death to death'. Tagore inherited this Upanishadic 'double consciousness,' which calls for a recurrent synthesis of body and soul, physical and spiritual, mind and matter. As he maintains in "Construction versus Creation," 'Life is a continual process of synthesis'. In spite of his cardinal faith in the cult of the soul, he was not disdainful of the material and practical side of life. He knew that body and spirit, visible and invisible, within and without are interdependent for their mutual realisation — they are one and the same, and one is not without the other. Like

Emerson, he believed that 'Human life is made up of two elements, power and form, and proportion must be invariably kept if we have it sweet and sound'; and, like Whitman, he was an 'arbiter of the diverse' who sought to knit "the old knot of contrariety". In "My Religion," Tagore comments, 'I am not in favour of rejecting anything, for I am only complete with the inclusion of everything. I want to accept all excluding nothing, for it is I, my friend, that waits outside to meet me!' This is his inclusive, multilateral ideology; he was realistic enough not to look for the soul outside the body, or for God outside nature and the world. In "Voice of Humanity," he explains:

> I do not cry down the material world. I fully realise that this is the nurse and the cradle of the Spirit. By achieving the Infinite in the heart of the material world you have made this world more generous than it ever was.

The poem that was quoted earlier (In the deep of the night...), also testifies to this view, where God urges that his devotee need not seek Him outside the daily realities of life but in the midst of everyday happenings. He should attend to his crying child and his lonely, affectionate wife in order to realise God and his own self; only by attending to the practical affairs of life and bestowing love upon his family can he pacify his thirst for God.

Contrary to Tagore's inclusivism and multilateralism, balance and equilibrium, modern civilization, he suggests, thrives on a partial and unilateral outlook. It is totally indignant of the moral and the spiritual side of life, of beauty and truth, of love and sympathy, of 'the music of soul' and the great rhythm of 'symphony' that lies 'at the very heart of the world'. It aspires solely and shamelessly to a life of material fulfilment and bodily comfort. Instead of goodness, it champions greed; instead of self-sacrifice, self-aggrandisement; instead of giving, possessing; instead of spiritual human unity, collective worldliness; instead of moral freedom, material bondage; instead of magnanimity, vindictiveness; instead of being, becoming. It replaces feelings, spontaneity and imagination with a bloodless, mechanical logic, based on the principles of usefulness and need. It looks upon the world like a grammarian who is singularly absorbed in the functional side of language in the study of a poem, instead of appreciating the full poem in its rhythm, harmony and meaning. Its interest ranges between the human stomach and the human head, leaving out the heart where the soul dwells, giving rise to a culture of mere production and consumption, buying and selling, pomp and pageantry, with no peace, understanding and amity in sight for the human race.

If civilization is a site of contention for Tagore, so is the nation, which he considers as the main institutional/political machinery through which the current materialistic and capitalistic civilization manifests and fulfils itself. Tagore was born at a time when nationalist movement in India against the British Raj was gaining ground. The Sepoy Mutiny of 1857, which was the first organised uprising by the Indian soldiers against their colonisers, took place only four years before the poet was born.

In 1905, the Swadeshi Movement (swadeshi meaning, literally: of one's own country — buying local products and boycotting foreign goods, especially the British) broke out at the very door steps of the poet, when the British, in keeping with their policy of divide and rule, partitioned Bengal, an Indian province inhabited by the same Bengali speaking people for centuries, into two: East Bengal (presently Bangladesh) and West Bengal. Initially, Tagore was infuriated by the British injustice and insanity in this action, and became actively involved in the Swadeshi Movement, writing patriotic songs to unite and inspire the people against British oppression, with such fury that Ezra Pound quipped, 'Tagore has sung Bengal into a nation'.

Soon after, he withdrew from the movement, never to have anything to do with nationalism again, except to launch a systematic diatribe against it in a series of lectures and essays, most prominently, "Nationalism in India," "Nationalism in Japan" and "Nationalism in the West." His departure from the Swadeshi Movement of 1905 made him vulnerable to wild criticisms from many of his contemporaries and compatriots, to which Tagore responded through his novel The Home and the World, published in 1915 — a political allegory that dramatises the writer's pacifist, universalist ideology vis-à-vis the nationalism of Realpolitik, in which Radhakrishnan poignantly capsulised, 'self-interest is the end; brute force, the means; conscience is taboo'. Even Gandhi's repeated urgings, during his Satyagraha movements that eventually brought independence to India, in 1947, from cruel and conniving British rule, failed to persuade Tagore to return to the fold of nationalism or reinstate his faith in the idea of the nation.

Nationalism is no doubt a deeply ingrained idea in the modern imagination. Anderson suggests that it is 'the most universally legitimate value in the political life of our time'. Bill Ashcroft et al. are of the view that in spite of 'all its contentiousness, and the difficulty of theorising it adequately, [nation/nationalism] remains the most implacably powerful force in twentieth century politics'.

Despite its dominance and universal acceptance as a political institution, the idea of the nation is of course relatively new. In 1882, when Tagore was still a young writer, the French Orientalist, Ernest Renan, in an address at Sorbonne, "What is a Nation?," felt it necessary to explain the origins of the idea to his audience because of its relative obscurity:

> Nations... are something fairly new in history. Antiquity was unfamiliar with them; Egypt, China and ancient Chaldea were in no way nations. They were flocks led by a Son of the Sun or by a Son of Heaven. Neither in Egypt nor in China were there citizens as such. Classical antiquity had republics, municipal kingdoms, confederates of local republics and Empires, yet it can hardly be said to have had nations in our understanding of the term.

So, what is the nation? How and when did it come about? What are Tagore's objections to it? How justified is he in his fury against the nation? Why did he consider it a 'menace' to mankind and spurn it as 'a cruel epidemic of evil... sweeping over the human world of the present age and eating into its moral fibre'? Why did he castigate it as a source of human diminishment, war and carnage, as he did with utmost ferocity in "The Sunset of the Century," a poem written on the last day of the nineteenth century, even before he was drawn into the Swadeshi Movement of 1905 and subsequently withdraw from it as a result of a growing sense of frustration and disillusionment? Here are the opening lines of the poem as a preview to the intensity of Tagore's outrage against nationalism:

> The last sun of the century sets amidst the blood-red clouds of the West and the whirlwind of hatred.
>
> The naked passion of the self-love of Nations, in its drunken delirium of greed, is dancing to the clash of steel and howling verses of vengeance.
>
> The hungry self of the Nation shall burst in a violence of fury from its own shameless feeding.
>
> For it has made the world its food.

Nation is a socio-cultural-political formation — an 'imagined community,' as Benedict Anderson has described it — of a group of people, living within a certain geographical boundary, with either a unifying cultural signifier, such as language, as in the case of linguistic nationalism of Europe, or certain shared collective values and overarching ideologies, but no inherently homogenising signifier as, for example, in 'Creole nationalism.'

As an institution, it is of European origin and its provenance can be traced in European political and social heritage. Critics suggest that the nation is a product of the European Enlightenment and the Industrial Revolution. Benedict Anderson argues that the rise of nationalism in Western Europe was made possible by the decline, if not the death, of religious modes of thought, in the wake of the rationalist secularism of Enlightenment, or the Age of Reason.

The guiding principles of this intellectual movement were the glorification of reason and faith in human dignity, both of which were instrumental in breaking down old belief systems, which gave centrality to the church and the theocentric worldview, and gave rise to a more pragmatic and worldly socio-political system of the nation, that would suit the new post-religious, secular world, or the godless expanse of what Anderson describes as 'homogenous empty time'. Anderson explains, 'What was then required, [following the decline of cosmological consciousness] was a secular transformation of fatality into continuity, contingency into meaning ... few things were better suited to this end than an idea of the nation'.

Ernst Gellner attributes the emergence of nationalism to the rise of industrialism, or capitalist economies, in the eighteenth and nineteenth centuries. The epochal shift of human society from pre-industrial to industrial economies, he argues, set up the conditions required for the creation of larger social units and economies that would also be culturally 'homogenous' and cooperative as a workforce, thus paving the way for the formation of the more complex and intricate social organisation of the nation-state. Effectively, the expansion of the workforce and the market made the earlier pre-industrial, tribal societies and their structures both inadequate and redundant.

Tagore's objections to nation/nationalism lie in its very nature and purpose as an institution. The fact that it is a social construction, a mechanical organisation, modelled with certain utilitarian objectives in mind, made it unpalatable to Tagore, who always valued creation over construction, imagination over reason, 'expression' over want, natural and organic over the man-made and contrived. In Tagore's view, 'Construction is for a purpose, it expresses our wants; but creation is for itself, it expresses our very beings'. He believed that the nation as a formation, based on needs and wants rather than truth and love, could not contribute much to man's moral fulfilment or to the dignity of human beings. To Tagore, race was a more natural, and therefore acceptable, social unit than the nation and he envisioned a world where races would live together in amity, keeping their 'distinct characteristics but all attached to the stem of humanity by the bond of love'.

Tagore was of the view that since nationalism emerged in the post-religious laboratory of industrial-capitalism, it is but an 'organisation of politics and commerce', that brings 'harvests of wealth' by spreading tentacles of greed, selfishness, power and prosperity, and sacrificing in the process, 'the moral man, the complete man... to make room for the political and the commercial man, the man of limited purpose'. Nationalism, Tagore expressed, is not 'a spontaneous self-expression of man as social being,' where human relationships are naturally regulated, 'so that men can develop ideals of life in cooperation with one another', but rather a political and commercial union of a group of people, in which they come together to maximise their profit, progress and power. Tagore dismissed nationalism as 'the organised self-interest of a people, where it is least human and least spiritual'. He saw it as a recurrent threat to humanity because it trampled over the human spirit and 'upset man's moral balance, obscuring his human side under the shadow of soul-less organisation'.

Tagore also found the fetish nationalism a source of war, hatred, mutual suspicion between nations and militarism. As Sandip argues in The Home and the World, 'country's needs must be made into a god' and one must 'set aside... conscience... by putting the country in its place'. This deification of the nation, where it is made to occupy the place of god and conscience, breeds exclusivism, fanaticism, cultural particularism, paranoia and xenophobia, thus every nation considering another a threat to its existence and waging war against it for self-fulfilment and self-aggrandisement, a justifiable act. Tagore explains:

> The Nation, with all its paraphernalia of power and prosperity, its flags and pious hymns, its blasphemous prayers in the churches, and the literary mock thunders of its patriotic bragging, cannot hide the fact that the Nation is the greatest evil for the Nation, that all its precautions are against it, and any new birth of its fellow in the world is always followed in its mind by the dread of a new peril.

Tagore argued that British colonialism also found its justification in the ideology of the nation as the British came to India and other rich pastures of the world only to plunder and so prosper their own nation. They were never interested in developing the countries of occupation, as it would contribute little to their national cause to turn their 'hunting grounds' into 'cultivated fields'. Like predators, they thrived by victimising and looting other nations and never felt deterred by love, sympathy, fellowship, or humanity in perpetrating heinous crimes for the sake of their nation. In other words, in Tagore's view, there is an inherent discourse of victimisation/othering in the discourse of nationalism - in order to have rich and powerful nations, some nations ought be left poor and pregnable: 'Because this civilization is the civilization of power, therefore it is exclusive, it is naturally unwilling to open its sources of power to those whom it has selected for its purposes of exploitation'.

Of course, Tagore's critique of nationalism might seem a little lofty and farfetched — 'too pious,' as Pound might have said — but much of it is intellectually valid and some of it is borne out by contemporary post-colonial criticism. Critics, for example, hardly ascribe the nation with any moral authority but emphasise its practical necessity, its legitimacy on the ground that it has laboured on behalf of modernity, an outcome of the overlapping discourses of Reason, Modernity and History that serves as an underpinning to modern civilization.

In the view of Leela Gandhi, 'nationalism is the only form of political organisation which is appropriate to the social and intellectual condition of the modern world'. She does not, however, suggest how beneficial it is from a human point of view, how much it contributes to the moral and spiritual fulfilment of human beings. Interestingly, that does not seem to be part of the contemporary discourse, something that Tagore was so preoccupied with; modern discourse is monocular in its acceptance of progress, civilization and modernity as a material and intellectual process only, and not both material and moral, or intellectual as well as spiritual — precisely the criticism that Tagore, a multilateral thinker, directed at the current unilineal civilization.

Critics also view the constructed aspect of nationalism as a weakness in the ideology. They believe that nations are profoundly unstable formations and are always likely to regress into more natural social units of clan, tribe, and race, or language and religious groups; that this structural vulnerability, or self-deconstructing discourse, is the inevitable consequence of its being a social construction. The process of formation/invention of the nation further makes it a potent site of power discourse, as the signifiers of homogeneity/overarching ideologies in creating the myth of nationhood almost always fail to represent the diversity of the actual national community that they profess to represent, and express and consolidate instead the interests of the dominant group(s) of people, thus creating a new hierarchy, hegemony, domination and exclusion within the structures of the nation. Fanon describes this as one of the principle dangers of nationalism, especially in the post-colonial societies, where nationalism is a derivative discourse and is often faced with additional problems:

> National consciousness, instead of being the all-embracing crystallisation of the innermost hopes of the whole people ... [becomes] a crude and fragile travesty of what it might have been ... [when] the nation is passed over for the race, and the tribe is preferred to the state.

Critics furthermore concur with Tagore's arguments that nationalism breeds xenophobia and violence, and contains a discourse of binarism, which perpetuates the process of victimising and othering of nations by one another. It is simply horrifying to see the gruesome violence and number of deaths that have taken place in recent times in the name of the nation, whether in Chechnya, Russia, Afghanistan or the USA, and the alacrity with which citizens are willing both to kill and to die for the sake of their nations.

In some instances, the fanaticism and irrationality that nationalism generates is no less than the religious fanaticism that preoccupies some people in the underdeveloped parts of the world, countries that are not yet considered part of the elite league of nations, and where, in some instances, so-called civilization and modernity have not yet travelled. Gellner, Anderson and Tom Nairn have pointed out the irrationality, prejudice, hatred, sentimentality, collective egoism and aggression that nationalism generates, and Leela Gandhi explains it in the following words:

> East or West, we are now aware of the xenophobia, racism and loathing which attends the rhetoric of [national/cultural] particularism. Nationalism has become the popular pretext for contemporary disquisitions of intolerance, separating Croatians and Serbians, Greeks and Macedonians, Estonians and Russians, Slovaks and Czechs, Armenians and Azerbaijanis, Israelis and Palestinians, Hindus and Muslims.

Were Leela to write her book more recently, she might have included in her list the new strained relationships that have evolved in the wake of the most tragic and repugnant events of 9/11 and the Bali massacre; and as the monstrous, menacing, satanic figure of neo-imperialism emerges from the spiritus mundi and threatens to engulf the world in a suicidal conflagration.

Tagore is astute in equating the imperial discourse with the discourse of nationalism and asserting the process of othering colonised nations by the Lacanian grande-autre, the great Other, or the colonising Other, to fulfil its imperial ego. A nation can construct itself only by constructing its others in such a way as to confirm its own reality. Thus, every nation is given to an inherent discourse of self and other, each finding its identity by positing itself against the other, thereby making each potentially an enemy of the other. This vindicates Tagore's statement, quoted earlier, 'that the Nation is the greatest evil for the Nation, that all its precautions are against it, and any new birth of its fellow in the world is always followed in its mind by the dread of a new peril'.

If nations are given to a binary relationship, so are the coloniser and the colonised. The business of creating an Empire is a business of creating the enemy, of drawing the opposition that must exist, in order that the Empire might define itself against those it colonises/excludes/marginalises. A colonising nation can never be benevolent to the colonised nation - it is there to ascribe its authority on the 'mastered' subjects through a discourse of power, and plunder them of their wealth and culture, like 'predatory creatures,' using Tagore's phrases, prowling through 'its hunting grounds,' which they would never like to convert 'into cultivated fields'. As Amy Cesaire starkly put it 'colonisation = "thingification"'. Or as Fanon has more elaborately stated:

> Colonialism is not satisfied merely with holding a people in its grip and emptying the native's brain of all form and content. By a kind of perverted logic, it turns the past of the oppressed people, and distorts, disfigures, and destroys it.

Tagore was intensely opposed to India joining the bandwagon of nationalism. It would compromise India's history and identity as a culture and bring her under the shadow of the West. In "Nationalism in India," Tagore cautioned:

> We, in India, must make up our minds that we cannot borrow other people's history, and that if we stifle our own we are committing suicide. When you borrow things that do not belong to your life, they only serve to crush your life ... I believe that it does India no good to compete with Western civilization in its own field ... India is no beggar of the West.

Tagore's warnings have come true because although India has attained freedom from the British Raj by appropriating the coloniser's own political discourse, thus using the master's tools to dismantle the master's house, it has ironically made the country follow the destiny that the West has thrust on her. The incorporation of the Western model of nationalism has erased the sense of difference of India as a society, capable of standing on its own, and created linkages that now allow neo-colonialist controls to operate over her both explicitly and implicitly, thus effectively reducing her to a 'beggar of the West.'

Tagore's lectures on nationalism drew many angry responses, even from those of kindred spirit, such as D. H. Lawrence, who spitefully declared Tagore, 'horribly decadent and reverting to all forms of barbarisms in all sorts of ugly ways' and denounced the 'wretched worship-of-Tagore attitude' as 'disgusting'. However, not all were offended; not everyone misunderstood him. The French Nobel Laureate, Romain Rolland, greeted him in a salubrious personal letter:

> The reading of Nationalism has been a great joy for me; for I entirely agree with your thoughts, and I love them even more now that I have heard them expressed by you with this noble and harmonious wisdom which, being your own, is so dear to us ... .

Tagore's animosity to nationalism should not make us think that he was not patriotic or that he was anti-West. He believed in a symbiosis of the East and West, a 'deep association' or a living relationship between the two cultures; a creative unity that was possible only when the East had discovered its soul and its separate identity. Moreover, his profound love for Bengal and India is manifest in his many immortal songs and poems. His love and intensity for the land transcended the bounds of a narrow, selfish and self-aggrandising nationalism and carried such depth, generosity and broadness that his compositions were adopted as national anthems in three countries. Despite the fervour, Tagore never allowed his love for his country to stand in the way of his love for truth, justice and humanity — he was not given to a national consciousness but a world-consciousness, a visvovod in which every country would keep alight its own lamp of mind as its part in the illumination of the world. As Nikhil says in The Home and the World, 'I am willing to serve my country; but my worship I reserve for Right which is far greater than my country. To worship my country as a god is to bring a curse upon it'. And as Atin says to Ela in Four Chapters:

> The patriotism of those who have no faith in that which is above patriotism is like a crocodile's back used as a ferry to cross the river ... That the life of the country can be saved by killing its soul, is the monstrously false doctrine that nationalists all over the world are bellowing forth stridently. My heart groans to give it effective contradictions ....

And, indeed, effective contradictions Tagore gave all through his life, through his paradisiacal imagination that envisioned a world of love, equality, honesty, bravery and spiritual unity of all mankind — of sympathy and fellowship across race, religion and gender — the world of sattva (light), to put it in a phrase from The Bhagavad Gita, rising from its current *tamasik* (dark) state, that the present humanity, infatuated with greed, wealth and power may not choose to tread, but it is there for them to choose when they rise from their long and horrific moral slumber. Tagore's following prayer for India is also his prayer for the rest of humanity:

> Where the mind is without fear and the head is held high;
>
> Where knowledge is free;
>
> Where the world has not been broken up into fragments by narrow domestic walls;

Where words come out from the depth of truth;

Where tireless striving stretches its arms towards perfection;

Where the clear stream of reason has not lost its way into the dreary desert sand of dead habit;

Where the mind is led forward by thee into ever widening thought and action -

Into that heaven of freedom, my Father, let my country awake.

To attain this state, of course, mankind will first need to break away from the 'mind-forged manacles' of modern civilization, and its main apparatus, the nation, and restore the soul to its rightful place, because only the soul can help us realise our true universal bond by redeeming us from the tyranny of matter, machine and money, and revitalising our inherent bond with God. Needless to say that Tagore's universalism is essentially different from the emerging globalisation which is variously described by sociologists as 'the second phase of modernisation,' 'metaphysics of the world market,' 'economic internationalisation,' and that shares the industrialist-capitalist premise of the nation-state, with a bias towards the intellectual realisation of human potential. Tagore's was a more poetical approach, rooted in comradeship and love; he sought to pave an intuitive, spiritual path for a world that is increasingly becoming prosaic and pragmatic, wilfully espousing a 'head culture' and the culture of, what Wordsworth would call, 'getting and spending'.

The Summary

In My Reminiscences, Tagore humorously recollects that when he was young he was brought up under the rule of the servants, who were not only negligent but also oppressive. To avoid their responsibility, they would often put the young Tagore at a spot in the servants' quarter, draw a chalk line around him, and warn him "with a solemn face and uplifted finger of the perils of transgressing the circle". Tagore, aware of the fate of Sita in Ramayana, for overstepping a similar circle by her husband, would accede to the forceful confinement, but would feel a defiant wish to wipe out the chalk line and find the horizon. This childhood experience became the poet's lifelong companion; he would feel muffled by any confining circle and challenge it with utmost vigour. The national boundary was another such arbitrary "circle" for him that circumscribed his wish to be one with the rest of mankind. He would not accept such thorny hedges of exclusion or the labels and divisions that stood on the way to the formation of a larger human community. He said that if nationalism is something imaginary, humanity has to readjust their imagination by being more inclusive and encyclopaedic, or by extending the horizon of their mind's eye, so that the fellowship of the species does not stop at a geographical border, like commodities. He affirms:

> Therefore, man will have to make another great moral adjustment which will comprehend the whole world of men and not merely the fractional groups of nationality. The call has come to every individual in the present age to prepare himself and his surroundings for this dawn of a new era, when man shall discover his soul in the spiritual unity of all human beings.

Tagore's process calls for a two-way ambiguous negotiation so that nations or communities can flourish and find their own fulfilment and yet rise above exclusivism and provincialism to forge an international community. It is like finding an axial line or a middle ground by shunning excesses, somewhat similar to the Emersonian "double consciousness," where the individual is required to keep his independence and yet not lose his sympathy; or the Whitmanesque celebration of the "self" and the "*en masse*," or "I" and "you," in one breath. The moment we spurn national narcissism or chauvinism, and rise above the dichotomous reasoning of self/other, we become part of the Tagoresque "one world," through a recurrent dialogic process.

But to attain that stage, a more fundamental change is required. Currently, the nation is but an organisation of "politics and commerce," focused on power and wealth. As an institution, its chief interest lies in the material well being of its people but not their moral or spiritual health. It reckons the individual's head and stomach but not his heart, where the soul dwells. This will need to be altered through the restoration of the soul to its rightful place. Without the soul, the individual is like a torn-away line of verse looking for the other line that could give it fullness through a rhyme but has been smudged. Soul is what brings creativity and sympathy to the self, and makes the individual human and humane. In an interview with Einstein, Tagore said, "My religion is in the reconciliation of the supernatural man, the universal human spirit, in my own individual being". This three way reckoning of the self-in the individual, in humanity and in god, all connected by an invisible thread-brings the world together in one nest. This is the higher unity of humanity, which is different from corporate globalisation or what Tagore calls, the "mere political or commercial basis of unity" between nations. His vision is given to a "magnificent harmony" that he believes is the ultimate destiny of humankind: the enlightened individuals and nations coming together to form an enlightened global society. Tagore explains this process, using a metaphor similar to Whitman's "grass" in "Song of Myself":

> As the mission of the rose lies in the unfoldment of the petals which implies distinctness, so the rose of humanity is perfect only when the diverse races and nations have evolved their perfect distinct characteristics but all attached to the stem of humanity by the bond of love.

Tagore's vision might seem idealistic but it is not unattainable. It calls for a humanitarian intervention into present self-seeking and belligerent nationalism, through the introduction of a moral and spiritual dimension in the institution. It also requires us to step out of history to reinvent a new future for ourselves that respects human dignity and sees every individual and nation as equals, in a true democratic spirit.

The risks for us not to take up Tagore's trajectory are too high. The current form of nationalism that works rationally within a "lunatic" doctrinal framework is threatening our very survival. Violence is spreading around the world like virus. Our vast killing power is multiplying everyday with the introduction of yet more sophisticated ammunition in our arsenal. Paul Hirst, a leading international social theorist, has predicted that with the prospects of climate change that might attenuate our resources and result in mass migration from a loss of "habitable land in highly populated areas like Bangladesh or the southern coast of China," or "desertification or water shortages in the Middle East or Southern Europe"; increase in the global income inequality; accretion of human rights violation worldwide; America's quest for global dominance and challenges from "new 'beggars' armies" to the military hegemony, as well as the general selfishness of the developed nations, threatens the world with a "conflict ridden international environment" in the twenty-first century, with the prospects of several conventional wars, "to limited nuclear war".

Such a prospect casts gloom and doom on humanity. Perhaps it is not too late for us to wake up from our horrific moral slumber and accept the path of international solidarity, peace, harmony and justice paved by the Indian enlightened humanitarian poet, Rabindranath Tagore; by challenging the reigning ideological system of self-seeking nationalism and jingoism, we could still avert the all consuming nightmare before us and alter the damning course of history.

4

Literary Contribution

The Works of Rabindranath Tagore consist of poems, novels, short stories, dramas, paintings, drawings, and music that Bengali poet and Brahmo philosopher Rabindranath Tagore created over his lifetime.

Tagore's literary reputation is disproportionately influenced by regard for his poetry; however, he also wrote novels, essays, short stories, travelogues, dramas, and thousands of songs. Of Tagore's prose, his short stories are perhaps most highly regarded; indeed, he is credited with originating the Bangla-language version of the genre. His works are frequently noted for their rhythmic, optimistic, and lyrical nature. However, such stories mostly borrow from deceptively simple subject matter — the lives of ordinary people.

Short Stories

Tagore began his career in short stories in 1877 — when he was only sixteen — with "*Bhikharini*" (The Beggar Woman). With this, Tagore effectively invented the Bangla-language short story genre. The four years from 1891 to 1895 are known as Tagore's "Sadhana" period (named for one of Tagore's magazines). This period was among Tagore's most fecund, yielding more than half the stories contained in the three-volume Galpaguchchha, which itself is a collection of eighty-four stories. Such stories usually showcase Tagore's reflections upon his surroundings, on modern and fashionable ideas, and on interesting mind puzzles (which Tagore was fond of testing his intellect with). Tagore typically associated his earliest stories (such as those of the "Sadhana" period) with an exuberance of vitality and spontaneity; these characteristics were intimately connected with Tagore's life in the common villages of, among others, Patisar, Shajadpur, and Shilaida while managing the Tagore family's vast landholdings.

There, he beheld the lives of India's poor and common people; Tagore thereby took to examining their lives with a penetrative depth and feeling that was singular in Indian literature up to that point. In particular, such stories as "*Cabuliwallah*" (The Fruitseller from Kabul, published in 1892), "*Kshudita Pashan*" (The Hungry Stones) (August 1895), and "*Atithi*" (The Runaway, 1895) typified this analytic focus on the downtrodden. In "The Fruitseller from Kabul", Tagore speaks in first person as town-dweller and novelist who chances upon the Afghani seller. He attempts to distil the sense of longing felt by those long trapped in the mundane and hardscrabble confines of Indian urban life, giving play to dreams of a different existence in the distant and wild mountains: "There were autumn mornings, the time of year when Kings of old went forth to conquest; and I, never stirring from my little corner in Calcutta, would let my mind wander over the whole world.

At the very name of another country, my heart would go out to it ... I would fall to weaving a network of dreams: the mountains, the glens, the forest .... ". Many of the other "Galpaguchchha" stories were written in Tagore's Sabuj Patra period (1914-17, again, named after one of the magazines that Tagore edited and heavily contributed to). Tagore's *Golpoguchchho* (Bunch of Stories) remains among the most popular fictional works in Bangla literature. Its continuing influence on Bengali art and culture cannot be overstated; to this day, Golpoguchchho remains a point of cultural reference. Golpoguchchho has furnished subject matter for numerous successful films and theatrical plays, and its characters are among the most well known to Bengalis.

The acclaimed film director Satyajit Ray based his film *Charulata* (The Lonely Wife) on *Nastanirh* (The Broken Nest). This famous story has an autobiographical element to it, modelled to some extent on the relationship between Tagore and his sister-in-law, Kadambari Devi. Ray has also made memorable films of other stories from Golpoguchchho, including Samapti, Postmaster and Monihara, bundling them together as *Teen Kanya* (Three Daughters). Atithi is another poignantly lyrical Tagore story which was made into a film of the same name by another noted Indian film director Tapan Sinha. Tarapada, a young Brahmin boy, catches a boat ride with a village zamindar.

It turns out that he has run away from his home and has been wandering around ever since. The zamindar adopts him, and finally arranges a marriage to his own daughter. The night before the wedding Tarapada runs away again. *Strir Patra* (The Letter from the Wife) has to be one of the earliest depictions in Bangla literature of such bold emancipation of women. Mrinal is the wife of a typical Bengali middle class man. The letter, written while she is travelling (which constitutes the whole story), describes her petty life and struggles. She finally declares that she will not return to his patriarchical home, stating *Amio bachbo. Ei bachlum* (And I Shall Live. Here, I Live).

In Haimanti, Tagore takes on the institution of Hindu marriage. He describes, via Strir Patra, the dismal lifelessness of Bengali women after they are married off, hypocrisies plaguing the Indian middle class, and how Haimanti, a sensitive young woman, must — due to her sensitiveness and free spirit — sacrifice her life. In the last passage, Tagore directly attacks the Hindu custom of glorifying Sita's attempted self-immolation as a means of appeasing her husband Rama's doubts (as depicted in the epic Ramayana).

Tagore also examines Hindu-Muslim tensions in Musalmani Didi, which in many ways embodies the essence of Tagore's humanism. On the other hand, Darpaharan exhibits Tagore's self-consciousness, describing a young man harbouring literary ambitions. Though he loves his wife, he wishes to stifle her literary career, deeming it unfeminine. Tagore himself, in his youth, seems to have harboured similar ideas about women. Darpaharan depicts the final humbling of the man via his acceptance of his wife's talents. As with many other Tagore stories, *Jibito o Mrito* provides the Bengalis with one of their more widely used epigrams:

Kadombini moriya proman korilo she more nai (Kadombini died, thereby proved that she hadn't).

Kabuliwala

Kabuliwala is a story written by Rabindranath Tagore. Two films have been produced based on this story, both named Kabuliwala. The first was filmed in Bengali in 1956 by Tapan Sinha, and the second in Hindi, also titled, Kabuliwala in 1961, directed by Hemen Gupta, produced by Bimal Roy.

At the 7th Berlin International Film Festival the film won the Silver Bear Extraordinary Prize of the Jury award.

Rehmat (Chhabi Biswas), a middle-aged fruit seller from Afghanistan comes to Calcutta to hawk his merchandise and befriends a small Bengali girl called *Minnie* (Tinku Thakur) who reminds him of his own daughter back in Afghanistan. He puts up at a boarding house along with his countrymen. One day Rehmat receives news of his daughter's illness through a letter from his country and he decides to leave for his country. Since he is short of money he decides to sell his goods on credit for increasing his business.

Later when he goes to collect on his money one of his customers abuses him and in the fight that ensues Rehmat warns that he will not tolerate abuse and stabs the guy when he does not stop the abuse. In the court Rehmat's lawyer tries to obfuscate the facts but in his characteristic and simple fashion Rehmat states the truth in a matter of fact way. The judge pleased with Rehmats honesty gives him 10 years rigorous imprisonment instead of the death sentence. On the day of his release he goes to meet Minnie but discovers that she has grown up to a 14-year old girl and is about to get married. Minnie does not recognise Rehmat, who realises that his own daughter must have forgotten him too. Minnie's father gives Rehmat the money for travel out of Minnie's wedding budget to which Minnie agrees, she also sends a gift for Rehmat's daughter.

Novels

Among Tagore's works, his novels are among the least-acknowledged. These include Chaturanga, Gora (1910), Shesher

Kobita, Ghare Baire, Char Odhay, and Noukadubi. Ghare Baire or The Home and the World, (which was also released as the film by Satyajit Ray, Ghare Baire) examines rising nationalistic feeling among Indians while warning of its dangers, clearly displaying Tagore's distrust of nationalism — especially when associated with a religious element. In some sense, Gora shares the same theme, raising questions regarding the Indian identity. As with Ghore Baire, matters of self-identity, personal freedom, and religious belief are developed in the context of an involving family story and a love triangle.

Shesher Kobita (translated twice, as Last Poem and as Farewell Song) is his most lyrical novel, containing as it does poems and rhythmic passages written by the main character (a poet). Nevertheless, it is also Tagore's most satirical novel, exhibiting post-modernist elements whereby several characters make gleeful attacks on the reputation of an old, outmoded, oppressively-renowned poet (named Rabindranath Tagore).

Though his novels remain under-appreciated, they have recently been given new attention through many movie adaptations by such film directors as Satyajit Ray, Tapan Sinha and Tarun Majumdar. The recent among these is a version of Chokher Bali directed by Rituparno Ghosh, which features Aishwariya Rai. A favourite trope of these directors is to employ rabindra sangeet in the film adaptations' soundtracks.

Among Tagore's notable non-fiction books are *Iurop Jatrir Patro* (Letters from Europe) and *Manusher Dhormo* (The Religion of Man).

Chokher Bali

Chokher Bali, literally Sand of the Eye, equivalent to eye-sore, is a Bengali novel written by Rabindranath Tagore in the early-20th century.

Plot: Binodini is a young widow left to her own devices when her husband dies soon after they are married. She returns to her village and lives there for a couple of months until she accepts the invitation of Rajlakshmi to live with her and her son, *Mahendra* (who had rejected a former marriage proposal with Binodini). He is newly married to *Ashalata* (a naive, gentle girl), but soon begins to feel a strong sexual attraction for Binodini. The story details the relationships of these three and Mahendra's best friend Bihari as they deal with issues like distrust, adultery, lies, and numerous fallings-out between them.

Binodini is a convent educated young girl who has been widowed and hence reduced to living very badly (like all widows of that period). He husband had died soon after their marriage. When Rajalakshmi — a wealthy widow living in Calcutta where thanks to philosophers — widows are much better off (This is in the late-1800s — the Era of Ishwar Chandra Visdyasagar) — invites Binodini to stay with them, Binodini accepts.

Meanwhile, Rajalakshmi's son Mahendra claims to have no interest in marriage (he rejected Binodini's marriage proposal once) and accompanies his close friend 'Bihari' when Bihari goes to see a girl for himself. Mahendra falls for the girl — Ashalata and marries her.

Initially Mahendra is besotten with his wife and forgets the world for her — but after Binodini arrives, Mahendra and Binodini begin to have an affair. Binodini is delighted to be sexually active again — being able to enjoy passions of a young woman.

Critical Acclaim: Tagore elaborately records early-20th century Bengali society, through his central character, the rebellious widow, who wants to live a life of her own. In writing this novel he exposes the custom of perpetual mourning on the part of widows, who were not allowed to remarry and were condemned to a life of seclusion and loneliness. It is a melancholy, stirring tale of the deceit and sorrow that arise from dissatisfaction and sorrow. Tagore has said about the novel, "I have always regretted the ending".

The Home and the World

The Home and the World 1916 (in the original Bengali, *Ghare Baire*, lit. "At home [and] outside") is a 1916 novel by Rabindranath Tagore. The book illustrates the battle Tagore had with himself, between the ideas of Western culture and revolution against the Western culture. These two ideas are portrayed in two of the main characters, Nikhil, who is rational and opposes violence, and Sandip, who will let nothing stand in his way from reaching his goals. These two opposing ideals are very important in understanding the history of this region and its contemporary problems. There is much controversy over whether or not Tagore was attempting represent Gandhi in Sandip but many argue that Tagore would not even venture to personify Sandip as Gandhi because Tagore was a large admirer of Gandhi and Gandhi was anti-violence while Sandip would use violence in any respect to get what he wanted. The book shows "the clash between new and old, realism and idealism, the means and the end, good and evil" (p xxiv) within India and southern Asia.

Background Context:

Political Movement: The novel's setting is in early-20th century India. The story line coincides with the National Independence Movement taking place in the country at the time, which was sparked by the Indian National Congress. There were various national and regional campaigns of both militant and non-violent ideas which all had the common goal of ending British colonial rule. Militant nationalism had a strong showing in the early part of the 20th century, especially during the World War I period. Some examples of this movement are the Indo-German Pact and Ghadar Conspiracy, unfortunately both of these failed. The latter stages of the movement saw a transition to non-violent forms of resistance led by Mohandas Gandhi.

India remained a British colony until 1947, when Pakistan (August 14) and India (August 15) gained their freedom. On January 26, 1950, India adopted a Constitution and became its own republic. At the time of Indian Independence, the Muslim dominated north west and eastern parts of the country were separated to form West Pakistan and East Pakistan (which later became Bangladesh). Particularly important to the novel is an understanding of the Swadeshi Movement, as a part of the Indian Nationalist Movement.

The Swadeshi Movement started in response to the Partition of Bengal by Lord Curzon which occurred in 1905. The Swadeshi Movement was a successful resistance policy against the British colonisation. Indian citizens were encouraged to boycott British goods in order to foster Indian identity and independence. This movement was important in fostering the "the new spirit in India," and separating India from Britain, which was largely thought to be responsible for the subsequent widespread poverty.

Traditional Indian Household: Family structures in traditional India consists of not only the nuclear family but also grandparents, parents-in-law, and unmarried sister-in-laws as well. Though the joint-family is linked to ancient India, its still prevalent in modern day India. Traditionally, baby boys were preferable to baby girls since boys were able to earn money and support the family. Girls on the other hand, were expensive to raise. They didn't bring home the bread and the girl's marriage dowry required a hefty amount of money and other luxury goods such as valuable jewellries and saris. Once girls were married-off to the other families, they would have to address their new parents-in-law as "father" and "mother". As home maker of the family, the wife's duty was to supervise the household and take care of the children, she also had to try hard to please her new in-laws.

The Home and the World tells us not only the personal struggles of the three main characters, but also little details of the family structure and how traditional Indian households were like. In the book, Bimala starts off as a traditional, obedient house wife who is faithful to her husband and even forces herself to be respectful towards her nagging sister-in-law. "I would cautiously and silently get up and take the dust of my husband's feet without waking him, how at such moments I could feel the vermilion mark upon my forehead shining out like the morning star".

However, as she falls "in love" with Sandip, she slowly weens away from her traditional housewife role. She becomes more daring, more confidently brushes off her sister-in-law's criticisms, and crosses outside the women's quarter of the house, and easily converses with another man, Sandip, who is not her husband. Through her dilemma, the readers are able to learn about the traditional ways of the Indian household through Bimala's change from the good house wife to an independent, more modern woman.

Plot Summary: The novel is set in early-20th century India in the estate of the Bengali zamindar Nikhil. He marries Bimala, a woman who is both of a lower status and of a darker complexion, which is contradictory to his family traditions. Their love is idyllic and both are dedicated to one another until the appearance of his friend and radical revolutionist, Sandip.

Sandip, a passionate and active man, is a contradiction to the peace-loving and somewhat passive Nikhil. His charismatic speech, support of the Swadeshi Movement, and a renewed appreciation of everything Indian while denying everything British garnered support from local natives across the province. After hearing Sandip speak at a rally, Bimala insists that Sandip visit Nikhil's estate. While visiting, Sandip's influential nature easily attracts the innocent and unsuspecting Bimala, and she suggests he make his headquarters at their house.

Once empowered by the inside world, knowing only her husband and home, she becomes engaged with the outside world, taking part in the Swadeshi Movement by working with Sandip. As the novel develops, Bimala is drawn to Sandip's passion and the attraction between the two becomes inevitable, producing a love triangle. She begins to question her marriage with Nikhil and finds in Sandip what she has always sought after in a man: zeal, ambition, and a hint of danger.

She begins to help Sandip by stealing money from Nikhil's treasury, convinced that if it is not equally his money as well as hers, then it belongs to the country. While Bimala claims her national duty as motivation, her true intentions lie in pleasing Sandip. Nikhil subsequently discovers their actions, but grants Bimala freedom to grow and choose what she wants in her life (as their marriage was arranged when she was a young girl). Meanwhile, Bimala experiences love for the first time, which ultimately helps her understand that it is indeed her husband Nikhil who really loves her.

The novel ends with a secular riot, resulting in Sandip fleeing the city. Nikhil is mortally wounded in the head. Amulya, a young follower of Sandip's movement who considered Bimala as his sister, and whom Bimala thinks of as her son (since she has no children), dies by a bullet through his heart.

Major Events:

The Rally: Near the beginning of the novel, Nikhil brings his wife Bimala to a political rally in an attempt to get her to join the outside world and get in touch better with "reality." Though Bimala had heard of Sandip before this time, and developed a somewhat negative opinion of him, this was the first time she heard Sandip speak. This event not only changes her opinion of Sandip, but affects her entire outlook on her life both at home and in the outside world. "I was no longer the lady of the Rajah's house, but the sole representative of Bengal's womanhood," Bimala says. "I returned home that evening radiant with a new pride and joy." After returning home, Bimala asks her husband to invite Sandip to their home for dinner, setting the plot of the novel in motion.

Bimala's Realisation: Towards the end of the book Sandip convinces Bimala to steal from her husband, Nikhil. While in the act of stealing 6,000 rupees, she comes to a realisation of the terrible crime she is committing, "I could not think of my house as separate from my country: I had robbed my house, I had robbed my country. For this sin my house had ceased to be mine, my country also was estranged from me". This represents a character turning point for Bimala: While in the act of thieving, she realises that Sandip is not only corrupting and robbing the nation, but encouraging her and others to do the same. Ultimately, she ends up giving the money to Sandip and receives unceasing praise from both Sandip and Amulya for her newly recognised sin.

However, Bimala realises that she has made a mistake by stealing the money from Nikhil and attempts to have Amulya pawn off some of her jewellery in order to replace the money. Amulya attempts to give the box back, but Sandip steals it and gives it back himself. This event allows both Amulya and Bimala to see that Sandip is concerned only with himself, thus allowing them to break free from part of his web. It is during this time that Bimala realises her power over Sandip by being able to easily make him jealous.

Characters:

Nikhil - Husband of Bimala: Nikhil is seen and described as an educated and gentle man. The reader can see that as the story is told from his point of view. His words flow more poetically, as if possessing a higher proficiency of language. He is from an aristocratic family of landlords, and his family prides themselves in beautiful women. However, Nikhil is different in that he married not only a poor woman, but also one who was not particularly attractive. Nikhil loves his wife very much as he likes to buy her

European style dresses and other modern gifts. He also tries to educate her about the outside world and bring her away from the traditional female life in India. However, due to his gentle and soft nature, he cannot do anything but watch and standby as he sees a relationship unfolding between his wife and his old friend, Sandip. He is also unpopular in the town because he has not joined them stating, "I am not running amuck crying Bande Mataram."

In light of this, the police also suspect him of harbouring some "hidden protest." In reality, Nikhil considers himself to be more aware of his country's role in a broader sense, and refuses to take part in Swadeshi. He claims that " '[He] is willing...to serve [his] country; but [his] worship he reserves for Right which is far greater than [his] country.' " In traditional texts Nikhil's full name reads as Nikhilesh. Its literal translation is "Lord of the Universe" with Nikhil being literally translated to '"whole" and insinuating harmony, wisdom, and awareness.

Bimala - Wife of Nikhil: Bimala is described as not very pretty and from a much more humble background than Nikhil. She loves her husband dearly, and enjoys being completely devoted to him. At the beginning of the novel, she seems to be confined to the traditional female role, and has no thoughts of entering the real world, even with persuasion from her husband. Her feelings make a rapid change with the occurrence of the Swadeshi Movement. "My sight and my mind, my hopes and my desires, became red with the passion of this new age". When she meets Sandip, her new ideals are fuelled by his zealous nature and a fiery, shameless side of her emerges.

As time goes on she becomes more interested and involved in the Swadeshi Movement; it is at this time that she starts to develop romantic feelings for Sandip. Literally translated Bimala means "without mal or blemish". It is often used to mean clean, pure, and immaculate. Often times the name is shortened to Bimal. Although Bimala is married to Nikhil and their marriage was arranged since she was a little girl, Nikhil believes that Bimala is free to make her own decisions to her life. "I was married into a Rajah's house. When I was a child, I was quite familiar with the description of the Prince of the fairy story". Therefore, Bimala is very dedicated to her husband, her marriage, and most importantly, her family values. However, Nikhil sometimes questions her view of him, basically that of a traditional woman. She cannot stand her husband's idleness, and unwillingness to participate in more "patriotic" endeavours. "Bimala has no patience with patience. She loves to find in men the turbulent, the angry, the unjust. Her respect must have its element of fear. "Bimala was not raised the way her husband was raised: well and educated. However, she understands the social differences between her and her husband. "My husband's grandmother and mother were both renowned for their beauty... only the auspicious marks with which I was endowed gained me an entry into this family — otherwise, I had no claim to be here".

Sandip: Sandip is the third major character in the novel, completing the love triangle. He is a guest in the home of Nikhil and Bimala and his revolutionary ideas and speeches have a significant impact on Bimala. He is very vocal in his anti-imperialistic views and is a skilled orator. Sandip represents characteristics that are directly opposite to those Nikhil possesses, thus drawing Bimala to Sandip. Bimala gets caught up in the ideas that Sandip presents as well as the man himself. Her seemingly increasing patriotism causes her to spend more and more time with Sandip, thereby solidifying the love triangle conflict. Where her husband is reserved and proper, Sandip is impassioned and stirs the emotions not only of Bimala, but the people of Bengal.

He spreads the notion of "Swadeshi", or using goods made locally and boycotting British goods. However, his character is far from the ideal patriot. His motivations are selfish at times, prompted by the need to better himself socially. He fools people with his mask of goodness, something that Nikhil sees through at the beginnings of Sandip's relationship with his wife. "I have been noticing for some time that there is a gross cupidity about Sandip. His fleshly feelings make him harbour delusions about his religion and impel him into a tyrannical attitude in his patriotism. His nature is coarse, and so he glorifies his selfish lusts under high-sounding names". At one point he convinces Bimala to steal from her house and her husband for the "cause". Sandip's presence in the novel concludes with him fleeing while his speeches and ideas result in communal riots. Sandip's full name is Sandip Babu. His first name is translated to "with dipa (light fire flame)". According to the notes in the novel this is used to describe him as "inflaming, exciting, arousing". Sandip's last name "Babu" originated as an aristocratic title however has come to describe Bengali's educated in the west, or comparable settings. The British used "Babu" as a patronising term however, its usage as an honorific title still survives in India today.

Bara Rani (Bimala's Sister-in-law): Bimala and her sister-in-law's relationship is strained at best. Bimala's sister-in-law causes a lot of tension in the household. Bara Rani also uses Nikhil to get the material items that she desires. Bimala constantly complains about her to Nikhil. Bara Rani taunts Bimala for her mingling with Sandip Babu.

Amulya: Bimala considers Amulya to be her adoptive son, whom she met from the Swadeshi Movement. When first they meet, Bimala asks him to acquire money for their cause. He lists wild schemes and plans, to which Bimala replies "you must not be childish" After pondering their situation, Amulya resolves to murder the cashier for the money. Tagore uses him to symbolise the raw emotion and passion, yet lack of sympathy for others often encompassed by group or riot mentality.

Tagore also characterises Amulya as the typical idealistic youth when Amulya rationalises the murder with a phrase from the Bhagavad Gita stating "Who kills the body kills naught!" Amulya is used as a parallel to Sandip, comparing follower to leader. When Bimala shows such sympathy by calling him "little brother", he is caught off guard, suggesting that the youth is even more impressionable with emotions than Sandip's ideals. Amulya struggles, as any youth, between completing the goals of the movement and developing strong relationships on an individual level, such as with Bimala; this is made extremely difficult by Sandip's powerful influence. Amulya frequently accepts Sandip's motives by rationalising the necessary actions. In a sense, he can be considered a pawn used by Bimala and Sandip in their strategic power struggle, particularly when Bimala requests he sell her jewels.

Important Themes:

Nationalism: While the entire novel centres around the Swadeshi Movement, the author of the novel is not advocating it but rather warning his audience of the dangers of such a movement. Tagore knows that it is possible for even a seemingly peaceful movement to turn quickly into aggressive nationalism. Such a change would do the country more harm than good. The character named Sandip is the vivacious and ardent leader of Swadeshi. He knows that his movement has the potential to turn ugly. He fervently believes however that freedom must be achieved no matter the cost.

On page 123-4, Sandip cites a story from the Bhagavad Gita in support of his own path. The story tells of the Hindu Lord Krishna advising Arjuna to perform his duty as a warrior regardless of the result. Sandip's use of the Hindu epic poetry to support his movement illustrates the tendency of individuals to use religion as a basis for nationalism. The use of excerpts from the Indian epic poem was indicative of the blending tradition elements of Indian culture with the ideals and goals of modern Indian Independence Movement. As both have the potential to yield individuals claiming an unshakable fervour for their cause, this can be a rather dangerous combination, a fact clearly acknowledged by the novel's author.

Nationalism is also expressed through the rejection of foreign goods, which was a part of the Swadeshi Movement. Sandip was strongly against the sale of foreign goods as Bimala stated that "Sandip laid it down that all foreign articles, together with the demon of foreign influence, must be driven out of our territory". Nikhil on the other hand felt the opposite. He stated that in terms of banishing foreign goods from his Suskar market that he "could not do it" and he refused to "tyrannise". Bimala even pleaded with her husband to "order them to be cleared out!". She also stated that banishing foreign goods "would not be tyranny for selfish gain, but for the sake of the country".

Tradition vs Modernism: As the title suggests, a major theme is the relationship of the home with the outside world. Nikhil enjoys the modern, western goods and clothing and lavishes Bimala with them. However, Bimala, in the Hindu tradition, never goes outside of the house complex. Her world is a clash of western and traditional Indian life. She enjoys the modern things that Nikhil brings to her, but when Sandip comes and speaks of nationalism with such fire, she sees these things as a threat to her way of life. Bimala's struggle is with identity. She is part of the country, but only knows the home and her home is a mix of cultures. She is torn between supporting the ideal of a country that she knows she should love, or working towards ensuring that her home, her whole world, is free from strife and supporting her husband like a traditional Indian woman should. Bimala is forced to try to understand how her traditional life can mix with a modern world and not be undermined. This theme ties in with the nationalism theme because it is another way that Tagore is warning against the possibility that nationalism can do more harm than good.

Sandip vs. Nikhil: Nikhil and Sandip have extremely different views for the growth of the nation. Nikhil believes in a nation that is peaceful, demonstrates the equality of individuals, and respects social harmony. Nikhil demonstrates these beliefs in him marrying Bimala, an "unattractive" women because of her skin colour. In the novel, Nikhil talks about disliking an intense patriotism nation, "Use force? But for what? Can force prevail against Truth?". On the other hand, Sandip has contrasting views for the growth of the nation believing in power and force, "My country does not become mine simply because it is the country of my birth. It becomes mine on the day when I am able to win it by force". The contradicting views of Nikhil and Sandip set up the story and constructs an interesting dilemma for Bimala. Unfortunately for Nikhil, he has already tried to show Bimala the outside world, and stir some sort of emotion within her since the beginning of the novel, and failed. Sandip possesses great oratory skill, that wins Bimala over simply because of his passion and ferocity, something that her husband may lack.

Illusions: The constant forming of illusions in the novel grows to be a major recurring theme. Sandip tends to create illusions that almost always have negative affects on his followers and on the nation of Bengal. He builds an illusion of his beliefs that sucks the people of Bengal into a sort of cult. His illusion is complete sovereignty, free of all other worlds, and an endless supply of wealth and self enjoyment. This illusion, as many are, is a fake and a lie. It ultimately sells these people a front row ticket to watch their nation fall into complete chaos and civil war among people with different beliefs. He constructs an illusion for Bimala to believe, saying she is the future, women are the future, they are the chosen path to salvation. Bimala builds an illusion that she is to blame for this war, it is solely her doing. That she has done all wrong and no right. She refuses to accept that she too was a victim of Bande Mataram. "I now fear nothing-neither myself, nor anybody else. I have passed through fire. What was inflammable has been burnt to ashes; what is left is deathless. I have dedicated myself to the feet of him, who has received all my sin into the depths of his own pain." The biggest illusion of all of is his mask of caring and passion, while he hides his own selfishness and desire for the world.

Truth: In more than one way, this novel is a comparison of different views of truth. Which reality is truer is up to the reader's interpretation. Nikhil maintains an idealistic view of the world while Sandip takes a radical, nature-worshipping view. He feels Nikhil's view of the world is inferior to the real, raw world in which he lives as a radical leader. Bimala as well must compare truths. Through her interactions with Sandip, she is introduced to the truth of "*shakti*" (female power), yet her life with Nikhil is centered on the truth of conjugality. Each of these instances is a comparison of truth as being something simply objective to being something with a more spiritual or moral dimension. While the story ends in tragedy, both views of truth are important players in the story's outcome, and it is left to the reader to ponder with which he or she agrees or disagrees.

Love/Union: From page one of the novel, the love and union between Nikhil and Bimala is illustrated as something sacred. Nikhil proved throughout the story that he was undeniably devoted to his wife. He proved this first by marrying a woman who hailed a poor family, along with accepting her darker skin. He made great effort to not only educate her, but also for her to understand her place in the world and not just her place in the captivity of their house. He shows his love by giving her freedom. Bimala also adores her husband, but in a less material manner. This is demonstrated in Bimala's daily ritual of "taking the dust", an Indian ritual of reverence not usually performed by a wife to her husband.

Due to Bimala's extreme devotion to Nikhil, In the beginning of the novel, the union between the two of them is seen as one that cannot be broken. However as, the story progresses, Bimala is slowly overcome by her feelings for Sandip. She eventually realises that she has found in Sandip what she longed for in Nikhil, fierce ambition and even violent defence of ones ideals. Her deep desire for Sandip led her to completely break her scared union with Nikhil, going as far as to steal money from her household funds. Sandip shows his love for Bimala through idolisation. This idolisation comes about due to her freedom though.

The tale clearly presents the theme of love and union time and time again, going from Nikhil and Bimala's marriage, through the love triangle created by Sandip, and once again returning to Bimala's love for Nikhil at the very end. This story tests the boundaries of the union of marriage. It stretches and twists it to the point where a 9 year marriage is nearly destroyed simply because of a raw temptation. In addition to the idea of romantic love, there is a sense of love of owns country depicted throughout the novel. Questions such as, is it best to love ones country through action, perhaps even violence, or by passive tolerance are posed in the arguments of Nikhil and Sandip. While love and worship seem parallel in marriage, Nikhil believes these feelings cannot apply to ones country. "To worship my country as a god is to bring a curse upon it".

The Role of Women: Throughout the novel as stated earlier a strong sense of devotion is seen in the relationship between Bimala and Nikhil. It is key to notice that an indirect evaluation of the role of women is seen in this novel also, in a very subtle manner. In the society described, Bimala, like most women, blindly worships her husband. This can be seen when, Bimala is described, "taking the dust of my husband's feet without waking him," and when she is caught doing this act of kindness, her reaction is, "That had nothing to do with merit. It was a woman's heart, which must worship in order to love." This seen shows the average woman in this society who believes love will happen and worship is a given in a marriage. She blindly respects her husband without understanding or having a grasp of who he is. Another one of the many scenes that alludes to a woman's place in this society is when Nikhil and Sandip Babu argue and Bimala is asked her opinion, which she finds unusual, in addition to "Never before had I [Bimala] had an opportunity of being present at a discussion between my husband and his men friends".

This line shows how there is a strong disconnect and there is no place, usually, for a woman in real world conversations. To further prove this, in Nikhil's story, the role of a woman is seen clearly, "Up till now Bimala was my home-made Bimala, the product of the confined space and the daily routine of small duties". The indirect references and descriptions are quite frequent throughout the novel and clearly allows the reader to get a sense of what women were subject to and their overall role in the society.

Religion versus Nationalism: One major theme in the novel is the importance of religion and on the other hand nationalism. In this novel, religion can be seen as the more "spiritual view" while nationalism can be seen more as the "worldly view." Nikhil's main perspective in life is by the moral and intangible while Sandip is more concerned about the tangible things, which to him is reality. Sandip believes that this outlook on life, living in a way where one may follow his or her passions and seek immediate gratification, is what gives strength and portrays reality, which is linked to his strong belief in nationalism.

From Sandip's point of view, "when reality has to meet the unreal, deception is its principal weapon; for its enemies always try to shame Reality by calling it gross, and so it needs must hide itself, or else put on some disguise". To Sandip, reality consists of being "gross," "true," "flesh," "passion," "hunger, unashamed and cruel". On the other hand, Nikhi's view is more concerned with controlling one's passions and living life in a moral way. He believes that it is, "a part of human nature to try and rise superior to itself," rather than living recklessly by acting on instinct and fleshly desires.

Nikhil argues that a person must learn to control their passions and "recognise the truth of restraint" and that "by pressing what we want to see right into our eyes we only injure them: we do not see". All these moral precepts tie in with his faith. Nikhil also speaks from a more religious perspective when he speaks of how "all at once my heart was full with the thought that my Eternal Love was steadfastly waiting for me through the ages, behind the veil of material things". This shows that Nikhil does not live morally just for the sake of trying to be good but that it is grounded in his religious views. Sandip reiterates the fact that in their country, they have both "religion and also our nationalism" and that "the result is that both of them suffer".

Film, TV or Theatrical Adaptations: Ghare Baire was first released at the Cannes Film Festival in France on May 22, 1984, under the direction of Satyajit Ray. It was also nominated for the Golden Palm award, one of the highest awards received at the Cannes Film Festival. It was later released in the United States on June 21, 1985. The scriptwriters were Satyajit Ray (writer) and Rabindranath Tagore (novel). Sandip was played by Soumitra Chatterjee, Nikhilesh was played by Victor Banerjee and Bimala was played by Swatilekha Chatterjee. At the beginning of the movie a woman tells the story of the events in her life and how they changed her perspective on the world. She recalls how her husband challenged traditions by providing her with education and letting her, a married woman, out of seclusion. Her husband's friend is a leader in the rebellion against the British when they come to visit and the movie takes off from there.

Historical Context: The story of The Home and the World takes place in 1916 in the Bangladesh Region. From the period of 1858 to 1947, the British Empire ruled 8 major provinces throughout the region of India. These regions include Pakistan, Bangladesh, Singapore, and Burma. Drawn to region for trading purposes, the British soon had set up an expansive Empire most noteworthy the East India Trading Company. Not only was it one of the biggest trading powers in the world, it also allowed Britain to enlarge its already huge Navy. The majority of the local people in India did not like being under Colonial Rule resulting in many rebellions. These uprising became known as the Indian Independence Movement. This movement included a variety of political parties, ideas, and movements that all strived to end British rule. Perhaps the greatest influence on the people of India came from the ideas and beliefs of Mohandas Gandhi who stressed that non-violence was the ultimate tool to opposing foreign rule.

Nastanirh

Nastanirh (1901), (English: The Broken Nest) is a Bengali novella by Rabindranath Tagore. It is the basis for the noted 1964 film, Charulata by Satyajit Ray.

According to Mary Lago in the introduction to the English translation of Nashtanir (translated by Lago and Supriya Sen), the novella was released three times: in 1901 in serial format, in 1909 as part of a special short story collection, and in 1926 as part of Tagore's standard collection of fiction.

Scholarship indicates that this story might have been based upon the relationship between Tagore's elder brother Jyotirindranath; his brother's wife, Kadambari Devi (who committed suicide shortly after Tagore's marriage); and Tagore (who spent a great deal of time with Kadambari, reading and writing poetry).

Nastanirh takes place in late-19th century Bengal and explores the lives of the "Bhadralok", Bengalis of wealth who were part of the Bengal Renaissance and highly influenced by the Brahmo Samaj. Despite his liberal ideas, Bhupati is blind to the loneliness and dissatisfaction of his wife, Charu. It is only with the appearance of his cousin, Amal, who incites passionate feelings in Charu, that Bhupati realises what he has lost.

Charulata (The Lonely Wife) is a 1964 film by Bengali director Satyajit Ray, featuring Soumitra Chatterjee, Madhabi Mukherjee and Sailen Mukherjee and is based upon Nastanirh.

Jogajog

Jogajog is a novel by Rabindranath Tagore. It was published in book form in 1929 (Asharh 1336). It was first serialised in the magazine Bichitra from Ashwin 1334 to Choitro 1335. In the first two issues the novel was titled Tin Purush. In the third issue in Ogrohayon 1334, Rabindranath changed the name to Jogajog.

The story revolves around the underlying rivalry between two families - the Chatterjees, aristocrats now on the decline (Biprodas) and the Ghosals (Madhusudan), representing new money and arrogance. Kumudini, Biprodas' sister, is caught between the two as she is married off to Madhusudan. She was brought up in a sheltered home where she had followed the traditional way of life and observed all the religious rituals like all the other womenfolk in the family. Her mental image of the husband is as someone who embodies all the qualities of the God she worships. Now, she is rudely shaken by the crude display of wealth and power by Madhusudan.

Even if brought up to be a good, submissive wife, she balks at the idea of sharing the conjugal bed. "Madhusudan repeatedly used (this) money-worshipping strain to sneer at Kumu's family. His natural vulgarity, the coarseness of his speech, his arrogant discourtesy, the uncouthness of his body and mind that so deeply characterised his life: all this was something from which Kumu's whole being shrank every moment." The novel also highlights marital rape. Kumudini is subjected to marital rape by Madhusudan. There is also a sexual liaison between Madhusudan and Shyamasundari, the widow of Madhusudan's elder brother. Biprodas is a vociferous supporter of equal dignity and rights for women.

The novel was translated by Supriya Chaudhuri (Oxford University Press, 2006) as part of the Oxford Tagore Translations.

Shesher Kobita

Shesher Kobita is a novel by Rabindranath Tagore, widely considered a landmark in Bengali literature. The novel was serialised in 1928, from Bhadro to Choitro in the magazine Probashi, and was published in book form the following year. It has been translated into English as The Last Poem (translator Anandita Mukhopadhyay) and Farewell song (translator Radha Chakravarty).

The novel recounts the love story of Amit Ray, a barrister educated at Oxford, whose virulent intellectualism reveals itself in its opposition to all forms of tradition. He meets Labannya in a car accident and the romance builds up in the misty hills of Shillong. Though the novel is primarily set in Shillong, it was written when Rabindranath was in Bangalore. Amito's iconoclastism meets Labannya's sincere simplicity through a series of scintillating dialogues and poems that they write for each other.

The novel also contains a self-reference of significance in Bangla literature. By the late-1920s, more than a decade after his

Nobel Prize, Tagore had become a towering presence in Bengal, and was facing criticism:

> A younger group of writers were trying to escape from the penumbra of Rabindranath, often by tilting at him and his work. In 1928 he decided to call a meeting of writers at Jorasanko and hear them debate the issues.

Shortly after this meeting, while writing this novel, Tagore has Amito railing against a much revered poet, whose name turns out to be Rabi Thakur — Rabi is a common short form of Rabindranath, and Thakur is the original Bangla for Tagore. Amito remarks: "Poets must live for at most five years. ... Our severest complaint against Rabi Thakur is that like Wordsworth, he is illicitly staying alive." These remarks aroused much mirth among the reading public, but the novel is also a serious attempt at demonstrating his versatility, at age 67, and the glittering wordplay, interwoven with poems in a modern free-verse style (written by Amito Ray under the fictitious name Nibaran Chakrabarty), underlines Tagore's command of the modernist ethos.

Even the theme was novel — after building up their affair and obtaining the blessings of Labannya's aunt, the lovers decide to marry other suitors, without the air of tragedy. In the text, the reason appears to be that they feel that daily chores of living together will kill the purity of their romance:

> Most barbarians equate marriage with the union, and look upon the real union thereafter with contempt.... ketaki and I — our love is like water in my *kalsi* (jug); I fill it each morning, and use it all day long. But Labannya's love is like a vast lake, not to be brought home, but into which my mind can immerse itself.

However, this surface text is subject to many interpretations. Rabindranath biographer Krishna Kripalini, writes in the foreword of his translation of Shesher Kabita (Farewell my Friend. London 1946):

> [Labannya] releases releases [Amit's] own submerged depth of sincerity, which he finds hard to adjust to... The struggle makes him a curiously pathetic figure...

The tragedy is understood by the girl who releases him from his troth and disappears from his life.

The poem 'Nirjharini' from the book was later published as a separate poem in the collection of poems known as Mohua.

Dramas

Tagore's experiences with drama began when he was sixteen, when he played the lead role in his brother Jyotirindranath's adaptation of Moliere's Le Bourgeois Gentilhomme. Tagore wrote his first original dramatic piece when he was twenty — *Valmiki Pratibha* (The Genius of Valmiki), which was shown at the Tagore's mansion. His works — emphasising fusion of lyrical flow and emotional rhythm tightly focused on a core idea — were unlike previous Bengali drama. Tagore stated that his works sought to articulate "the play of feeling and not of action". In 1890 he wrote *Visarjan* (Sacrifice); it has been regarded as his finest drama. In the original Bangla language, such works included intricate suplots and extended monologues. Later, Tagore's dramas used more philosophical and allegorical themes. For example, his 1912 *Dak Ghar* (Post Office) received rave reviews in Europe and was shown in London (at the Irish Theatre), Berlin, and Paris. Lastly, Tagore's *Chandalika* (Untouchable Girl) was modelled on an ancient Buddhist legend describing how Gautama Buddha's disciple Ananda asks water of an *Adivasi* (tribal girl, probably of the numerous Santal tribes found throughout western regions of Bengal.

Tagore's plays also are important to Bengali literature. All of his plays have been repeatedly staged and reinterpreted over the years. His most famous play, perhaps, is *Raktakaravi* (Red Oleanders) — the name of a red flower. It tells of a King who lives behind an iron curtain while his subjects have cruelty and death delivered upon them at the slightest pretext. People are forced to work in the mines so that the kleptocratic King and his cronies may render themselves even more wealthy. The play follows the heroine Nandini, who leads the people and finally the King himself towards the destruction of this artifact of subjugation. However, this ultimate victory is preceded by numerous deaths, most importantly that of Ranjan, Nandini's lover, and Kishore a young boy devoted to her. Tagore devoted much effort to

Raktakaravi, with (at least) eleven extant revisions. However, Tagore's motivation in writing Raktakaravi is disputed, with some suggesting negative opinions formed during his visit to the mines of Bombay. Others attribute it to dislike of the West, while others think that a woman motivated him to create Nandini. Tagore's other notable plays include Chitrangada, Raja, Valmiki-Pratibha, and Mayar Khela.

Poetry

Internationally, Gitanjali is Tagore's best-known collection of poetry. Tagore was awarded the Noble Prize in 1913 for his book 'Gitanjali' . Song VII from Gitanjali reads as follows:

> Free-verse translation by Tagore (Gitanjali, verse VII):
>
> "My song has put off her adornments. She has no pride of dress and decoration. Ornaments would mar our union; they would come between thee and me; their jingling would drown thy whispers."
>
> "My poet's vanity dies in shame before thy sight. O master poet, I have sat down at thy feet. Only let me make my life simple and straight, like a flute of reed for thee to fill with music."

Besides Gitanjali, other notable works include Manasi, *Sonar Tori* (Golden Boat), Balaka ("Wild Geese" — the title being a metaphor for migrating souls), and Purobi. Sonar Tori's most famous poem — dealing with the ephemeral nature of life and achievement — goes by the same name; it ends with the haunting phrase "*shunya nadir tire rahinu pari/jaha chhilo loye gelo shonar tori*" (all I had achieved was carried off on the golden boat — only I was left behind).

In *Dui Bigha Jomi* (A Strip of Land), Tagore explores the plight of a sharecropper whose meagre parcel of farmland is taken over — using falsified papers — by a moneylender; the poem concludes: "*rajar hosto kore shomosto kangaler dhon churi*" (it is the King's hand that steals from the downtrodden). Sonar Tori also contains Hing Ting Chhot. Although comic in form, it illuminates what Tagore saw as Bengali society's crippling lack of vision, originality, and wisdom: *durbodh ja chhilo kichu hoye gelo jol, shunno akasher moto ottonto nirmol* (Oh yes, now all has been explained, like the empty expanse of the open sky). Throughout his life, Tagore experimented with different poetic styles. For example, in his early years, he occasionally wrote his works in Shadhu Bhasha (a Sanskritised dialect of Bangla); later, Tagore moved seamlessly to using Chalit (a more popular dialect). Lastly, the poems in Balaka mark the start of an epoch; the most notable of these reads:

> Oh youth, oh the tender,
>
> Oh green, oh unknowing,
>
> hit the bodies of the halfdead to bring them back to life.

Later, with the development of new poetic ideas in Bengal — many originating from younger poets seeking to break with Tagore's style — Tagore absorbed new poetic concepts, which allowed him to further develop a unique identity. Examples of this include Africa and Camalia, which are among the better known of his latter poems.

Gitanjali

Gitanjali is a collection of 103 English poems, largely translations, by the great poet Rabindranath Tagore. This volume became very famous in the West, and was widely translated.

Gitanjali is also the title of an earlier Bengali volume (1910) of 157 mostly devotional songs. The word *Gitanjoli* is composed from "*git*", song, and "*anjoli*", offering, and thus means — "An offering of songs"; but the word for offering, anjoli, has a strong devotional connotation, so the title may also be interpreted as "prayer offering of song".

The English collection is not a translation of poems from the Bengali volume of the same name. While half the poems (52 out of 103) in the English text were selected from the Bengali volume, others were taken from these works (given with year and number of songs selected for the English text): Gitimallo (1914), Noibeddo (1901), Khea (1906) and a handful from other works. The translations were often radical, leaving out or altering large chunks of the poem and in one instance even fusing two separate poems.

The translations were undertaken prior to a visit to England in 1912, where the poems were extremely well received. A slender volume was published in 1913, with an exhilarating preface by W. B. Yeats. In the same year, based on a corpus of three thin translations, Rabindranath became the first non-European to win the Nobel Prize.

Poetry: The poems of Gitanjali express a largely metaphysical outlook, talking about a union with the "supreme"; but like much western poetry that explores similar themes, the language suggests the union of two earthly lovers. This type of anthropomorphic depiction of celestial love is quite common in the Vaishnava literature of India since the 12th century. Rabindranath Tagore encountered it also in his interactions with the Baul community in rural Bengal.

For example, poem 7 in the English volume renders poem 125 from the Bengali Gitanjali, *Amar e gan chherechhe tar shokol olongkar* and talks of heavenly love in terms of the lover taking off her jewellery, which is getting in the way of the union.

Some poems involve themes related to nature, but here, too, the spiritual is subtly present, as in this poem (no. 57), given here along with the Bangla text in Roman script:

> Light, my light, the world-filling light, the eye-kissing light, heart-sweetening light!
>
> Ah, the light dances, my darling, at the centre of my life; the light strikes, my darling, the chords of my love; the sky opens, the wind runs wild, laughter passes over the earth.
>
> The butterflies spread their sails on the sea of light. Lilies and jasmines surge up on the crest of the waves of light.
>
> The light is shattered into gold on every cloud, my darling, and it scatters gems in profusion.
>
> Mirth spreads from leaf to leaf, my darling, and gladness without measure. The heaven's river has drowned its banks and the flood of joy is abroad.

Legacy: In the English-speaking world, the writings of Tagore are no longer widely read. Nonetheless, for millions of Bangla speakers, the Bengali originals continue to resonate, as in this verse:

I stand mesmerised,

wondering how you sing

your notes hold the world spellbound -

the light of your music

lights up my universe.

Music

Tagore was also an accomplished musician and painter. Indeed, he wrote some 2,230 songs; together, these comprise Rabindra sangeet, now an integral part of Bengali culture. Yet, Tagore's music is inseparable from his literature, most of which — poems or parts of novels, stories, or plays alike — became lyrics for his songs.

These ran the gamut of human emotion, and are still frequently used to give voice to a wide range of experiences. Such is true of two such works: Bangladesh's *Aamaar Sonaar Baanglaa* and India's Jana Gana Mana; Tagore thus became the only person ever to have written the national anthems of two nations. Tagore also had an artist's eye for his own handwriting, embellishing the cross-outs and word layouts in his manuscripts with simple artistic leitmotifs.

At age sixty, Tagore took up drawing and painting; successful exhibitions of his many works — which made a debut appearance in Paris upon encouragement by artists he met in the south of France — were held throughout Europe. Tagore — who likely exhibited protanopia (colour blindness), or partial lack of (red-green, in Tagore's case) colour discernment — painted in a style characterised by peculiarities in aesthetic and colouring style. Nevertheless, Tagore took to emulating numerous styles, including that of craftwork by the Malanggan people of northern New Ireland, Haida carvings from the Pacific Northwest region of North America, and woodcuts by Max Pechstein.

Rabindra Sangeet

Rabindra Sangeet, also known as Tagore Songs in English, is a form of music composed by Rabindranath Tagore who added a new dimension to the musical concept of India in general and Bengal in specific.

Rabindra Sangeet use Indian classical music and traditional folk music as sources. Tagore wrote some 2,230 songs.

Influence and Legacy: Rabindra Sangeet has had a very strong influence in bengali cultural. These songs are regarded as cultural treasures of Bengal in both Bangladesh and West Bengal (India).

The Rabindrasangeet, which deal with varied themes are immensely popular and form a foundation for the Bengali ethos that is comparable to, perhaps even greater than, that which Shakespeare has on the English-speaking world. It is said that his songs are the outcome of 500 years of literary and cultural churning that the Bengali community has gone through.

In his book Caste and Outcaste, Dhan Gopal Mukherjee has said that these songs transcend the mundane to the aesthetic and express all ranges and categories of human emotion. The poet had given a voice to all-big or small, rich or poor. The poorest boatman on the Ganges as well as the rich landlord find expression for their emotional trials and tribulations in Tagore's songs.

Rabindrasangeet has evolved into a distinctive school of music. Practitioners of this genre are known to be fiercely protective of tradionalist practice. Novel interpretations and variations have drawn severe censure in both West Bengal and Bangladesh. And like Beethoven's symphonies or Vilayat Khan's sitar, Rabindrasangeet demands an educated, intelligent and cultured audience to appreciate the lyrical beauty of his compositions.

He was among the first to recognise that cinema should have its own language. In 1929 he wrote, "The beauty and grandeur of this form in motion has to be developed in such a way that it becomes self-sufficient without the use of words." The inherent beauty and depth of Tagore's songs have persuaded a number of filmmakers to use Tagore's songs in their films including Satyajit Ray, Ritwik Ghatak, Mrinal Sen, Nitin Bose, Tapan Sinha and

Kumar Shahani. His songs were also used in British, European and Australian movies just to capture the mood of a cinematic situation and to reveal a delicate interplay of relationships. Similarly, Hollywood film Siddhartha (1972) had Tagore's "O Nadi Re" sung by Hemant Kumar.

Ritwik Ghatak said of Tagore, "That man has culled all my feelings from long before my birth...I read him and find that...I have nothing new to say." In his Meghe Dhaka Tara (The Cloud-capped Star) and Subarnarekha, Ghatak uses Rabindrasangeet to express the poignancy of post-Partition Bengal.

Two of the songs written by Tagore are the national anthems of India and Bangladesh. These are:

- *Bangladesh:* "Amar Shonar Bangla"
- *India:* "Jana Gana Mana"

Uniqueness of Rabindrasangeet: Tagore died in 1941, but his sublimity and effect of his songs are eternal. In his songs, pure poetry has integrated the creator, nature and love. Human love (Prem) transforms into love and devotion for the creator (Bhakti). The collection of his 2000 odd songs is known as Gitabitan (garden of songs). The four major parts of this book are Puja (worship), Prem (love), Prakriti (Nature) and Bichitra (Diverse). However, the categorisations melt away in many songs. A song about rains may reveal longing for the lover. A love song may turn out to be love of the creator. Here are first two lines of one song:

> You are standing beyond my song. My melody reaches your feet, but I cannot reach you (Translation).

Amar Shonar Bangla

Amar Shonar Bangla (My Golden Bengal) is a 1906 song written and composed by the poet Rabindranath Tagore.

The word shonar literally means 'made of gold', but in the song shonar Bangla may be interpreted to either express the preciousness of Bengal or a reference to the colour of paddy fields before harvest. The song was written in 1906 during the period of Bongobhanga (Bongobhongo — 1905 Partition of Bengal) — when Bengal was divided in two halves by the British government based on religion. This song, along with a host of others, was written to rekindle the unified spirit of Bengal.

It is said that the music of this song was inspired by the Baul singer Gagan Harkara's song "*Kothay Pabo Tare*".

The first 10 lines of this song constitute the national anthem of Bangladesh. It was adopted in 1972 after the independence of Bangladesh. The English translation was done by Syed Ali Ahsan.

Lyrics: Literal translation:

My beloved Bengal
My Bengal of Gold,
I love you.

Forever your skies,
Your air set my heart in tune
As if it were a flute.

In spring, O mother mine,
The fragrance from your mango groves
Makes me wild with joy,
Ah, what a thrill!

In autumn, O mother mine,
In the full blossomed paddy fields
I have seen spread all over sweet smiles.

Ah, what beauty, what shades,
What an affection, and what tenderness!
What a quilt have you spread
At the feet of banyan trees
And along the banks of rivers!

O mother mine, words from your lips
Are like nectar to my ears.
Ah, what a thrill!

If sadness, O mother mine,
Casts a gloom on your face,
My eyes are filled with tears!

Chitto Jetha Bhayshunyo

Chitto jetha bhayashunyo (Where the mind is without fear) is among one of the most quoted poems in India and Bangladesh.

Written by Rabindranath Tagore before India's independence, it represents Tagore's dream of how the new, awakened India should be. The original Bengali poem was translated by the poet himself and was included in the Nobel Prize winning Gitanjali in 1912.

The English version is:

> Where the mind is without fear and the head is held high;
>
> Where knowledge is free;
>
> Where the world has not been broken up into fragments by narrow domestic walls;
>
> Where words come out from the depth of truth;
>
> Where tireless striving stretches its arms towards perfection;
>
> Where the clear stream of reason has not lost its way into the dreary desert sand of dead habit;
>
> Where the mind is led forward by thee into ever-widening thought and action ...
>
> Into that heaven of freedom, my father, let my country awake.

The last two lines of original Bengali version are harsher. They state:

> "Lord Father, strike {the sleeping} Bharat (India) without mercy, so that it may awaken into such a heaven.

While Tagore was not a politician, his poem has continued to inspire Indians to create a free-thinking, united and dynamic nation. The poem is also very popular among the liberals in Bangladesh.

Tagore died on August 7, 1941, six years before an independent India came into existence.

Ekla Chalo Re

Jodi Tor Dak Shune Keu Na Ashe (If they answer not to thy call), often shortened to *Ekla Cholo Re* (Walk Alone) is a song written by the Nobel Prize winning poet Rabindranath Tagore, and is a part of the Rabindra Sangeet canon.

It exhorts the listener to continue his or her journey, despite abandonment or lack of support from others. The song is often quoted in the context of political or social change movements; Mahatma Gandhi cited it as one his favourite songs.

Lyrics: Tagore's English translation:

If they answer not to thy call walk alone,

If they are afraid and cower mutely facing the wall,

O thou of evil luck,

open thy mind and speak out alone.

If they turn away, and desert you when crossing the wilderness,

O thou of evil luck,

trample the thorns under thy tread,

and along the blood-lined track travel alone.

If they do not hold up the light when the night is troubled with storm,

O thou of evil luck,

with the thunder flame of pain ignite thy own heart

and let it burn alone.

In Popular Culture:

- A part of the song was used in the 2005 film Netaji Subhash Chandra Bose: The Forgotten Hero. It was sung by Sonu Nigam and composed by A. R. Rehman video search.
- "*Ekla Chalo Re*" is the title of a book by the Jain Acharya Mahaprajna

- The song was famously sung by Vinoba Bhave during the beginnings of his Bhoodan Movement, with "blessed" substituted for "unfortunate".
- It inspired "*chal akelaa, chal akelaa, chal akelaa*" by Pradeep in movie Sambandh, 1969 video search.

Jana Gana Mana

Jana Gana Mana (Bengali: *Jono Gono Mono*) is the national anthem of India. Written in highly Sanskritised Bengali, it is the first of five stanzas of a Brahmo hymn composed and scored by Nobel laureate Rabindranath Tagore. It was first sung at the Calcutta Session of the Indian National Congress on 27 December 1911. Jana Gana Mana was officially adopted by the Constituent Assembly as the Indian national anthem on January 24, 1950.

A formal rendition of the national anthem takes fifty-two seconds. A shortened version consisting of the first and last lines (and taking about 20 seconds to play) is also staged occasionally.

Lyrics: Although written in Bengali, the pronunciation of the anthem varies considerably across India due to the country's extensive linguistic diversity. The transcription below reflects the original Bengali pronunciation, in both the Bengali script and romanisation. Many of the silent letters found in the lyrics are pronounced by speakers of other Indian languages, reflecting a spelling pronunciation of the Bengali text, and often matching the pronunciation of the cognate words in the speaker's native language.

Translation into English: The following translation, attributed to Tagore, is provided by the Government of India's national portal:

Thou art the ruler of the minds of all people,

Dispenser of India's destiny.

Thy name rouses the hearts of Punjab, Sind,

Gujarat and Maratha,

Of the Dravida and Orissa and Bengal;

It echoes in the hills of the Vindhyas and Himalayas,

mingles in the music of Jamuna and Ganges and is
chanted by the waves of the Indian Ocean.
They pray for thy blessings and sing thy praise.
The saving of all people waits in thy hand,
Thou dispenser of India's destiny.
Victory, victory, victory to thee.

Controversies: Controversy exists regarding the appropriateness of Jana Gana Mana as the national anthem of an independent India. The poem was composed in December 1911, precisely at the time of the Coronation Durbar of George V, and is considered by some to be a paean in praise of "the overlord of India's destiny". The composition was first sung during a convention of the then loyalist Indian National Congress in Calcutta on Dec. 16, 1911. It was sung on the second day of the convention, and the agenda of that day devoted itself to a loyal welcome of George V on his visit to India. The event was reported thus in the British Indian press:

"The Bengali poet Babu Rabindranath Tagore sang a song composed by him specially to welcome the Emperor." (Statesman, Dec. 28, 1911)

"The proceedings began with the singing by Babu Rabindranath Tagore of a song specially composed by him in honour of the Emperor." (Englishman, Dec. 28, 1911)

"When the proceedings of the Indian National Congress began on Wednesday 27th December 1911, a Bengali song in welcome of the Emperor was sung. A resolution welcoming the Emperor and Empress was also adopted unanimously." (Indian, Dec. 29, 1911)

The belief gained ground that the poem has been written in honour of the visiting monarch. Others aver that the newspaper reports cited above were misguided, the confusion arising since a different song, written in Hindi by Rambhuj Chaudhary, was sung on the same occasion in praise of the monarch. However, the two poems were written in different languages; Tagore already enjoyed much fame in India, and newspaper reports are both consistent and categorical on the point of Tagore having himself sung his composition on the occasion.

Other explanations for the motivations that informed the creation of the poem have been proposed. On a visit to India, the poet Yeats received a visit from an Indian admirer who was also, in Yeats' words, "an Indian devotee" of Tagore. In a letter to a lady friend, Yeats quoted this unnamed devotee as giving him a 'strictly off the records' version of events dealing with the writing of Jana Gana Mana. Thus, Tagore is said to have written the poem in honour of God. In a letter to Pulin Behari Sen, Tagore himself wrote:

> "A certain high official in His Majesty's service, who was also my friend, had requested that I write a song of felicitation towards the Emperor. The request simply amazed me. It caused a great stir in my heart. In response to that great mental turmoil, I pronounced the victory in Jana Gana Mana of that Bhagya Vidhata [ed. God of Destiny] of India who has from age after age held steadfast the reins of India's chariot through rise and fall, through the straight path and the curved. That Lord of Destiny, that Reader of the Collective Mind of India, that Perennial Guide, could never be George V, George VI, or any other George. Even my official friend understood this about the song. After all, even if his admiration for the crown was excessive, he was not lacking in simple common sense."

In 2005, there were calls to delete the word "Sindh" and substitute it with the word Kashmir. The argument was that Sindh was no longer a part of India, having become part of Pakistan as a result of the Partition of 1947. Opponents of this proposal hold that the word "Sindh" refers to the Indus and to Sindhi culture, and that Sindhi people are an integral part of India's cultural fabric. The Supreme Court of India declined to change the national anthem and the wording remains unchanged.

In July 1985 in the state of Kerala, some of the Jehovah's Witnesses' children were expelled from school under the instructions of Deputy Inspector of Schools for having refused to sing the national anthem, Jana Gana Mana. A parent, V. J. Emmanuel, appealed to the Supreme Court of India for legal remedy. On August 11, 1986, the Supreme Court overruled the Kerala High Court, and directed the respondent authorities to re-admit the children into the school. The decision went on to add: "Our tradition teaches tolerance, our philosophy teaches tolerance, our Constitution practices tolerance, let us not dilute it".

There are few set rules about reciting the Jana Gana Mana which includes not singing it under any cover, not singing it under any imperfect state of mind. Not doing so is to show disrespect to the national anthem. Rule related to not singing Jana Gana Mana under any cover corresponds to the freedom of yourself and hence of your country while the other rule justifies that not being in proper state of mind may lead in incorrect recitations which is again a disregard to your country.

English Composition in Madanapalle: Rabindranath Tagore translated Jana Gana Mana from Bengali to English and also set it to music in Madanapalle, a town in Andhra Pradesh.

Though the Bengali song had been written in 1911, it was largely unknown except to the readers of the Brahmo Samaj journal, "*Tatva Bodha Prakasika*", of which Tagore was the editor.

During 1918-19, Tagore accepted an invitation from friend and controversial Irish poet James H. Cousins to spend a few days at the Besant Theosophical College, of which Cousins was the principal. On the evening of February 28, he joined a gathering of students and upon Cousins' request, sang the Jana Gana Mana in Bengali. In the days that followed, enchanted by the dreamy hills of Madanapalle, Tagore wrote down the English translation of the song and along with Cousins' wife, Margaret (an expert in Western music), set down the notation which is followed till this day.

The library of Besant Theosophical College in Madanapalle, the framed original English translation is displayed.

Paintings

Over one thousand poems; nearly two dozen plays and play-lets; eight novels; eight or more volumes of short stories; more than two thousands songs, of which he wrote both the words and the music; and a mass of prose on literary, social, religious, political, and other topics. On top of these, his English translations; his paintings; his travels and lecture-tours in Asia, America, and Europe; and his activities as educationist, as social and religious reformer, and politician. The life's work of Ravindranath Tagore is the accomplishment of a titan. Gurudev Rabindranath Tagore — mystic, visionary, painter and Nobel laureate for literature — was India's grand old man of letters. But Tagore has been immortalised not only by his poetry but also by his paintings and his important contribution to Indian Art through Vishwa Bharati.

Born in Jorasanko on 7th May 1861, seventh in a family of fourteen. The Tagores were a cultured and wealthy family, and Rabindranath's father, Devendranath, was one of the leaders of the Brahma Samaj. The poet's early life was spent in an atmosphere of religion and arts, principally literature, music and painting. In religion his inspiration was derived from the Vedas and the Upanishads, but with him as with many Hindus the Upanishadic monoism was diversified by the Vaisnava dualism.

Rabindranath learnt drawing in his childhood and was attracted to the sketches drawn by his elder brother Jyotirindranath. At the age of seventeen, his first book of poems was published. In 1878, he went to England for further studies but returned back in just seventeen months as he was disappointed with the studies. In music Tagore's training was classical Indian, though as a composer he rebelled against the tyranny of classical orthodoxy, and introduced many variations of form and phrase, notably from Bengali folk-music.

In 1911, on revisiting England, Tagore brought the English Gitanjali, which was published in 1912. Gitanjali saw him winning, in 1913, at the age of 52, the Nobel Prize for literature. The first Nobel Prize ever awarded to an Asiatic, made him world-famous. Following this, he was knighted by the British in 1915.

In 1917, Tagore founded the innovative 'Vishwa Bharati' university in the rural settings of Shantiniketan, thus realising a life-long dream to create a context for a genuine all-round development of human faculties. Far from the neurosis of the city life, this was not to be a degree-oriented establishment, but an attempt, in his own words "to study the mind of Man in it's realisation of different aspects of truth from diverse points of view."

Two years later, in protest against the ghastly massacre of hundreds of innocent Indians at the 'Jalianwala Bagh' by General Dyer, Sir Ravindranath returned his title to the British and quietly opened the art wing of his university called '*Kala Bhavan*'. He invited the like-minded painter Nandlal Bose to run the wing with a free hand, thus encouraging the evolution of an original vision, reflecting the intuition and expression of the students, unleashed from the bounds of tradition and the stifling rigours of conventional training. The opening of the 'Kala Bhavan' proved to be a decisive landmark in the history of evolution of Indian Art.

Tagore spent the rest of his life at Shantiniketan, except for several travels and lecture-tours in which he carried his message of human integrity to many countries in Asia, America and Europe.

In 1924, while writing "Purabi" he started doodling on the pages of his manuscript. However, Rabindra Nath Tagore's famous world appearance as painter in France in 1930 was not sudden. Long before the Paris exhibition which vaulted him to worldwide painterly fame, in 1926, Tagore had long discussions on his art with Romain Rolland. Himself a Nobel laureate Romain Rolland wrote in his book 'Inde-journal', on 3rd July, 1926 "......other day Tagore was discussing on his application of colour in paintings. He likes very little red colour, the dominance of red colour in Italian village did not attract him. His love goes violet and blue and he has more liking for green." Tagore had discussions about art with another Nobel Laureate, French poet Saint John Perse over their several meetings in 1920s.

Rabindranath transformed his lack of formal training of art into an advantage and opened new horizons in the use of line and colour. He was prolific in his paintings and sketches as he was in his writing, producing over 2,500 of these within a decade. Over 1,500 of them are preserved in Vishwa Bharati, Shantiniketan.

It is evident that in his search of newer form of expression in line and colour Rabindranath was trying to express something different from what he did in his poetry and songs. If he sought peace and enlightenment in his songs, he seems to explore darkness and mystery in his drawings. Dark creatures and haunting landscapes of another, primordial and marvellous world, which constituted Tagore's works puzzle and delight the world. With the passage of time, critics and art lovers have been discovering in these outpourings from the depths of his fanciful mind a more modern and disquieting Tagore than they see elsewhere.

Tagore himself, in his article 'My Pictures', explains his paintings as follows "The world of sound is a tiny bubble in the silence of the infinite. The Universe has its only language of gesture, it talks in the voice of pictures and dance. Every object in this world proclaims in the dumb signal of lines and colours, the fact that it is not a mere logical abstraction or a mere thing of use, but it is unique in itself, it carries the miracle of its existence. In a picture the artist creates the language of undoubted reality, and we are satisfied that we see. It may not be the representation of a beautiful woman but that of a common place donkey or of something that has no external credential of truth in nature but only in its own inner artistic significance.

"People often ask me about the meaning of my pictures. I remain silent even as my pictures are. It is for them to express and not to explain. They have nothing ulterior behind their own appearance for the thoughts to explore and words to describe, and that appearance carries its ultimate worth. Then they remain, otherwise they are rejected and forgotten even though they may have some scientific truth or ethical justification. Love is kindred to art, it is inexplicable. Duty can be measured by the degree of its benefit, utility by the profit and power it may bring, but art by nothing but itself. There are other factors of life which are visitors that come and go. Art is the guest that comes and remains. The dithers may be important, but Art is inevitable."

In spring 1930, when on a tour to France, Tagore was advised, by some art critics of local newspapers who saw his paintings, to hold an exhibition in Paris. He held the first public and international exhibition of his paintings in Paris in May 1930, at the Gallerie Pigalle. The exhibition was later held in different countries in Europe in the same year. But India and his home town Calcutta had the honour of hosting it only in 1931, a year later of Paris exhibition.

The exhibition remained open to public from the 5th to the 19th May, 1930. Duchess Anna de Noailles, in her introductory remarks in the catalogue of the exhibition of Tagore's paintings "To me it is like climbing a staircase of dreamland"

After the conclusion of Paris exhibition, exhibitions were held in England, Denmark, Sweden, Rome, Germany and Russia in Europe. Later exhibitions were also held in USA and Canada. The exhibition of paintings drew an unprecedented overwhelming admiration in Germany.

It was shown in Berlin, Munich, Hamburg, Dusseldorf, Stuttgart and other places in Germany. The then German President and ministers and also Albert Einstein, the great scientist, attended Tagore's exhibition.

Tagore's paintings and sketches fascinated young German students to mass hysteria. Among them a student of the Art Academy of Munich Oswald Malura, at the age of 20, received a Mond travel scholarship of the academy to study Indian art and philosophy.

Malura stayed in India for three years (1929-32) and visited Bombay, Agra, Delhi, Kashmir, Benaras, Himalayas, Shantiniketan and Calcutta and he met Annie Besant, Mahatma Gandhi and poet Tagore.

At Shantiniketan, this amateur cinematogarpher recorded a 12 minute-film on Tagore as a painter and teacher in the open-air classes. There are some still photographs that showed how Tagore drew and painted but this movie film or cinema on Tagore as an artist is indeed rare.

Malura revisited Calcutta in 1986 and presented this short silent film on Tagore as painter to the Vishva Bharati University in December 1986. Malura said, "my impression was that Tagore was to me like a Godsent man. I liked so much his sketches and colouring that I could not resist myself to photograph it. But alas! it was in black and white."

In Tagore's own words, "The world speaks to me in colours, my soul answers in music". Obviously, the soul was very articulate with colours too.

In later years, as Tagore reached his sixties, he tried to finance his Vishwa-Bharati University personally, relying on royalties and proceeds from his lecture tours. By 1941, Tagore's health had seriously deteriorated. Tagore died peacefully, after an operation in Calcutta on August 7, 1941.

In his life, he embodied the quintessence of Indian culture, combining an abundant intellect with a devout passion to his cause, and his inspirational compositions have stood the passage of time. Tagore's contribution to the art of India remains one of the most important till date.

5

Tagore's Spiritualism

Rabindranath Tagore the bard of Bengal immaculately brought out the essence of Eastern spirituality in his poetry like no other poet. His spiritual vision, as he himself said, is imbued "with the ancient spirit of India as revealed in our sacred texts and manifested in the life of today."

The Guru of Indian Poets

During the days of freedom movement, several poets and writers of India produced creative works capable of inspiring nationalism and patriotism among the people. Among the poets Rabindranath Tagore was a great Indian poet, who contributed enormously to the nation's freedom movement.

The Guru of Indian poets, Rabindranath Tagore was born in Calcutta on 7th May 1861. The Tagore family had a long tradition of culture and yet was not closed to the new winds coming from the west to India at that time. And what is more, the family was ready to provide its children every thing that was congenial to the flowering of their inherent talents.

Rabindranath Tagore ran away from a traditional school during his early teens and had his education seen to and supervised by his father. He was sent to England in 1878 for further education under Henry Morley at London University College. At the threshold of his youth, he had already been initiated into Indian classical literature, Indian and western music and had begun to write verse. In his making as a poet, Tagore was greatly influenced by the inspirations from Brahmo Samaj. His books of poems, dramas, short stories and novels in Bengali soon gave him a distinctive place in that literature.

Initially a raconteur, his compendium 'Letters from a Sojourner in London' which was based on his life and times in London was published in book form in 1881. During the same year he wrote the play 'Valmiki Prativa' and it was a rare stage appearance when Tagore appeared in the title role. Tagore's genius entered a new phase when he composed the poems of 'Manasi', the musical play 'Mayur Khela' and the drama 'Raja Rani'. He was the editor of the monthly magazine 'Sadhana'. He ultimately published his works 'Sonar Tari' and 'Panchabhuta' in the same journal.

It is the powerful patriotic spirit of Tagore's literary works that brought him in the mainstream of the freedom struggle and earned him national wisdom. He captured the depth of the nation's feelings in his poem 'Into That Heaven of Freedom' a poem that moved many nationalists to tears.

> Where the mind is without fear
> And the head is held high,
> Where knowledge is free,
> Where the world has not been broken up,
> Into fragments by narrow domestic walls,
> Where words come out from the depth of truth,
> Where tireless striving stretch its arm towards
> perfection,
> Where the mind is led by thee into ever-widening,
> Thought and action into that heaven of freedom,
> My Father, Let my country awake.

As a patriot poet and a nationalist, Rabindranath Tagore influenced not only the leaders of the national movement but also the masses. His works generated a spirit for liberating India from colonialism. He was on a poetic mission to save India from slavery. His works ignited passion and united people to dedicate themselves to the national struggle. He opposed the Partition of Bengal along communal lines and resented the concept that would divide his beloved state. He preached swadeshi, composed soul-stirring songs, wrote incisive essays, addressed meetings and led protest marches.

Tagore gifted to India her national anthem, a prose paraphrase of which he read at Over Town Hall as part of his world famous essay 'My Interpretation of India's History. The national anthem was composed for the Brahmo Samaja anniversary in 1912. The inspiration and patriotic spirit generated by this song was considerable and immeasurable. The song generated a sense of national unity during the days of freedom struggle which made India stronger than ever before. That poem made one of the makers of modern India. He was a seer and national builder. He was given importance for revival of Hinduism.

Tagore was a great poet. In 1874 his first poem 'Abhilash' was published in 'Tattobodhini Patrika'. During his life his entire writings include 1,000 poems, 2,000 songs and large number of short stories. In 1912, Tagore sailed for England, where the translation of the 'Gitanjali' (Song-Offerings) created a literary sensation among the British poets. Gitanjali established Tagore as a world poet. In 1913, Tagore's Gitanjali was nominated and selected by the Swedish Academy for the Nobel Prize for literature.

For his literary activities, he was Knighted by the British government in 1915. But protesting the Jalianwala Bagh tragedy, Rabindranath Tagore gave up his 'Knighthood' in 1919. During this time he declared, "When the badges of honour make our shame glaring in their congruous context of humiliation, and I, for my part, wish to stand, shorn of all special distinctions, by the side of my country men who for their so-called insignificance are liable to suffer degradation not fit for human beings."

Rabindranath Tagore had started his own school at Shantiniketan in West Bengal in 1901, which grew up gradually to be named as the Vishva Bharati or the centre of the world learning in 1971. The place is now one of the recognised Universities of India and has been a place especially for the study of art, music, literature and cultures of the world. Today this university at Shantiniketan sought to provide a place where children could grow up in freedom, amidst an environment of nature's beauty and warm human relationships.

Tagore was not only a good litterateur, but also was a good painter. In his time each painting of his life was very individualistic. He had given tunes to his songs and having a style and a nuance of their own, they form now a separate category in Indian music called Rabindra Sangeet.

Tagore was a pioneer in the experiment with rural reconstruction in India. The contribution of his songs to the national freedom movement was immense. In short, he is an example of the multifarious ways the excellence hidden within a person can express itself, provided the proper environment is there and provided the centre within the individual is awake to take advantage of that environment.

To conclude, Tagore's life time achievements can be put in Iqbal Masud's words "In Tagore we have a culture going back 2,000 years-it is what one can call the Hindu Culture. But a point that is often missed is that Tagore was a product of the Bengal Renaissance, which in turn was a product of 19th century liberalism."

Tagore's Work to Live for Generations

If one individual is to be singled out for representing the values and traditions of India from the ancient times to the modern age, it cannot be any one other than Rabindranath Tagore.

He was the one person who incorporated the wisdom of the past, reflected in the spiritual and intellectual attainments of the Vedas and the Upanishads. Yet, he was never so immersed in India's seemingly other-worldly heritage, underlined in the philosophical concept of the world being an illusion (*maya*), as to negate rationalism. To use a cliche, he combined the best of both worlds.

Tagore scored in this respect over his other great contemporary, Mahatma Gandhi, for the Mahatma placed a far greater emphasis on the spirit of renunciation marking a rejection of the Western industrial civilization.

To a large extent, it is this attitude extolling the 'simple living, high thinking' outlook that is still favoured in India, even if it is not infrequently identified with hypocrisy.

Tagore set his face against such a rule of thumb approach to life if only because his horizon was much wider than Gandhi's. He had no time for Gandhi's rejection of European machines and preference for primitive Indian ones like the '*charkha*', or the spinning wheel.

> 'If a man is stunted by big machines', Tagore wrote, 'the danger of being stunted by small machines must not be lost sight of. The charkha in its proper place can do no harm ... but where ... it is in the wrong place, then the thread can only be spun at the cost of a great deal of the mind itself. The man is no less valuable than the cotton thread.'

Poet, thinker, playwright, novelist, writer of short stories, dance dramas and songs, painter and educationist — Tagore's versatility was matched only by his genius. Truly, he was Gurudev, the epitome of the preceptor idealised in Indian myths and folklore.

Not surprisingly, Gandhi bestowed the title on Tagore — an honour that befits him even today — just as Tagore called Gandhi the Mahatma, recognising the sterling qualities of a saint in the politician, who is embroiled in the heat and dust of quotidian battles.

It was left to Nehru to say that although Tagore and Gandhi were 'entirely different from each other, and yet both of them (were) typical of India, both in the long line of India's great men'.

If Tagore's legacy remains as relevant today as it was in his time, the reason is that he cherished certain ideals that have come to distinguish India in the present-day world. Hence, perhaps, the statues, busts and university chairs named after him which dot the world.

The first and foremost concept of Indian nationhood that he lauded was its inclusiveness. He recounts in one of his poems how the streams of Aryans, non-Aryans, Sakas, Huns, Pathans, Mughals *et al.* have merged to give India its distinctive identity. It is not impossible that he developed this concept from a study of his own family, which he regarded as a product of the 'confluence of three cultures, Hindu, Mohammedan and British'.

It is this ideal of an integrated and vibrant multicultural society, a rainbow nation, which India holds up today as the only valid model which can ensure the survival and advancement of all. Otherwise, the so-called civilizational clashes between ethnic, religious and linguistic groups will tear the world apart.

It is perhaps just as well that the great man died before India itself fell prey in 1947 to one such murderous conflict based on religion. And, then, the broken nation saw another divisive conflict in 1971 based on language and sub-nationalism, which led to the creation of Bangladesh.

Tagore would probably have been even more mortified by the second rupture because he came from that part of the subcontinent — East Bengal. In his time, he witnessed the colonial rulers partition Bengal in 1905, a traumatic upheaval for his Sonar Bangla. Fittingly, it is his song of love and reverence for the land where he was born (Amar Shonar Bangla) which is now the national anthem of Bangladesh.

Tagore recognised the seeds of the conflicts that tore apart India in Gandhi's use of religious symbols, both Hindu and Muslim as in the concept of Ram Rajya and the exhortation in favour of the Caliphate. He was as opposed to Gandhi's love for 'small machines', with their numbing effect on the mind, as to his idealisation of religious emblems, which can exert an equally stifling impact on the largely illiterate masses.

> 'I blamed Mahatmaji', Tagore wrote, 'for exploiting (the) irrational force of credulity in our people.' While Gandhi defended the Hindu idols, as the English clergyman and admirer of India C. F. Andrews recalled, 'believing the masses (to be) incapable of raising themselves immediately to abstract ideals', Tagore could not 'bear to see the people eternally treated as a child'.

Many will see Tagore's depiction of the crafty politician mouthing nationalistic slogans to mobilise the credulous in his novel Gharey Barey as a mirror image of the present political scene, just as his prescient vision that a revolution devours its own children, as in Char Adhyay, will be appreciated today although it was written in the context of the much-lionised anti-British revolutionaries and anarchists of his time.

Tagore wasn't without his critics at home and abroad. Even while accepting the Nobel Prize for Literature in 1913, he referred to the 'calumnies and insults' he had received from his countrymen. The West, too, lost its interest soon enough. Graham Greene thought in 1937 'I cannot believe that anyone but Mr. Yeats can still take his (Tagore's) poems very seriously'. And Yeats himself had come to the conclusion by then that Tagore wrote 'sentimental rubbish'.

Notwithstanding these ups and downs, as in the life of all individuals, big and small, Tagore's thinking had a stamp of modernity which can act as guideposts for India and the world — just as his song, '*Ekla Chalo Re*' (Walk Alone), inspired Gandhi during the communal violence of 1946-47.

And nowhere is Tagore's modern outlook more evident than in his paintings, with their remarkable stark originality, quite in contrast to the mellifluous nature of his verse. Perhaps more than any other aspect of his vast artistic output, it is in his paintings that apparently depict his real self — 'I am by nature a savage' — that Tagore will live for generations.

Tagore's Mystical Quest

Swami Adiswarananda of the Ramakrishna-Vivekananda Centre of New York, in his preface to 'Tagore: The Mystic Poets' writes, "The inner-seeking spirituality of India infused all of Tagore's writing. He wrote in many genres of the deep religious milieu of Hinduism. The values and core beliefs of the Hindu scriptures permeated his work."

Says the Swami: "Rabindranath Tagore's philosophical and spiritual thoughts transcend all limits of language, culture, and nationality. In his writings, the poet and mystic takes us on a spiritual quest and gives us a glimpse of the infinite in the midst of the finite, unity at the heart of all diversity, and the Divine in all beings and things of the universe."

Tagore's Spiritual Beliefs

Tagore believed that "True knowledge is that which perceives the unity of all things in God." Tagore through his vast body of immortal literary works taught us that the universe is a manifestation of God, and that there is no unbridgeable gulf between our world and God's, and that God is the one who can provide the greatest love and joy.

Tagore's Poetry Teaches Us How to Love God

Tagore's 'Gitanjali' or 'Song Offerings' that contains his own English prose translations of Bengali poetry was published in 1913 with an introduction by the Irish poet W. B. Yeats. This book won Tagore the Nobel Prize for Literature that year. Here's an excerpt from his introduction that helps us realise that "We had not known that we loved God, hardly it may be that we believed in Him..."

The Ubiquity of God in Tagore's Works

Yeats Writes: "These verses ... as the generations pass, reveller will hum them on the highway and men rowing upon the rivers. Lovers, while they await one another, shall find, in murmuring them, this love of God a magic gulf wherein their own more bitter passion may bathe and renew its youth... The reveller in the read-brown clothes that he wears that dust may not show upon him, the girl searching in her bed for the petals fallen from the wreath of her royal lover, the servant or the bride awaiting the master's homecoming in the empty house, are images of the heart turning to God. Flowers and rivers, the blowing of conch shells, the heavy rain of the Indian July, or the moods of that heart in union or in separation; and a man sitting in a boat upon a river playing lute, like one of those figures full of mysterious meaning in a Chinese picture, is God Himself..."

Select Poems from Tagore's Song Offerings

The following pages contain a selection of his best poems that are steeped in Indian mysticism and the omnipresence of the Almighty as someone so close to our heart.

Leave this chanting and singing and telling of beads! Whom dost thou worship in this lonely dark corner of a temple with doors all shut? Open thine eyes and see thy God is not before thee!

He is there where the tiller is tilling the hard ground and where the pathmaker is breaking stones. He is with them in sun and in shower, and his garment is covered with dust. Put of thy holy mantle and even like him come down on the dusty soil!

Deliverance? Where is this deliverance to be found? Our master himself has joyfully taken upon him the bonds of creation; he is bound with us all for ever.

Come out of thy meditations and leave aside thy flowers and incense! What harm is there if thy clothes become tattered and stained? Meet him and stand by him in toil and in sweat of thy brow.

When the creation was new and all the stars shone in their first splendour, the gods held their assembly in the sky and sang 'Oh, the picture of perfection! the joy unalloyed!'

But one cried of a sudden — 'It seems that somewhere there is a break in the chain of light and one of the stars has been lost.'

The golden string of their harp snapped, their song stopped, and they cried in dismay — 'Yes, that lost star was the best, she was the glory of all heavens!'

From that day the search is unceasing for her, and the cry goes on from one to the other that in her the world has lost its one joy!

Only in the deepest silence of night the stars smile and whisper among themselves — 'Vain is this seeking! unbroken perfection is over all!'

In one salutation to thee, my God, let all my senses spread out and touch this world at thy feet.

Like a rain-cloud of July hung low with its burden of unshed showers let all my mind bend down at thy door in one salutation to thee.

Let all my songs gather together their diverse strains into a single current and flow to a sea of silence in one salutation to thee.

Like a flock of homesick cranes flying night and day back to their mountain nests let all my life take its voyage to its eternal home in one salutation to thee.

When it was day they came into my house and said, 'We shall only take the smallest room here.'

They said, 'We shall help you in the worship of your God and humbly accept only our own share in his grace'; and then they took their seat in a corner and they sat quiet and meek.

But in the darkness of night I find they break into my sacred shrine, strong and turbulent, and snatch with unholy greed the offerings from God's altar.

I know thee as my God and stand apart — I do not know thee as my own and come closer. I know thee as my father and bow before thy feet — I do not grasp thy hand as my friend's.

I stand not where thou comest down and ownest thyself as mine, there to clasp thee to my heart and take thee as my comrade.

Thou art the Brother amongst my brothers, but I heed them not, I divide not my earnings with them, thus sharing my all with thee.

In pleasure and in pain I stand not by the side of men, and thus stand by thee. I shrink to give up my life, and thus do not plunge into the great waters of life.

What divine drink wouldst thou have, my God, from this overflowing cup of my life?

My poet, is it thy delight to see thy creation through my eyes and to stand at the portals of my ears silently to listen to thine own eternal harmony?

Thy world is weaving words in my mind and thy joy is adding music to them. Thou givest thyself to me in love and then feelest thine own entire sweetness in me.

[illegible]

Tagore was of the view that [illegible] of the post-religious laboratory of industrial capitalism. It is but the organisation of politics and commerce that brings 'harvests of wealth by spreading tentacles of greed, selfishness, power and prosperity, and sacrificing in the process, the moral man, the complete man, to make room for the political and the commercial man, the man of limited purpose'. Nationalism, Tagore expressed, is not 'a spontaneous self-expression of man as social being', where human relationships are naturally regulated, so that men can

6

The Great Genius

Rabindranath Tagore is one of those few iconic personalities whom the people of India hold very close to their heart. A literary genius and a humanist, he did not leave any facet of life untouched until it bloomed into an unforgettable creation of supreme beauty and charm. A people's bard, his heart never stopped wrenching at the sight of human misery. For this he would compose and stage drama and stretch out a helping hand to bring succour to the needy. A thorough nationalist, he would not brook any narrow sentimentalism coming in the way of universal human values. An uncompromising lover of freedom, he would be resolute in raising his voice even against trifle attempts at its stifling. He was the muse who could transfix the garrulous currents of river Padma in a notebook sitting on its bank. He remains as yet a gem of a man to be surpassed in whatever he did. Not surprisingly, the greatest tribute to him came from none else than the Mahatma in his own lifetime, who called him 'Gurudev'.

Tagore, the Genious

As a child Rabindranath's natural curiosity to know the world in which he lived had suffered immeasurably at the hands of those who tried to educate him. In a household that was humming with all kinds of activities, it was but natural for the fourteenth child of a generously expanding joint family to be relegated to the sidelines of its attention. He had thus been left almost to the care of what he later termed as "servocracy." The one who was appointed to feed him would be happy if he ate less and the other in charge of keeping him engaged would in the first opportunity make good while leaving him alone in a room.

It was not that he grudged the lack of family attention. For him it was indeed a blessing in disguise. He could then revel at the marvels of the nature's ways "through the venetian shutters of the window he would gaze below" and play with his own imaginations. The only problems he had to put up with were however the tyrannical elementary lessons, which the tutor at home was ever so eager to impart him. Going to school like other children from the family thus appeared to him as a possible option that could bring outings from home. But the first school, Oriental Seminary, where he went to as a toddler, left him with only bitter memories of physical disciplining and how not to study. All that he would remember of this early experience later was about "how much easier it is to acquire the manner than the matter".

The second school, which he went to, likewise turned out to be abysmally abnormal in its treatment of children, though ironically it was named Normal School. Whereas the first school excelled in various "ingenious methods of punishment", this one specialised in a routine that had little to cheer about. There was no respite even at home from megalomaniac tutors. They came one after another like scheming characters in a play as it were to change his world of consciousness.

The only joyous experience through all these miseries was his initiation into the actual world of learning by his elder brother Hemendranath, who insisted on grooming the children's inherent potential through their mother tongue. The net result of it all was not only that he realised how fruitful this approach was as a child, but also that how worthwhile it was socially and culturally after he had advanced well into his life and had begun experimenting with children's education at Shantiniketan. As he wrote later in his remarkably candid style: "Learning should as far as possible follow the process of eating. When the taste begins from the first bite, the stomach is awakened to its function before it is loaded, so that its digestive juices get full play. Nothing like this happens, however, when the Bengali boy is taught in English ... While one is choking and spluttering over the spelling and grammar, the inside remains starved, and when at length the taste is felt, the appetite has vanished."

Then there came the most exciting experience of his childhood while accompanying his father to the high Himalayas, particularly those first few days, which they spent at Shantiniketan on their way. Left largely to his own, there grew in him the natural instinct to compose verses and join the Maharishi in reading "select pieces from Sanskrit, Bengali and English literatures" during the day and reciting hymns in the evening. Such was the keenness in adhering to this routine even at Dalhousie that upon his return he could sing extempore the whole of the Valmiki Ramayana in Sanskrit at the request of his mother at her "open-air gatherings on the roof-terrace in the evening."

The long term effect of it was such that despite the insistence of the elders at home to tie him down to the school regimen, he dropped out of it altogether. In the words of his biographer: "The tutors soon found to their cost that while it was easy to take the horse to the water's edge, it was not easy to make it drink."

Rabindranath's childhood experiences in the company of his father had a very soothing and lasting impact on his mind. It had welled up in him the visions of young disciples chanting Vedic hymns in the presence of inspired rishis in those ancient hermitages, which nestled quietly in the midst of nature. With five children and in the prime of his life now, he thus resolved to realise that vision in his father's retreat at Shantiniketan. In this attempt, to use his biographer's words again, he sought to "replace the soulless and mechanical system of education which the British rulers had imported from their Victorian slums by a new and creative one in which both teaching and learning would be pleasurable."

Very receptive to the creative impulses from his childhood, he was quite eager from the very beginning to encourage his pupils in the school to develop natural abilities in an ambience of tender felicity and learn by doing things themselves rather than relying on teachers, who in turn must not indulge in hurling lessons at them from high platforms "like hailstorms on flowers."

Rabindranath always knew nature to be the best teacher. Therefore, moving away from the contemporary practice of erecting walls both metaphorically as well as practically around children, he earnestly began the practice of holding classes in the open with trees to provide the shade and the distant horizon to provide the ingredients of learning for children. In an environment so surcharged with the raw elements of nature, education could take place both in arts and sciences naturally.

Education for Rabindranath had to be rooted in the soil where it germinates and hence a symbiotic relationship had to be nurtured between what is being learnt in the school and what is there to be learnt from outside it. Ruing the fact that contemporary educational institutions in the country in their keenness to imitate the West had been encouraging a culture of "foolish display" of borrowed etiquettes and knowledge, he passionately emphasised on the utility of extension activities and community service. This for him formed the basis of all education — a creative continuum between life and learning.

And therefore his clarion call to the people was to prepare for a system of education that "should be in full touch with our complete life, economical, intellectual, aesthetic, social and spiritual," and in which institutions should be located "in the very heart of society, connected with it by the living bonds of varied cooperations." He did not have the slightest doubt that "the best and the noblest gifts of humanity cannot be the monopoly of a particular race or country." Therefore, he would urge everyone to "give up for ever the habit of swearing by Europe," and find out "what ideal has long been admired and cherished by our countrymen and what means should be adopted to inspire the heart of our people."

Vision of Life and View of Literature

The fact that Rabindranath Tagore is a Versatile literary prodigy is universally acknowledged. He is indisputably a poet of global reputation. He is also a playwright of great stature. He was familiar with the dramatic tradition in India. He had drunk deep at its fountain. He was a gifted actor and had endeavoured to give a new direction, tone, and stature to the Bengali stage, He was also familiar with the European dramatic tradition and great dramastists like Shakespeare and Ibsen.

Tagore's conception of life, literature and art is so vast and varied that his social philosophy has been completely submerged by them. He was a great poet and philosopher. He had seen the rise and growth of liberalism, extremism, socialism and formalism in the country. He was a great patriot. Had I died begging for my country, even unsuccessfully, that would have been worship, acceptable to the Gods. He stood for political freedom of India as well as for the preservation of the spiritual individuality of each and every nation of the world, Tagore was a strong believer in the dignity of the individual and the value of freedom and initiative for all nations.

It was his passionate belief that India's special contribution to human civilization lies in her exaltation of the principle of unity in diversity. Tagore was not an active politician, but he took part in Indian politics by using his pen. He had deep love for his country as he had love for humanity and God, Man abiding happiness is not in getting anything but in giving himself upto what is greater than himself, to the ideas which are larger than hid individual life, the ideas of his country, of humanity, of God. He was a lover of truth and non-violence. It is very clearly presented in his play Mukta Dhara.

He sees truth in nature, Everything in nature is truth for him. He rejects the view that man can get salvation by renouncing this world. Nature is the supreme reality for him. An intense love of the earth and of human joys and sorrows are the most salient feature of his writings. In his writings, we can see his love for nature. His play the cycle of spring celebrates nature's plenty and beauty. He shows that not only human being, but birds, trees and flowers all are singing and dancing with joy and full of life, The worlds is nor denial of God It is his living image, so there is no inherent antagonism between man and natural harmony with nature, that one can use the forces of nature for his own purpose only because his power is in harmony with the power which is universal, and that is the long run his purpose never can knock against the purpose which works through nature.

The spirit of man resides in the physical organism which is the part of the nature. Tagore thinks that the fulfilment of these earthly pleasures is also necessary.

Man can find paradise here on earth. There is no need to renounce the world but to see paradise by bringing oneness with nature and with God, Tagore says, I believe that the vision of paradise is to be seen in the sunlight and the green of earth, in the beauty of the human face and the wealth of human life, even in objects that are seemingly insignificant and unprepossessing. He knows that none can achieve the spiritual without the temporal, He loves nature and wants that all human beings should but and bloom like it.

Because it is nature in which and can get joys, fullness of his life goodness and fufilment. He sees beauty and plenty everywhere in nature. Tagore's ideal was not the satisfaction of sensuous nature of man only, but also the realisation of the self or infinite in him through love. Man's knowledge does not end with the biological necessities of life but it also concerns itself with love emotions passions and is necessary for the survival of humanity. Tagore says : To be truly united in knowledge, Love and service with all beings and thus to realise one's self in the all pervading God is the essence of goodness.

The individual is a part of God, through the realisation of true-self one is trying to become one with God, which is the ultimate truth of life, As Tagore observes: To live in perfect goodness, is the relax one's life in the infinite. An individual can not be happy by the extinction of his self but by the expansion of his soul. Man seeks enjoyment in exchanging thoughts and feeling with all: Pleasure is for one's own self, but goodness is concerned with the happiness of all humanity and for all time.

Tagore rejected the puritanical attitude of life and ridiculed those who seek *Moksha* liberation of the soul by the subjugation of their desires. The hero of the play *Sanyasi* who tried to realise the infinite by crushing his natural desires and feelings of the heart is brought back into the world of men and affairs by girl, who suggests that salvation lies not in the ramification of the world but in love and survival of humanity. Tagore is a lover of mankind. He maintains that love of man as man is the supreme ideal. He believes that emotions, passions and beauty are the everlasting truths. He shows this in the play Chitra. Tagore's view of love is based on the Vedantist concept of unity in all created things. The life which is full of greed, pride, cruelty, self-seeking and full of false ambitions is a sort of spiritual sleep. It makes man forget the supreme reality that surrounds him. As we see in his plays Mukta Dhaṛa, Red Oleanders' and Gandhari.

Real freedom lies in deliverance from this ignorance. This can be achieved only by conquering all passions, desires for self-gratification and self-aggrandisement: The chick knows when it breaks through the self centred isolation of its egg. However, pleasantly perfect and rounded it may be, it must be given a blow to, it must be burst through and there by the freedom of light and air be won, and the complete purpose of bird life be achieved.

Love is free because it comes from within. It is a quality of the soul itself. But at the same time it is noose bound because it implies complete surrender to the joy and freedom of the object of the love. Love is independent of anything else, For him, the entire universe is essentially one. The relation between the individual and the universe is not one of the conflict and enmity by one of harmony and love, Sexual passion is selfish and destructive, but when controlled by the ideal of love it becomes a symbol of man's spiritual affinity with the infinite.

The tragedy of human life consists in our vain attempt to stretch the limits of things which can never become unlimited, to reach the infinite by absurdly adding to the rungs of the ladder of the finite. Tagore is not a pessimist. Death and evil are not the ultimate reality for him. His view about death is that, death is a negative aspect of life. So it can have no permanent hold on the minds of man. He brings out this idea in the play the cycle of spring. The King on seeking two grey gears behind his ear, is totally disturbed and takes it as a messenger of death.

But when the post makes him understand that this is his rebirth, but after a certain period, changes will come in every thing in nature. Tagore is an optimist. He sees novelty in the death also. He welcomes it as other things in his life, he say pessimism is a form of mental dispsomania' it disdains healthy nourishment, indulges in the strong drink of denunciation and creates an artificial dejection which thirsts for a stronger death. The existence of evil in the world can not detract from the supreme value of life, it is the positive element of good that he dominated life through the ages and given it a meaning and momentum. Society is a spontaneous self-expression of man as a social being. It is important in the every nature of man. For Tagore, society is not an outcome of man's necessity. He rejects the view that man is a social animal by necessity. According to him, human society is the best expression of the inner-self of man of the creative joy in him. That expression leads him to the full relaxation of the divine humanity. It is collective creation of God, through which his social being tries to find itself in its truth and beauty.

In this large life of social communism, man come to the sense mutual accommodation and the law of proportions. Society is natural and spontaneous. The power of society does not reside in any part of it but is distributed among the people. His ideal is a free society of really true individuals. Social units are living personalities and they have inner ideals and self expressions. This leads to their distinctive creations is the fields of literature, art religion, philosophy, social symbols and ceremonials. This adds to the beauty and variety of the life, to richness of our enjoyment and understandings of truth.

Tagore is not merely a writer but more than that. Through his writings. He does or small by his deeds. Tagore was not an orthodoxy, traditionalism, ritualism and false religion in many of his writings. He presents the same view in his plays Sacrifices and Malini. Raghupati of Sacrifice and Kshmankar of Malini both are fanatic worshipper of God.

He hates materialism. Because in this sate, man forgets all humanity, values and kind heartedness. He is more cruel and wicked to achieve more in his life, Tagore rejects science and technology, because according to him we can maintain a standard by these things but we get poverty, hunger and other new problems like unemployment.

He rejects man made social values and bondages. Because they are not true and permanent, but man made them according to his necessity. He presents the idea in the play Karna and Kunti, Kunti had to leave her son under the compelling conditions of society at the time of his birth, and the result, her two sons, Karna and Arjuna, are against each other and bitter enemy. He rejects the law of man and he accepts the nature's law which is permanent and free of all bondages.

Tagore's poems, plays, novels and short stories faithfully mirror the spirit of the age and are the Jarbinger a new era, The barriers between castes and creed had started showing signs of decline to rapid industrialisation and development in every field. He wrote songs to propogate his views among the people, he used his pen to enable people to distinguish between good and bad, tradition and values. He made literature a powerful vehicle of expressing his views on society.

Tagore used literature as a means of creating a better world in which virtues like goodness, truth, beauty and freedom will prevail. All will be free from exploitation, fear, slavery and thralldom of every kind. There is perfect harmony between his social vision and literary creed.

The Fire

Born on 7 May 1861 to noble parents Rabi, as Rabindranath Tagore used to be affectionately called by members of his family and friends had exhibited astonishing signs of creative talents from his very childhood. Perhaps, the extraordinary circumstances of his birth were not least responsible for that initial germination and subsequent fruition of such creative potential.

Beginning with Raja Ram Mohan Roy's path breaking endeavours at socio-religious reforms from about 1828, when he established the Brahmo Sabha and in an organised way set out on a course of relentless campaign to rid the country of pernicious social customs like Sati and awakening his fellow men and women "from their dreams of error" through rightful acquaintance with the virtues of their scriptures. Bengal at the centre of a strong renaissance wave that was sweeping across the country had already galloped a long way to take the fervour on to its next higher plane by the time Rabindranath arrived on the scene.

That Ram Mohan had left a lasting imprint in the mind of Rabindranath is borne out by his own estimation of that towering prophet of modernism, a veritable bridge between the East and the West. In his resounding words, "Ram Mohan was the only person in his time, in the whole world of man, to realise completely the significance of the Modern Age. He knew that the ideal of human civilization does not lie in the isolation of independence, but in the brotherhood of interdependence of individuals as well as nations in all spheres of thought and activity". This singular thought of essential "human unity" never took leave of Rabindranath's consciousness until he breathed his last in 7 August 1941. In the domain of educational thinking, likewise, he held on to the essence of Ram Mohan's earnest arguments for "a more liberal and enlightened system of instruction."

But unlike Ram Mohan, who had no precursor to look up to, Rabindranath in many ways represented the zenith of the nineteenth century renaissance spirit. Whereas in case of the former life began in Bengal and ended in Bristol, the latter journeyed throughout the world several times over and yet passed into eternity in the soils of his birth, in the present day city of Kolkata. At a philosophical level such truisms of life bear testimony to the missions of individual births.

Making his Place

Even as Rabindranath was about twelve years old, he accompanied his father, the illustrious Maharishi Debendranath Tagore for a Himalayan sojourn at Dalhousie. It was the kind of magical place, where his natural contemplative mind would soak itself not only in the profundity of the Upanishadic philosophy and the highly aesthetic works of Kalidasa, but also in the wondrous world of phenomenal subjects like history, astronomy and modern science. Away from the "grind of the school mill", it was here that he forever understood concretely what true freedom holds for the efflorescence of the human personality. Despite being a stern disciplinarian that his father was, he would never stand in the way of any of his progeny's natural expression of being. Rabindranath would later reminisce: "Many a time have I said or done things repugnant alike to his taste and his judgement; with a word he could stop me; but he preferred to wait till the prompting to refrain came from within. A passive acceptance by us of the correct and the proper did not satisfy him; he wanted us to love truth with our whole hearts; he knew that mere acquiescence without love is empty. He also knew that truth, if strayed from, can be found again, but a forced or blind acceptance of it from the outside effectually bars the way in." And so, with a mountaineer's spike in hand, he would wander about "from peak to peak" bemused at the resonance he had with the spectacle of nature.

Back at home, he could still conjure up those exalting experiences when put to task by his Bengali tutor and rendered into lilting verse scene after scene from Macbeth in his mother tongue. Further, fatigued by the "dismal class hours" in school, he composed his first ever solo poem, *Abhilash* (Yearning) with the footnote in the family journal Tattvabodhini Patrika merely describing the author as a twelve year old boy. In any case, the composition heralded the coming to an end of his formal schooling two years later.

Freed from what he subsequently described as a "combination of hospital and gaol," that is the school, Rabindranath found ample time and opportunity to delve deeper into the realm of creativity. There already was a certain nip in the air of Bengal and in the family home existed a perfect setting for his creative impulse to ascend to its full glory. When he was all of fourteen, he recited his first patriotic poem in the Hindu Mela, then organised annually in Calcutta with liberal patronage from the Tagores. Being an event with political overtones, anything uttered from its platform was bound to make ripples in the public domain. So, his poem was published for the first time under his own name in the then widely subscribed Anglo-Bengali weekly, the Anand Bazar Patrika. It happened at a time, when the novels of Bankim Chandra Chatterji, then being serialised in the literary journal Bangadarshan, were already "taking the Bengali heart by storm."

This public attention was to further usher him on the path of creativity far more intensely than he could have previously thought of. And in his doing so his brother Jyotirindranath and sister-in-law Kadambari Devi did not play a less significant role. What was most encouraging for the budding poet was the "stimulating companionship," which the duo offered him, shorn of any big brotherly stance, in gay abundance.

This is a theme, which Rabindranath would come back to again and again in his reminiscences. "But for such snapping of my shackles, I might have become crippled for life. Those in authority are never tired of holding forth the possibility of the abuse of freedom as a reason for withholding it, but without that possibility freedom would not be really free. And the only way of learning how to use properly a thing is through its misuse." Thus, Rabindranath's first long narrative poem *Banaphul* (The Wild Flower) came out during this time describing the tragic tale of a young girl Kamala, who sought refuse in death being denied the love by the conformist society that she so sincerely longed for.

The nationalist stirring of the period coupled with Jyotirindranath's romantic idea of regaining the country's lost freedom through secret society parleys also roused him to dabble with satirical writing. The new Viceroy, Lord Lytton's pompous Durbar held in Delhi in 1877 coinciding with the tragic occurrence of a heart-rending famine in rural Bengal provided him with the perfect material for his first such satirical composition, which he read out to a large gathering of people again on the occasion of the Hindu Mela in that year.

His next spell of creative expressions came in the form of his first short story *Bhikarini* (The Beggar Maid), a historical drama in blank verse Rudrachanda, another long narrative poem Kavi Kahini and several other articles and translations all of which were published in the new literary monthly Bharati started by his brother Jyotirindranath. These effusive creations, in the words of his biographer Krishna Kripalini, spoke eloquently "not only of his genius but of that literary period in Bengal when the old forms and values were dead or dying and the new ones had yet to take shape with this new star."

As a matter of fact, within the horizon of Bengal's literary world nothing at this stage captured better a mystical understanding of nature harmonised as it were by an amazing degree of scientific temperament than his Kavi Kahini, which only matched his quintessential love for beauty. Subsequently this triune would stand him always in good stead. But such was his love for the allegorical Vaishnava poetry of medieval Bengal that he could not resist the urge to pour out "his own vague yearnings in the same mould." Hence, the work that was produced under the name Bhanusimha Thakurer Padavali, created such a genuine excitement among orientalist scholars of the time that the author's name in the poem semantically alluded to an imaginary fifteenth century poet, was taken to be true.

Firming in the Literary Field

Despite the renaissance fervour of those days, it was inconceivable for any one, and least of all the family patriarch, to expect that a career could be made out of literary pursuits and still fit into the family tapestry. Rabindranath's grandfather Dwarkanath Tagore was a man of fabulous resources, who "lived lavishly and entertained regally."

His father Debendranath Tagore "was even more remarkable" being known popularly as the Maharishi. Of his 13 elder siblings the eldest, Dwijendranath was "a man of gigantic intellect;" the second one, Satyendranath was "the first Indian to break into the stronghold of the Indian Civil Service," from the third, Hemendranath he learned his first lesson which remained firmly etched in his mind; the fifth, Jyotirindranath "a genius of uncommon versatility" was the source of his inspiration, his sisters, both Saudamini and Sarala excelled in arts and letters. And, he was the fourteenth child. Naturally, the Maharishi was concerned about his future and therefore readily agreed to his elder son Satyendranath's suggestion that Rabindra should accompany him to England, where he could harness his "impetuous talents" to become either a civil servant like his brother or, if not that, at least a barrister.

It was on his way to England, at his brother's official residence at Ahmedabad that on the banks of river Sabarmati "the lonely boy read voraciously of English literature and through English of European literature." From this intellectual engagement a stream of critical essays and free translations from European authors ensued, which were all published in Bharati. Besides, works of celebrated European poets like Goethe and Dante also prompted him to ponder over the way people in the West looked upon life. Some of these witty observations found place in his writings of this time. On the issue of love, on which the medieval bhakti lore had always had a major influence on him, he observed: "They say, love is blind. Does that mean that to see more is to be blind? For love sharpens the eye and enlarges the understanding." Likewise, on a certain perception of beauty, he observed: "Our ancients said that modesty is woman's best ornament. But women put on so many ornaments that there is little room left for this one."

At a more technical level, these writings formed what can be supposedly stated as the first nucleus of his prose compositions invariably though these compositions remained always "overshadowed by his reputation as a poet." One more notable creation from this genius during this period came in the domain of music, which "lasted till the end of his life" and in due course came to be popularised as Rabindra Sangeet all over Bengal.

In September 1878, he finally sailed off to England with brother Satyendra, leaving far behind the roots of all his inspiration. Sea voyage for him was sickening. And, on arrival in London, sadly, what he found was a "dismal city", the like of which he had never seen before — "smoky, foggy and wet, and everyone jostling and in a hurry." This ominous observation coming from Tagore might have sent shock waves among many youth of his age aspiring to go to England in search of a better future. However, his Yurop Pravasir Patra, which he wrote from there for publication in Bharati captured a young Indian's candid observations on English life and manners of late-19th century and offer historically significant early specimens of literary prose in colloquial Bengali. Be that as it may, no sooner did he start appreciating the strength of English social life after staying there for a few months and particularly viewed from the perspective of a woman's role and status in it, he was called back home, mercifully for him to "the light of my country, the sky of my country." Thus, that incessant lonely feeling of pravas came to an end.

The Efflorescence

Back at home in February 1880 Rabindranath poured himself out "in a cascade of songs" named *Sandhya Sangeet* (Evening Songs) and wrote his first musical plays *Kal Mrigaya* (The Fateful Hunt) and *Valmiki Pratibha* (The Genius of Valmiki) breaking down the longstanding barrier between the classical and folk idioms.

Whereas the evening songs definitively bore "the unmistakable stamp of his genius," he did not shirk from even experimenting with a few strands of western music in his two musical plays. As with every other experience of his life in this context too, he would later reminisce, "as the stream does not flow straight on but winds about as it lists, so did my verse ... Freedom first breaks the law and then makes laws which brings it under true self-rule."

Public adulation followed this creative flow as before and so followed his desire to come out more emphatically into the public domain. In a public lecture on 'Music and Feeling' in Calcutta he successfully defended his thesis that "the function of music was to express what the words fail to express." That apart, Rabindranath's human concern also began touching those burning issues of the time that caused noticeable distress around the world. Thus, in a scathing treatise he laid bare the monstrosity of Britain's opium trade in the then China. His first complete novel *Bou-Thakuranir Hat* (The Young Queen's Market) of this time too harboured a similar thought process.

A natural inheritor of prodigious spirituality both at home and outside, Rabindranath also had his first brush with a luminous experience of the self around this time. Later in life The Religion of Man became a natural outgrowth of this intense experience. Besides, with spiritual awakening there also flowed literary creations of a different kind. Those were at once replete with a certain sense of exultation and "a rediscovery of the wonder of this world and the joy of living." *Nirjharer Swapnabhanga* (The Fountain Awakes) and *Prabhat Sangeet* (Morning Songs) bore the surer imprint of that new mood. It was, as it were, the obsession with rational explanation of phenomena that was a characteristic fixation with his age, which no longer troubled his creative impulse. At any rate, the enterprise to search for meaning in nature had always appeared to him as meaningless. As he would later put it: "If someone smells a flower and says he does not understand, the reply to him is: there is nothing to understand, it is only a scent ... That words have meaning is just the difficulty."

In the summer of 1883, at Karwar on the western seaboard, Rabindranath played out this contest between "spirit and life," between "truth and beauty," and "between reason and love" in his first ever poetic drama, *Prakritir Pratishodh* (Nature's Revenge). Thus, when he picturised in songs the myriad trysts of folk life in his *Chhabi O Gaan* (Pictures and Songs), glimpses of this metaphysical insight poured into his poetic narration. His outpourings in versatile prose also touched a vast array of issues ranging from the social to political and from the literary to philosophical.

Then there came Balak, another monthly magazine from the family stable, the pages of which were filled by his pen. This was a magazine for children. Not long before he had faced two most potent and yet opposing faces of life's truism — one was his marriage with *Bhavatarini* (renamed Mrinalini), and the other, his sister-in-law Kadambari's death under tragic circumstances. As he had earlier mused in his two most stirring poems, Endless Life and Endless Death, these two contrary events provided him with far deeper philosophical insight into the meanings of life and death — the process of embodiment and dissolution.

Thereafter, as secretary of the Brahmo Samaj he wrote several essays dwelling on the theme 'Religion and Spirituality.' In those essays he could find the right space and context to objectively asses those myriad views and counter views, which surrounded the questions of whether western education augured well for the country or holding fast to the country's age-old heritage served it better. But in the end, as his biographer puts it: "His imaginative sympathy and understanding of human nature enabled him to appreciate the passionate partiality of both the outlooks and he himself entered the list only when he felt that justice and humanity were at stake." However, despite engagement with such disquisitory exercises, his sense of muse did not become torpid. Rather his poetic heart throbbed through many a sonnets and some translations of English and Japanese poems all of which were published in a compilation named, Kari O Kamal.

His successive works came of his wider travels both within and beyond the shores of India and hence from a far larger canvas of human concern and civilizational enterprise. During this course he made his second visit to London in 1890 and in a letter to niece Indira wrote back: "Is man a mere machine made of metal that he should function in strict accordance with rules? So vast and varied is the mind of man, so many its hunger and so diverse its claims that it must now and again swerve and reel and toss. This indeed is what makes man human, the proof that he lives, the refutation that he is not a mere bundle of matter ...One who has never known the turbulence of life, in whom the petals of the mysterious flower within have not opened, such a one may seem happy, may seem a saint, his single track mind may impress the multitude with its power — but he is ill-equipped for the life's true adventure into the infinite." Undoubtedly he was aghast at the way humanism was being trampled down by the so-called civilization. And, thus "tired of the place" and even "tired of the beautiful faces" there, he decided to return.

Upon his return was published his fąmous collection of poems, *Manasi* (Of the Mind). If in one of these poems he captured the fateful capsising of a boat going to Sri Jagannath at Puri and taking with it the lives of 800 pilgrims, in another he lashed out at the "Banga Bir", the new-age heroes of Bengal who read all about the valiant acts of Cromwell and Mazzini but often chose at ease to rest at home with the deceptive thought that they "were as good as the best."

The Solid Earth Beneath

Rabindranath's acquaintance with the grist and grind of people's life and the social and economic ills which had the country in its grip grew far more intimate as he was entrusted with the task of looking after the vast family estates in north Bengal and Orissa. His dissections of these ills were later published under the title, Chhinna Patra and were translated into English as Glimpses of Bengal. Naturally, his writings from here on were to carry a much more rigorous "impress of maturity" notwithstanding tentalisingly creative outpourings like the beautiful drama Chitrangada, which he composed in 1891. This dominant mood was also exhibited upfront in his actions on the ground and pretty much dismissed the over-bearing public perception of him as only a romantic litterateur.

Being true to the people he loved so much, Rabindranath began experimenting with community development in right urnest. And then there was no looking back. He was acutely aware of the erratic nature of Indian seasons, and particularly, that of the monsoon. He was also aware of the unpredictable nature of Indian agriculture and arising out of it, the swings in the hopes and despair of the Indian peasant community. He was certainly not unaware of the basic exploitative nature of the colonial administration. He knew that for the drudgeries of life to be lifted, age-old dependence on nature couldn't be converted into another kind of deprecating dependence — that is to look up to the State for succour. So the fundamental premise on which he based his community development programme came to be "self-help and enlightenment."

While the first had to do with the economic reinvigoration of the life of an ordinary peasant, the second assumed far greater significance in his scheme of things. It occupied "his lifelong passionate interest," an interest that led him to "working out his educational experiments in Shantiniketan." In the words of his biographer, Kripalini: "He strove to build up, through social participation and service, a living communication between the students of his school, the budding intelligentsia who might become the active leaders of tomorrow, and the peasants rooted in the soil, the solid core of Indian economy and society. So long as the core remained unchanged India would remain static, whatever the seeming progress among the intelligentsia in a few big cities like Calcutta or Bombay."

Thus, for half a century, from the day his father entrusted him the duty of looking after their family estates till he breathed his last, Rabindranath remained preoccupied with these twin tasks of uplifting rural life through the agency of Shantiniketan and bringing enlightenment to his people through the agency of creative education at Shantiniketan. Both these institutions were deservingly invested with not only what he received as Nobel Prize for his effervescent work Gitanjali in 1913, but also his unrestrained personal service and care as long as he lived.

It was not as if his passionate engagement with the life of Indian peasantry was all a mirage and there was nothing for the latter to offer him in return. On the contrary, in his engagement with them he found a form of literary expression that was as yet unavailable in the country. And it was the short story. As his biographer writes, "though the short story is now very popular with Indian writers, no one can be said to have equalled him in his art, much less surpassed him." In all fairness, from The Post Master to The Kabuliwallah, his stories portrayed so many oft-ignored though very fascinating characters from different planes of life that one wonders if these were real characters. Besides, in the dross of peasant life also Rabindranath found ample material to immortalise them in canvas.

However, for him the "joy of writing one poem far exceed(ed) that of writing sheaves and sheaves of prose." No wonder, the weight of experience in between brought a certain mystical sensibility to suffuse his poetry of this time. *Sonar Tari* (The Golden Boat), *Chaitali* (The Late Harvest) and *Nadi* (River) bear testimony to it.

These were also the days of surging nationalism. But every patriotic rumbling in India used to be mercilessly crushed by the ever-so-suspicious foreign regime. In 1898 a Bill against Sedition was brought in the Council to gag the rising chorus of nationalism. But forever a champion of personal freedom and political liberty, Rabindranath could not have reconciled to the idea of this Bill becoming an Act. Therefore, with a deep sense of outrage, he called for its immediate withdrawal in a public lecture entitled, *Kantharodh* (The Throttle) at Calcutta. Besides, he also helped raising funds for the defence of Lokmanya Tilak in a case that accused him of sedition. Then his natural instinct for the humanitarian cause too led him to assist Sister Nivedita in organising relief for the plague affected people of Calcutta.

However, these were smaller renderings at the service of his motherland in comparison to what he did during this period of crisis in terms of his contribution to the cause of national resurgence through his *Kathas* (Ballads) and *Kahanis* (Tales). In the years to come this engagement with the cause of national freedom was only to grow, be it on the issue of the Partition of Bengal in 1905 or the tragic massacre of innocent men, women and children at Jalianwala Bagh in 1919 or for that matter during the Non-cooperation and Civil Disobedience Movements of the 1920s and the 1930s. But what he essentially championed was not of a variety that can be confused with any self-serving or jingoistic sentiment, as he was a living witness to all those horrendous sins that had been perpetrated by nation states across the world in the name of self-love. His sense of India, to quote a few lines from a hymn he sang through his principal protagonist in Gora, was of a more inclusive, exulted kind.

It read:

> "Awake my mind, gently awake
> In this holy land of pilgrimage
> On the shore of this vast sea of humanity
> that is India.
>
> Here I stand with arms outstretched
> to hail man — divine in his own image —
> and sing to his glory in notes glad and free.
>
> No one knows whence and at whose call came pouring endless inundations of men
> rushing madly along — to lose themselves in the sea:
> Aryans and non-Aryans, Dravidians and Chinese,
> Scythians, Huns, Pathans and Moghuls —
> all are mixed, merged and lost in one body.
> Now the door has opened to the West
> and gifts in hand they beacon and they come —
> they will give and take, meet and bring together,
> none shall be turned away
> from the shore of this vast sea of humanity
> that is India."

7

Tagore's Philosophy of Humanism

Rabindranath Tagore has not failed to force the world to come with its magazine articles and monographs to expound his views. The world-wide interest and popularity of his writings are due as much to the lofty idealism of his thoughts as to the literary grace and beauty of his writings. Rabindranath's teaching, with its vital faith in the redeeming power of the spiritual forces and their up-building energy, has a particular value at the present moment, when the civilized world is passing through the crucible of a ghastly war which, whether or not it purges the nations of their pride and hate, lust for gold and greed of land, at least proclaims, in no uncertain tones, the utter bankruptcy of materialism.

To be great is not merely to be talked about, it is also to be misunderstood, and Rabindranath has not escaped this fate. The many attempts made to explain him contradict each other, for "from the words of the poet men take what meanings please them." There are two views regarding his philosophy of life. If we believe one side, he is a Vedantin, a thinker who draws his inspiration from the Upanishads. If we believe the other, he is an advocate of a theism more or less like, if not identical with, Christianity. Rabindranath inclines to the former view. "To me the verses of the Upanishads and the teachings of Buddha have ever been things of the spirit, and therefore endowed with boundless vital growth; and I have used them, both in my own life and in my preaching, as being instinct with individual meaning for me, as for others, and awaiting for their confirmation my own special testimony, which must have its value because of its individuality." Rabindranath's philosophy by life is viewed by this school as nothing but the ancient wisdom of India restated to meet the needs of modern times.

His writings are a commentary on the Upanishads by an individual of this generation on whom the present age has had its influence. The soul of ancient India is mirrored in them. His idealism is a true child of India's own past and his philosophy is thoroughly Indian both in origin and development.

In Dr. Kumaraswamy's words, "the work of Rabindranath is essentially Indian in sentiment and form." The other view holds that Rabindranath Tagore, like other regenerators of Hinduism, has freely borrowed from Christianity and Western teaching, and has woven these alien elements into the woof of his own faith. If he does not confess his indebtedness to the West, it is, in the words of the Spectator's reviewer, a case of "local patriotism, "ingratitude," and "insincerity." "We have Mr. Tagore employing his remarkable literary talents in teaching borrowed Ethics to Europe as a thing characteristically Indian."

"There is a fatal flaw of insincerity in its most seemingly elevated utterances." These critics believe that the morals and philosophy underlying Rabindranath's thought are essentially Christian. They identify the Vedanta philosophy with a doctrine that makes the absolute an abstract beyond, the world an illusion, contemplation the way of escape, and extinction of soul the end of man. Obviously Rabindranath is not all this. He gives us a "human" God, dismisses with contempt the concept of the world — illusion, praises action overmuch and promises fullness of life to the religious soul.

These are essentially the features of the Christian religion, and what is Rabindranath Tagore if not a typical Christian of the type spiritual India would produce in larger numbers in years to come? The Rev. Mr. Saunders remarks: "The God of Gitanjali is no impersonal, imperturbable absolute of Hindu philosophy, but in fact, whether He be explicitly Christ or not, He is at least a Christ-like God, and the experience of his suppliant and lover is one with the deep core of all Christian experience." The Rev. Mr. Urquhart observes: "He opened his soul to the ideas of the West and he has drawn from Christianity, especially, ideas the influence of which upon his whole trend of thought has not always been acknowledged. The Eastern dress which he has given to these ideas has often concealed both from his own eyes and those of his readers their true origin, and although truth is one and inhabits no particular clime, absence of indication here has sometimes led to consequences prejudicial to the development of truth itself. The ideas of Rabindranath, like those of so many thinkers of modern India, have often been quite wrongly assigned to Indian sources."

Mr. Edward J. Thompson, who calls it 'nonsense' to say that (Gitanjali represents 'true Hinduism', observes: "The man who henceforward must rank among the great religious poets of the world does not call himself a Christian: but in him we get a glimpse of what the Christianity of India will be like, and we see that it is something better than the Christianity which came to it."

There is no use dogmatising at the very outset, for that would be to attack the central question at issue. An impartial exposition of Rabindranath's views would set at rest all doubts and disputes. We do not find any systematic exposition of his philosophy of life in any of his writings. Even Sadhana is a book of sermons, or mystic hymns, or perhaps meditations. It is a sigh of the soul rather than a reasoned account of metaphysics; an atmosphere rather than a system of philosophy.

But we feel that the atmosphere is charged with a particular vision of reality. In his writings we have the reaction of his soul to the environment, his attitude in the face of life. His personality is completely revealed in his poems, which are the unconscious expression of his soul, the outpourings of his devotional heart, and the revelation of his poetic consciousness.

His writings must and do contain suggestions of his intellectual creed. Though poetry is not philosophy, it is possible for us to derive from Rabindranath's works his philosophical views.

Human Consciousness

Human consciousness is the starting-point of all philosophic enquiry. The contradictions of human life provoke the quest for truth. Man is a finite-infinite being. He combines in himself spirit and nature. He is earth's child but heaven's heir. "At one pole of my being I am one with stocks and stones .... but at the other pole of my being I am separate from all." As a link in the natural chain of events, man is subject to the law of necessity; as a member of the spiritual realm of ends, he is free.

It is this contradiction, which we come across in science, art, and morality, that demands a solution. The individual aspires after perfect truth, perfect beauty, and perfect goodness. But in the finite world he can only approximate to, but never completely possess, them. We can see the ideals as through a mist. Intellectually we aspire after an ideal of truth which is complete, harmonious, and all-comprehensive.

The world of isolated facts is at best finite and conditioned. Intellect, with its separatist tendencies and dissecting habits, finds itself unable to grasp the whole. On the moral side, we feel the break between ideal aspirations and actual facts. There is a struggle between the infinite within, which makes the soul yearn for an ideal, and the lower finite, which is the heritage from the past evolution. "O Great Beyond, O the keen call of thy flute! I forget, I ever forget, that the gates are shut everywhere in the house where I dwell alone."

There is a tension between the higher and the lower. The two elements have not attained a harmony. The higher self presents us with a moral imperative which we recognise to be right, but our actual lower self contests its higher birth and pays homage to the delights of sense.

Even if we identify ourselves with the higher and fight the lower, it sometimes happens that we feel worsted. The natural forces seem too much for the moral. In this distress the finite individual asks: Is the moral ideal a dream, and am I a fool to fight for it against the tremendous odds of nature? Have I a fighting chance of victory, or is the enterprise foredoomed to failure? Is the struggle between good and evil presided over by a higher

Being on whom I could depend, or is it a great hazard where the result can be anything? As a rational being he craves for a working probability. SO long as nothing definite is known, the finite soul, struck by the galling injustice and evil of the world, wrings his hands in despair and cries out to Heaven: What must I do to be saved? Wretched man that I am, who shall deliver me from the body of this death? The contradictions of finite life clearly establish that the finite individual is not the ultimate in the world but only an incomplete something requiring supplementation. The need for a philosophy which would reconcile the opposing elements of life, self and not-self, is felt to be urgent.

Free Man's Worship

If what our intellect reveals to us is true, if the world is a chance congeries of individuals attempting without success to fight and conquer nature, the best thing for the wise man would be to withdraw from the universe and contemplate the noble ideals in his cloister, leaving the world to rack and ruin. Mr. Bertrand Russell represents his tendency very forcibly in his brilliant article on "The Free Man's Worship": "That man is the product of causes which had no provision of the end they were achieving; that his origin, his growth, his hopes and fears, his loves and his beliefs are but the outcome of accidental collocations of atoms ; that no fire, no heroism, no intensity of thought and feeling can preserve an individual life beyond the grave; that all the labours of the ages, all the devotion, all the inspiration, an the noonday brightness of human genius, are destined to extinction in the vast depth of the solar system, and that the whole temple of Man's achievement must inevitably be buried beneath the debris of a universe in ruins — all these things, if not quite beyond dispute, are yet so nearly certain that no philosophy which rejects them can hope to stand." "Blind to good and evil, reckless of destruction, omnipotent matter rolls on its relentless way."

Spiritual tempers recognise the high worth of human aspirations and require of men a contemplation of the ideals sacred to humanity. The way to escape from the sway of fate lies in giving up the ties binding man to the external world. We are exhorted by Mr. Russell "to abandon the struggle for private happiness, to expel all eagerness of temporary desire, to burn with passion for eternal things. This is emancipation; this is Free Man's Worship." The pessimists of all ages demand an extirpation of desires and an attainment of inner freedom. The world is full of contradictions and human life is a great discord. The external world appears to be so awry that it drives man into the deepest solitudes of the soul. A sort of other-worldly mysticism which treats with contempt both nature and man develops.

The 'Absolute is said to be quite different from the world, just the opposite of the finite'. The characteristics we are acquainted with in the finite universe can only be denied of it. It alone is real and the world is unreal. Such an intellectualist philosophy will make the Absolute an abstract beyond, the world an unreality, contemplation the way of escape, and extinction of soul the end of man. But the Absolute will then be left in a perilous state, having nothing to do with the universe. This view is a confession of the defeat or discomfiture of man and can never satisfy his real needs. In this conflict of forces, self and not-self, right and might, there are thinkers who ask us to take up sides with might and wickedness. Nietzsche demands worship of force. The God of earth is a God of might and vengeance and not a God of right and conscience. This view is so patently absurd that we need not waste words over it.

A different view, meant especially to emphasise the religious needs of man, prevails in the West. According to it self and not-self are opposed. "The West seems to take a pride in thinking that it is subduing nature, as if we are living in a hostile world where we have to wrest everything we want from an unwilling and alien arrangement of things."

The world of nature is regarded as a refractory force hard in resisting and slow in giving in. Man in his battlings with matter presided over by Satan requires the help of God. God along with mankind struggles to over-come the forces of evil and darkness. All such theistic conceptions generally end in making God a finite being. Leibnitz, in his famous Theodicy, makes God a limited one. He says the existing world is the best of all possible worlds. Evidently all worlds were not possible to God; He selected the best possible, and it has turned out to be not quite a good one.

Mill holds to a limited God in his Essay on Religion. Doctors James, Schiller, and Rashdall postulate a finite and personal God. These thinkers hold to a pluralistic conception of the universe and find themselves unable to account for the unity of the world process. No religion can finally rest in a God who is engaged in a conflict with evil in which He requires the help of man. We can never be sure of the outcome of the struggle. It is quite possible that a God who is limited by the resisting evil may have, like man, defeat for His end; only, if man fails with the help of God, great is his fall indeed.

The defeat is more fearful when God has not deserted the side on which man is. A suffering God, a deity with a crown of thorns, cannot satisfy the religious soul. He is one among many, subject to the limitations of man. There is a great gulf fixed between humanity presided over by God and nature led by His opposite. So long as one principle has not universal sway, so long the basis of pessimism is sound and safe. How can man, without the joy of hope and confidence in victory, bear up against the pressure of alien force? The fear of what the unknown and the unknowable energy might do fills his life with doubt and misery, weakness and distraction.

Only a universal principle can deliver human life from despair. The Absolute is nothing short of the universe in its totality. It is the whole of perfection in which the opposition of good and evil is overcome. But the theist's God is identified with a part of the universe, the good, while the evil is left in its own independence. God is the virtue of the virtuous, and there is another opposing him,' the wickedness of the wicked. The God of theism is only an aspect of the Absolute, an appearance of a deeper reality. Modern theism, aware of this difficulty, lays stress on Divine immanence, thus watering down the personal God into the Absolute whole. The views here referred to 'read the world wrong' and do not give us a philosophic synthesis of God, world and self, for in a true synthesis we cannot have absolute divisions between man and nature. We need a principle, superior to them all, which would assign to each, self and not-self, its appropriate value, and give harmony to their mutual relations; a principle of synthesis which would comprehend both elements and transform their apparent antagonism into an organic relationship.

A closer scrutiny reveals to us the kinship of nature and spirit, not-self and self. The fact that we are able to interpret nature, know it, appreciate it, fight and conquer it, shows that it is akin to human consciousness: "We could have no communication whatever with our surroundings if they were absolutely foreign to us." Man is "reaping success every day, and that shows there is a rational connection between him and nature, for we never can make anything our own except that which is truly related to us." If we separate man from nature "it is like dividing the bud and the blossom into two separate categories, and putting their grace to the credit of two different and antithetical principles."

"The Indian mind never has any hesitation in acknowledging its kinship with nature, its unbroken relation with all." In India where civilization developed in forests near to nature, there was no thought of an antagonism between man and nature, no idea of forcibly wresting treasures from nature.

Human consciousness, animal life, and inanimate nature are different grades of the same energy, stages of the same development. Self and not-self into which the universe has been dichotomised are no rivals, but are the different expressions of the same Absolute, different modes of its existence. Nature is not antagonistic to spirit; not-self is there for the purpose of being used up by the spirit. It is fuel for the name of the spirit. The Taittiriya Upanishad calls matter annam or food.

The human will convert its environment into food. Objective nature is capable of being determined in accordance with the subject's wishes. The past progress of the Universe clearly establishes the success which has attended man's attempt to utilise the environment for the ends of life and spirit. The not-self is a means for the manifestation of spiritual power. Only through nature can spirit realise itself.

"The earth, water and light, fruits and flowers, to her were not merely physical phenomena to be turned to use and then left aside. They were necessary to her in the attainment of the ideal of perfection, as every note is necessary to the completeness of the symphony." If we adopt the right attitude to nature, we feel the pulse of spirit throbbing through it. A true seer sees in natural facts spiritual significance.

The poetic temper hears the voice of spirit crying aloud in nature. "The man whose acquaintance with the world does not lead him deeper than science leads him, will never understand what it is that the man with the spiritual vision finds in these natural phenomena. The water does not merely cleanse his limbs, but it purifies his heart; for it touches his soul. The earth does not merely hold his body, but it gladdens his mind; for its contact is more than a physical contact, it is a living presence. When a man does not realise his kinship with the world, he lives in a prison-house whose walls are alien to him.

When he meets the eternal spirit in all objects, then is he emancipated, for then he discovers the fullest significance of the world into which he is born ; then he finds himself in perfect truth, and his harmony with the All is established." The eye of an artist is needed to perceive the spiritual beauty of the things of nature. Only his eye can penetrate through the confusing chaos of shadows and appearances, and see the cosmos within. Rabindranath has the eye which pierces into the secret of which the natural fact is the sign and prophecy.

He is a poet of nature in whose hands the crudest stuff of existence acquires a poetic colouring. The spiritual phases of nature leap up to his God-filled eyes, kindle devotion in his heart, and set song on his lips. To his soul touched by God the physical world of science appears in all its sweetness and simplicity as to a child. It is a "fairy universe where the stars talk and the sky stoops down to amuse him, and all nature comes to his window with trays of bright toys." To him "the touch of an infinite mystery passes over the trivial and the familiar, making it break out into inerrable music." "The trees, the stars, and the blue hills" ache "with a meaning which can never be uttered in words."

A breath of divine passion passes over the whole world, making it pure and perfect. He feels "a thrill passing through the air with the notes of the faraway song floating from the other shore." He can never escape the divine presence, twist and turn as he will. The deep shadows of the rainy July and the stormy night suggest Gods presence. He is a mystic soul who can hear the voice of God in the tempest and see His hand in the stilling of the wave.

It is no wonder that Rabindranath advocates life in nature and in the open as the best means of spiritual progress, for in nature the religious eye will see the infinite lying stretched in silent smiling repose. Rabindranath sings not of the cloister or the retreat, but of the open highway and the King's Post Office. He revels in the open air and is not afraid to stand under the golden canopy. According to him the best way to derive divine inspiration is to lose oneself in the contemplation of nature. In silence and in solitude we have to enjoy the presence of the divine in nature.

He does not lay stress on religious instruction in the Bolpur school, but believes that religious feeling and piety will work their way into the life of the students if the environment is pure and noble. "We do not want nowadays temples of worship and outward rites and ceremonies. What we really want is an Ashram. We want a place where the beauty of nature and the noblest pursuits of man are in a sweet harmony. Our temple of worship is there where outward nature and human soul meet in union." Recognising the influence of environment upon temperament, the ancient teachers chose the forest shades or the banks of holy rivers as the sites for their Ashrams. When we are filled with the sense of the divinity that surrounds us, then we feel impelled to give ourselves up to reverie or meditation on God.

In moments of such exaltation when we silently adore the living presence that reveals itself through the grandeur of nature, which makes it heard in the soul through the contemplation of the world of immanent divinity, a great peace steals over us. The infinite then murmurs its secret into our ears, and tells the story of the soul and the legend of the earth. To commune with the unutterable, we should get away from the noisy world of action, escape from the machinery of life which kills the soul. Dull mechanical work degrades and brutalises the individual, while a life of nature elevates and purifies the soul. Rabindranath beautifully depicts how an enthusiastic surrender to the spontaneity of natural scenery leads a man to his goal.

We then lie exposed to all the winds of heaven that blow. We feel a presence, all love and peace. The load slips off our heart, and the soul is lifted above life, petty, vexatious, and harassing, and slides into a perfect harmony. The divine light Hoods the soul, the divine music ravishes it, and the soul expresses its joy by humming the hymn of the universe. So running "upon the dusty path of the despised" takes us nearer to God. In The Post Office, the child Amal, rid of the prejudices of the sophisticated Madhav, wistfully yearns to get away from the clank of crowds, the noise and glare of the town, into countryside with its hills and dales. Even though his continuance in the world is said to depend on his keeping indoors, the cage bird longs to be a free bird and enjoy the freedom of the woodland. For as it is put in The Cycle of Spring: "This outer world has been made with a lavish expenditure of sun and moon and stars. Let us enjoy it, and then we can save God's face for indulging in such extravagance."

Rabindranath's conception of nature is antagonistic to the view which makes nature opposed to the self and its aspirations. He has a positive view of the relation of spirit to nature. The two are aspects of the Absolute. Nature and society are revelations of the divine spirit. The same light dwells in the world outside and the world within. This ultimate oneness of things is what the Hindu is required to remember every moment of his life. "The text of our everyday meditation is the Gayatri, a verse which is considered to be the epitome of all the Vedas. By its help we try to realise the essential unity of the world with the conscious soul of man; we learn to perceive the unity held together by the one Eternal Spirit, whose power creates the earth, the sky, and the stars, and at the same time irradiates our minds with the light of a consciousness that moves and exists in unbroken continuity with the outer world." The song of the soul and the music of the spheres are but the expressions of the divine harmony.

The same spirit dwells in the most distant sun and in the darkest depths of the soul. Nature is not a hostile power harassing man at every turn; the universe is not foreign to us.

Rabindranath's conception of the unity of the world gives us the assurance that the ideals of Science and Morality are real, and sustains us on the path of right untempered by the grim realities of pain and crime. It makes us realise how the spiritual forces of the world cooperate with us in our endeavours. If the distinction of man and world, self and not-self, were the last thing, then "there would have been absolute misery and unmitigated evil in this world. Then from untruth we never could reach truth, and from sin we never could hope to attain purity of heart; then all opposites would ever remain opposites, and we could never find a medium through which our differences could ever tend to meet." Then our life would become a hideous tragedy of waste and wrong, fear and weakness. But progress in the realms of Science, Art, and Morality shows that self and not-self are only relatively opposed. It is the business of man to break down the opposition, and make both express the one spirit.

This view restores the balance between nature and spirit, and makes life worth living. "It were well to die if there be Gods, and sad to live if there be none." If there is the all-embracing spirit, the glooms and shadows of life lose their edge and bitterness. Then we feel that we are not battling with an unknown antagonist on a doubtful issue, but that we are trying to realise progressively a victory that is guaranteed to us. Perfect confidence takes the place of blank despair. The confused and shadowy world of experience becomes quite clear and transparent. Doubt is vanquished; the contradictions of life cease. "All that is harsh and dissonant melts into one sweet harmony."

Realisation of the Absolute

The creation of the universe is only the realisation of the Absolute, the revelation of its freedom. "God hands himself by creating." It is the creative joy that gives birth to the universe, which is not only separate from God but also united to Him. God is the basis of the whole universe. It is the self-sundering of the Eternal which calls into existence the universe of men and things. But this must have "duality for its realisation". The whole breaks up its individuality into the two aspects of self and not-self, Iswara and Maya, Purusha and Prakriti.

"When the singer has his inspiration he makes himself into two; he has within him his other self as the hearer, and the outside audience is merely an extension of this other self of his. The lover seeks his own other self in his beloved. It is the joy that creates this separation, in order to realise through obstacles the union." The not-self or Prakriti or Maya is generally conceived of as the passive and the self as the active principle. It is their mutual supplementation that promotes the unity of the universe. The Eternal One realises itself by the action and interaction of the two principles. The principle of negativity impels the Eternal One to realise itself in the world. It is the woman "in the heart of creation." "She who is ever returning to God his own outflowing of sweetness; she is the ever fresh beauty and youth in nature; she dances in the bubbling streams and sings in the morning light; she with heaving waves suckles the thirsty earth ; in her the internal One breaks in two in a joy that no longer may contain itself, and overflows in the pain of love."

The first existent out of the Absolute is Iswara with the not-self over against him. Iswara is the personal God who represents the ideal of goodness to the finite minds. He is the father, creator or governor of the universe. The not-self is the negative reflection of the affirmative Iswara. The whole universe develops in, through, and by means of, the interaction between these two.

The universe is the eternal sacrifice of the supreme. The Bhagvat Gita says: "The whole world rests on sacrifice. It is the law of the universe." He is sacrificing himself that nature and humanity may live. This self-sundering of the whole in which the world is contained is but the expression of his joy and the law of the universe. It is "the joy that makes the earth now over in the riotous excess of the grass, the joy that sets the twin brothers, life and death, dancing over the wide world, the joy that sweeps in with the tempest, shaking and waking all life with laughter, the joy that sits still with its tears on the open red lotus of pain, and the joy that throws everything it has upon the dust, and knows not a word." The outburst of joy is needed for the realisation of the concrete richness of the world. The universe is newborn continually, as a result of this joy.

This lesson that "the old is ever new" is the central theme of The Cycle of Spring. The Absolute realises through separation and union.

This separation is needed to make the eternal concrete. But the separation of the two is not the last word. The universe is not merely a going forth from God, but is also a coming towards Him. The union of the two is complete, but in the universe it is being made. The finite represents to us the tension of the self to become the infinite. The universe is the struggle of the finite to reach the infinite. It is a play of hide and seeks between the two, God and man. All objects of the world are finite-infinite, but the tension between the two is at its highest in the human consciousness. Man approximates to the ideal but never qua man reaches it. The world is the process of becoming infinite, but not the consummation. Should man completely realise the infinite, and should the world reach its goal of becoming the infinite, then there will be no universe and necessarily no Absolute.

Though God is everything, everything is not God. Wile the whole universe is regarded by Rabindranath as the expression of God, still different things express God in different degrees. He thus admits the conception of degrees of reality. "The revealment of the infinite in the finite, which is the motive of all creation, is not seen in its perfection in the starry heavens, in the beauty of the flowers. It is in the soul of man." Man, the animal with the upward look, is a higher revealment than the mere animal, and the animal is higher than the worm, which is higher than the clod. "To all things else you give; from me you ask." Subject to this reservation we can say that the objects of the universe are parts of God aspiring to be the whole.

God is the infinite ideal of perfection. Man has yet to become what he is. On account of his finiteness he does not realise his aim. The content of his ideal passes beyond his existence. It has a reach beyond his grasp. He strives towards it, but it eludes his effort. He sees it as a vision beheld in dreaming, something longed for. The finite universe of persons and things represents to us the passage from the imperfect to the perfect. We see the road, the end is not yet. Through the world, the opportunities it affords, "they are coming, the pilgrims, one and all — coming to their true inheritance of the world." The world is but the progress of pilgrims in their quest for the infinite. Every object m it cries out, "I want thee, only thee," and struggles to attain immortal life.

Realm of Finite Nature

Man cannot reach the ideal so long as fragments of finiteness stick to him, so long as his intellect, emotion, and will are bound in the realm of finite nature. The finite intellect reduces the universe to the opposites of self and not-self, organism and environment, and leaves us there without revealing to us the final unity in which these relative opposites rest. The ultimate unity breaks itself into the two factors of subject and object, man and nature. Intellect reads the manifestations, but misses the unity in which the two are gathered together. It exults in the strife of the opposites which is the play of the universe. The whole in which these distinctions are, not abolished, but overcome, the unity which is the final or the ultimate explanation of the things, is not grasped by it. What it does is to break up the world-poem and discover in it "the law of its rhythms, the measurement of its expansion and contraction, movement and use, the pursuit of its evolution of forms and character."

These are no doubt "true achievements of the mind," but Rabindranath says, "We cannot stop there." Our thought cannot finally rest in them. We are in the hands of opposites still. The Upanishad says: "You will have fear so long as there is dualism." The universe of intellect "is like a railway station; but the station platform is not our home." The world of intellect, with its distinctions of good and evil, truth and error, self and not-self, beauty and ugliness, is only a stage on the pathway to reality.

The intellectual vision is full of hard-and-fast lines of distinction. It makes the opposites absolute, and the system becomes full of contradictions; but if we pierce behind it we shall find that the rigid distinctions of intellect are fluid, and mingle in a wondrous whole. "This screen that thou hast raised is painted with innumerable figures with the brush of the night and the day. Behind it thy seat is woven in wondrous mysteries of curves, casting away all barren lines of straightness." Beyond the two, beyond the unite and the infinite, we have the Absolute, which the finite intellect cannot grasp. Our mind cannot reach it. Our soul looks into the dim unknown to catch sight of it, but cannot find it where we come across motor cars and aeroplanes. Our vision is external, and God is not there; our vision is turned inside, and God is not there.

We shall not see Him until we see Him everywhere, in and out, in darkness and in light. In the drama of Job it is put in the mouth of Zophar: "Canst thou by searching find out God? Canst thou find out the Almighty unto perfection? It is high as heaven;

what canst thou do? Deeper than Sheol; what canst thou know?" The intuitive insight by which we can see God, the intellect cannot give. The Absolute is the highest unity from which all being proceeds; but it is so exalted and so exquisite that none of our conceptions can adequately describe it. Its overflowing life breaks through all intellectual barriers. A simple childlike vision, purified and purged of all prejudices, can get at it. When the soul is absorbed in God, it sees Him. "The soul that knows Brahman becomes Brahman." Reasoning and argument are of no avail. Syllogism does not give us its spirit. It is deeper than demonstration. Intelligence cannot fathom the depths of that divine mystery. He is a God who hideth Himself. He can be "felt in the dark, but not seen in the day." He can only be known intuitively. Rabindranath says: "The vision of the Supreme One in our own soul is a direct and immediate intuition, not based on any ratiocination or demonstration at all."

To the eye of the finite intellect, it is darkness, impenetrable darkness. God is the King of the Dark Chamber. We are in a dark prison, surrounded by walls which our finiteness has raised, which separate us from others. Outside it there is light and no darkness. If suddenly the great vision appears to our untrained eyes, which can see objects only in the pleasure garden, if it reveals itself unexpectedly to our ordinary consciousness, sticking to the small strutting ego as if it were everything of consequence in the world, the vision will alarm the eyes and shake that consciousness to its foundations. Liven to the high-souled Arjuna, with his soul full of divine fire and heart full of devotion to God, the tremendous vision of the Universal Form of God was insupportable, too terrific and awful for him to look upon. By its exceeding brilliance it will dazzle the eyes of mortal man. God who shows himself in a moment of great suffering win look terrible.

For one awful moment the Princess saw into the heart of things with the eyes of eternity, and had visions of suns grown cold, universes frozen. We cannot see either in perfect darkness or in perfect light. Both are dark to us — one with the excess of brightness, the other with the lack of it. We want a mixture of opposites everywhere, and that we have in our solid-seeming world. The Princess in the drama of The King of the Dark Chamber, which describes the eternal quest of the soul for its kindred, wishes to see her husband and dear lord in the empirical world, where we have summer houses and motor cars, in the world of time, space, and causation. She wants to see him as an object among objects. She cannot reach him thus. The scientist says: You can sweep the wide heavens with the telescope but will not find God. Even so the Princess, when her vision is confined to the empirical world, may grow sceptic about the existence of God.

"It strikes me, Kaundilya, that these people haven't got a King at all. They have somehow managed to keep the rumour afloat." The existence of God is put down for a fiction or a hypothesis, contrived by the cunning, perhaps to keep the wretch in good order. Life becomes a despairing question and God a problem. He is near to her if she looks from the proper angle of vision, but it is far on if she adopts the empirical standpoint. The Absolute is a phantom that eludes her grasp. So long as the Princess wants to find God, who is ever in love with her, where she sees trees and animals, birds and stones, she cannot find Him.

The reason is that the Supreme is not an object which we can see with our finite eyes. It is the very light by which we see all objects. How can we see it as an object when it is both the subject and the object, when it is the light by which we see and the light which we see? There is nothing else than light to see it by. If we turn ourselves rightly, we shall see it everywhere. Ourselves and the whole universe are eternal witnesses to its presence. It is the life of life, the self of self. It is in our very heart.

We need not fathom the sea, or sweep the sky; we need not ascend into heaven or descend into the deep to reach it. A conversion of soul is what is needed. If we break through the ordinary gaze we shall find it. Our cherished illusions must go. The vulgar wisdom of the masses should be recognised to be vulgar. An inversion of the secular into the religious consciousness is needed. If we get rid of the finiteness, and rise above the intellectual level and pierce behind the veil, we shall see it face to face. To see God we should transfer ourselves to another dimension of reality. We should break down the barrier of individuality and relax the despotism of the senses; our ignorance will then be removed. We escape from the light of separation and see God as the transcendent darkness in which the whole universe is bathed. Surangama says: "A day came when all the rebel in me knew itself beaten, and then my whole nature bowed down in humble resignation on the dust of the earth. And then I saw ... I saw that he was as matchless in beauty as in terror. Oh, I was saved, I was rescued." We shall then see our ordinary consciousness to be the real darkness and the transcendent one to be the perfect radiance of Eternity. The Princess says: "Your sight repelled me because I had sought to find you in the pleasure garden, in my Queen's chambers: there even your meanest servant looks handsomer than you. That fever of longing has left my eyes for ever. You are not beautiful, my lord you stand beyond a comparisons!" While the supreme is bright and clear to the religious intuition, it is misty and dark to the cold intellect. It is "dark from its surpassing brightness ... as the shining of the sun on his course is as darkness to weak eyes."

To the finite consciousness God is far away; to the religious soul He is quite near. God is present, yet absent. The Bhagavad Gita says: "Near and far away is That." The Isa Upanishad says: "He is far and also near." "When you think that He is not here, then you wander farther and farther away, and seek Him in vain with tears. Where lie is far on, there He is unattainable: Where He is near, He is very bliss." "They have sung of Him as infinite and unattainable: but I in my meditations have seen Him without sight." Tukaram, the Indian saint, says: "O man, why do you travel from place to place to search God? As the deer does not know that it possesses an invaluable thing called *kasturi* (musk), so you do not know what is within you. Search God within you and you will find Him." Rabindranath says: "You were in the centre of my heart, therefore when my heart wandered she never found you."

In thus transcending intellect by intuition we become childlike in our simplicity and innocence of the world's ways. Our knowledge is transformed into wisdom. "God waits for man to regain his childhood in wisdom."

The eyes of the body are closed as in sleep for the eyes of spirit to open as in dreams. "Yea, when it sleeps, the mind is bright with eyes." Thus Rabindranath, in common with other mystics, discriminates between the path of intuition, which is the way of wisdom born of love, and the path of intellect, which is the way of knowledge born of observation. Intuition enables us to penetrate beneath outward appearances studied by science and see the life in things. It is a matter of experience or insight, which is coercive and certain. The design-argument, which makes God a matter of inference and not observation, is urged by Janardhan in The King of the Dark Chamber. "But look at the nice order and regularity prevailing all over the place — how do you explain it without a King?" This argument is put down for mere quibbling, as the question is to be decided by intuition. "Have you, or have you not, seen the King? Yes or no?" Kabir sings: "They are blind who hope to see it by the light of reason, that reason which is the cause of separation. The house of Reason is very far away." Reason, which can help us to weigh the dust or measure the air, cannot show us the face of God. The truly religious soul does not argue and infer, but meditates and waits for light. The poet, the artist, and the lover pursue this path of intuition; the mystic knows it, and lives in the full light of the vision.

Characterisations of God

In the characterisations of God in the Vedanta writings and Rabindranath's works we find an identity of thought. The popular idea that the Brahman of the Vedanta is an abstract beyond is incorrect. Rabindranath protests against such a misconception. He says: "The infinite in India was not a thin nonentity, void of all content. The Rishis of India, asserted emphatically, 'To know Him in this life is to be true; not to know Him in this life is the desolation of death'. How to know Him then? 'By realising Him in each and all.' Not only in nature, but in the family, in society, and in the state, the more we realise the world-conscious in all, the better for us. Failing to realise it we turn our faces to destruction."

The Vedanta thinkers do not place God in the solitude of a world beyond. The hymn or mantra, chanted every evening at the Bolpur school, "The God who is in fire, who is in water, who interpenetrates the whole world, who is in herbs, who is in trees, to that God I bow again arm again," is from the Upanishads. The Vedantic Absolute as much as Rabindranath's God is a concrete spirit.

The mystics of all faiths and creeds, from the Rishis of Upanishads downwards, are at one in this belief in the immanence of God. St. Paul says: "He is above all, through all, and in all." So too we read: "Raise the stone, and there thou shalt find me; cleave the wood, and there am I." It is meaningless to argue that the Vedantic Absolute is a barren nothing and R.abindranath's God a concrete something, and therefore Rabindranath is no Vedantin. The logic is irresistible; only the premisses are false.

Critics may urge that the Vedanta philosophy is ambiguous about the nature of God. True it says, God is All, but it also says God is nothing. "It is not this, not this." This dilemma of mysticism which makes God sometimes the All, sometimes nothing, is not peculiar to the Vedanta writings, but runs through all mystic literature. Rabindranath's poems are full of it. In some pages the Absolute is an abstract, formless, featureless unity, not a God who deserves to be adored and worshipped. It is "the inscrutable without name and form."

The Upanishads are full of such apparently contradictory descriptions, for they are only the records of the spiritual experiences of the sages of India. "He is not this, He is not that." "It is neither coarse nor fine, neither sharp nor long, neither red like fire nor fluid like water; it is without shadow, without darkness, without air, without water, without attachment, without taste, without smell, without eyes, without ears, without speech, without mind, without light, without breath, without mouth, without measure, having no within and no without; it devours nothing and no one devours it."

To represent the other tendency we have the Chandogya, which says: "All this universe has the Supreme deity for its life. That deity is truth. He is the Universal soul. Thou art He, Swethakethu." The Mundaka Upanishad says: "This immortal Brahma, to the right and the left, below and above, all pervading, Brahma is this All, this infinite world." The contradiction between the two accounts is only apparent and not real. If by means of our finite intellect we try to reach the Absolute we shall fail in our attempts. The Kena Upanishad says: "It is far from the known and above the unknown." The Taittiriya says: "Words together with the mind return without comprehending it." The Absolute unity is opposed to intellectual duality, and the intellectual account of the Absolute remains a negative one. But when we rise above the plane of intellect to religion, poetry, and philosophy we see it face to face. When we say that the Absolute is above the grasp of intellect, we do not mean that it is opposed to it. Only in the Absolute the intellectual is realised. "In love all the contradictions of existence merge themselves and are lost. Only in love are unity and duality not at variance." At the intuitional level the Absolute is the all-comprehending love with whom we can commune, whom we can love, adore, and worship. The Absolute is the whole Universe. The creation is the dance, leela, or the play of the Absolute. "The Creator brought into being the game of joy The Earth is his Joy. ... In play is the creation spread out. In play it is established." Rabindranath's God as much as the Vedantic Absolute is a concrete Universal.

God is a Trinity

Now the question arises, Is Rabindranath's God a person and not the impersonal Absolute of the Vedanta? Yes: Gitanjali makes of God a person. The Vedanta Philosophy in an its stages of development provides for such a conception. Art, philosophy and religion are the specialised modes in which the Absolute presents itself to mankind. God is a trinity because man is. The human individual is a unity of intellect, emotion, and will, and me Supreme Ideal, to satisfy sentiment, win, and reason, appears as Supreme Beauty, Supreme Good, Supreme Truth. And as the human individual is a unity of the three, and as these elements cannot conflict with each other, and as no one of them can complete its idea except as it gathers into itself the two others, even so there is no discord between the different aspects of truth, beauty, and goodness in the Supreme Ideal.

This ideal shows itself to man's capacity for joy as Supreme Beauty, to his capacity for knowledge as Supreme Truth, to his capacity to act, as Supreme Good. The contents of the three do not vary, though their form does. Art, philosophy, and religion are different forms and expressions of worship and different ways of approach to God. The particular method depends upon the temperamental characteristics with which the Creator has enriched human nature.

All souls — saints, sages, and seers — seek union with God. Mystic souls of an emotional and imaginative cast of mind express their devotion by love, worship, and adoration. They make a person of the object of their love. In Rabindranath the art aspect predominates. His wealth of imagination, force of feeling, and intensity of passion turn his words into music and poetry. The poems of Gitanjali are the offerings of the finite to the infinite. The relation between the two is conceived of as that between the lover and the beloved — an analogy employed by the mystics the world over. Throughout oriental literature, this analogy is constantly used to express the true relationship between the human soul and God. Radha's passionate devotion to Krishna is the symbol of the soul's yearning for God.

When Krishna, to draw all creation to him, sings the divine music of his flute, she listens to it and gives up her all for His sake. The analogy of human love holds, in that in perfect love we have two yet one, a single life led by a man and a woman. The surrender of the soul, the fulfilment of love, and the union with the other spirit, characteristic of human love, are present in the longing for the Absolute. But if we press this analogy too far we get all sorts of difficulties. Ultimately there will be no divorce between head and heart, reason and faith.

Rabindranath is intellectual enough to recognise that the Vedantic Absolute which he believes to be the ultimate philosophical unity does not lend itself to intellectual description. But being an artist, he translates his spiritual experience into material symbols. The language is metaphorical, and if literally interpreted would lead to absurdities and contradictions.

Miss Evelyn Underhill remarks in her admirable introduction to Kabir's Poems: "It is a marked characteristic of mystical literature that the great contemplatives, in their effort to convey to us the nature of their communion with the supersensuous, are inevitably driven to employ some form of sensuous imagery: coarse and inaccurate as they know such imagery to be, even at the best." If from the poems of Gitanjali we infer that God is a person over against man, we make a mistake. To Rabindranath God is not a being seated high up in the heavens, but a spirit immanent in the whole Universe of persons and things. Rabindranath's love is a spiritual love above sex, unintelligible to the world at large, a love which loses itself in the sea of the Absolute to "melt and vanish away in the dark, or it may be in a smile of the white morning, in a coolness of purity transparent."

The Absolute of philosophy becomes the God of religion, to all followers of the Bhakti school. Iswara, the highest manifestation of the Absolute, is the personal Lord of the Universe. The distinction of the lover and the loved is kept up till the last point, when in perfect love the two become one. The personal God is then dissolved in the Absolute. If Rabindranath is viewed as a worshipper of a personal God, he may be looked upon as the living example of the long and noble succession of religious devotees of whom India is justly proud, including among others Manikkavasagar, Ramanuja, Maddhwa, Ramananda, Vedanta Desikar, Jnaneswar, Namdev, Vallabha Charya, Kabir, Chandidas, Chaithanya, Nanak, Dadu, Tulsidas, and Tukaram.

This Bhakti school has had a continuous history from the very beginnings of reflection in India. A Christian critic, Dr. Macnicol, says: "Theism is both ancient in the land and indigenous to the soil. . . . No one need suppose that the ideas that bhakti connotes are a foreign importation into India." The critics who make Rabindranath a borrower from Christianity betray an astonishing lack of "historic conscience" — a charge generally urged against Indians. The Absolute of philosophy and the God of religion have both a place in the Vedanta system.

Those who draw a hard-and-fast line of distinction between the two will never be able to understand the Vedanta philosophy. What Richard Garbe says of the Bhagavad Gita is true of other Vedanta writings: "The doctrines which are here put into the mouth of Krishna present a remarkable combination of pantheistic and monotheistic ideas, of philosophical thoughts and of pure and deeply religious faith in God." The formless Absolute has to be conceived as a being of form by the unite individual. To put it the other way, we can say that the Absolute, which is above the pairs of opposites of beauty and ugliness, truth and error, good and evil, still appears for the sake of man as perfect Beauty, perfect Truth, and perfect Goodness. "The Perfect decks itself in beauty for the love of the Imperfect."

Acquisition of the True Insight

The acquisition of the true insight into things is the mark of religion. That insight we can have only when our souls have so expanded as to feel for the whole universe. This expansion of soul, this "widening of the range of feeling," can be achieved not by extending to our possessions, not by extending our dominions, but by giving up our unite self. "We have, however, to pay a price for this attainment of the freedom of consciousness. What is the price? It is to give oneself away. Our soul can realise itself truly only by denying itself. The Upanishad says, Thou shall gain by giving away, Thou shall not covet." "The consciousness of the infinite in us proves itself by our joy in giving ourselves out of our abundance. And then our work is the process of our renunciation, it is one with our life. It is like the flowing of the river, which is the river itself."

Spiritual attainment consists in giving away or renunciation. We have to conquer the world by caring naught for it. Self-denial is the path to self-realisation. This idea is brought out by the image of the lamp and the oil. "The lamp contains its oil, which it holds securely in its close grasp and guards from the least loss. Thus, is it separate from all other objects around it and is miserly. But when lighted it finds its meaning at once; its relation with all things far and near is established, and it freely sacrifices its fund of oil to feed the flame."

With the annihilation of self comes the fulfilment of love. The self-centred life becomes God-centred. Man shall not see God and live, goes the saying. Certainly not. So long as he is man he cannot see Him. When he sees Him he ceases to be man. Before that vastness and splendour man's individuality shrinks and crumbles into dust. The all-dwelling love invades, submerges, and overwhelms the individual consciousness. The whole individual — body, mind, and soul — is given up to God.

This, state of supreme bliss is not "death but completeness." It is the perfection of consciousness, where there is no dust or darkness to obscure the vision. It is an utter clearness and transparency through which God's rays pass and repass without let or hindrance. It is complete harmony, perfect love, and supreme joy. In that all-embracing consciousness the finite and the infinite are enfolded in one. "The inward and the outward are become as one sky, the Infinite and the finite are united." It is self-transcendence, not annihilation. It is life eternal. "It is the extinction of the lamp in the morning light; not the abolition of the sun." A passage in Nettleship hits the point well.

"Suppose that all human beings felt habitually to each other as they now do occasionally to those they love best. All the pain of the world will be swallowed up in doing good. So far as we can conceive of such a state it will be one in which there will be no individuals at all, but an universal being, in and for another; where being took the form of consciousness, it would be consciousness of another which was also oneself — a common consciousness. Such would be the atonement of the world." Mr. Bosanquet asks us to think of the attitude demanded of one by a masterpiece of art.

"You scarcely recognise yourself, when for a moment Shakespeare or Beethoven has laid his spell on you." In human life we soon slip back from this condition of self-forgetfulness; in the supreme state of mind we have a perpetuation of this condition. The final state is a total transformation of the personality into an explicit organ of the Absolute. The independent false will is destroyed; the perfect surrender of the will to God makes the will the Divine will. We obtain this condition, not by abstraction, but by comprehension, not by exclusion, but by inclusion. It is therefore fullness of life. "Life dies into the fullness."

The individual tries to realise the infinite within him, adore it, clasp it with affection, and ultimately become one with it. Till this goal is reached, man is caught in the world process. When it is reached the false individuality separating man from God becomes extinct. "When one knows thee, then alien there is none, then no door is shut." The soul is then prepared to meet death or anything even more fearful than that. For it then shares the life eternal which death cannot defeat. "My whole body and my limbs have thrilled with his touch who is beyond touch; and if the end comes here, let it come." The white radiance of eternity fills him, and puts fire into his heart and music into his soul. He becomes endowed with eternal youth and strength, and fills the world with light.

Doctrine of Reincarnation

With the Hindu philosophers, Rabindranath believes in the gradual perfection of individuals till the ideal is attained. The soul has to pass through many lives before the goal can be reached. "Thou hast made me endless, such is thy pleasure. This frail vessel thou emptiest again and again, and fillest it ever with fresh life. The time that my journey takes is long and the way of it long. I came out on the chariot of the first gleam of light, and pursued my voyage through the wildernesses of worlds leaving my track on many a star and planet." In the progress towards perfection, man, owing to the weakness of his flesh, has to renew his body, and this renewal is what we call death. "It is thou who drawest the veil of night upon the tired eyes of the day to renew its sight in a fresher gladness of awakening." Death is only a preparation for a higher and fuller life.

In the matter of future life, Rabindranath is at one with the Rishis of the Upanishads, who also hold the two views of immortality and reincarnation, the me of completeness and perfection and the life which continues endlessly. Both these views are valid in their respective spheres. So long as man is finite and does not give up his selfish nature, his destiny is not fulfilled, and the final consummation of becoming one with God is not attained, he is in the moral life struggling hard to attain the end which he does not get. He perpetually approximates to the goal, but never reaches it. For a unite being to achieve this impossible task, as Kant urges, infinite time is not enough.

So long as man identifies himself with his finite, fleeting personality, he is subject to the law of infinite progress and perpetual approximation. As Indians have it, he is bound in the cycle of births and deaths. He goes from life to life; death becomes only an incident in life, a change from one scene to another. But when the individual completely surrenders himself to the universal life, and the self becomes one with the supreme, then he gains the bliss of heaven and shares the life eternal.

He is lifted above the travail of births and deaths, and above mere succession in time, to which alone death is relevant. In the moral life, where we have the individual attempting to reach the goal, we have the endless succession in time which belongs to the finite; but when moral life is swallowed up in religion, then the spirit transcends time and attains a timeless immortality.

Absolute is the Organic Whole

The Absolute is the organic whole consisting of the different elements of matter, life, consciousness, and intellect. These are the expressions of the whole; but if they set themselves up for the whole, we are in the region of maya. As parts of the Absolute they are real; as unconnected with it they are illusory. Avidya or ignorance of the real nature of the world and man's place in it chains us in the bonds of maya. Then the finite existence becomes a pathos, and nature a bondage from which we should escape. In the world of maya our individuality appears to be ultimate; but if we overcome this illusion, we find our individual consciousness to, be a unique expression of the universal.

"Everything has this dualism of maya and satyam, appearance and truth. ... Our self is maya where it is merely individual and finite, where it considers its separateness as absolute; it is satyam where it recognises its essence in the universal and infinite, in the supreme self, in Paramatman." In the Devi Bhagavata it is said that when Shakti turns towards the world she is maya; when she turns towards the Lord she is seen to be himself. It is wrong to think that the world has an independent existence. "This world-song is never for a moment separated from its singer. Music and the musician are inseparable." The play of the universe is centred round God.

If we separate the two, we break up the real into the two abstracts of the finite and the infinite, which are both unreal and illusory. The mere finite is like "a lamp without its light," a "violin without its music." The mere infinite is "utter emptiness." The two are real in their union. "The infinite and the unite are one, as song and singing are one." It is only in marriage with the finite that the infinite can bear fruit; divorced from it, it remains barren. The unity of God is realised only through the many. "The real with its meaning read wrong and emphasis misplaced is the unreal." Maya, thus, is a phantom that is and is not.

Real Significance of Nature and Society

When we perceive the real significance of nature and society we find they are there for the purpose of enabling us to reach the infinite. The ideal is to be attained, not by escaping from the confusions of the world of sense, but by spiritualising them. Rabindranath does not look upon the body as the tomb or the prison of the soul from which it has to be liberated.

For him man is bound up with nature; the human spirit is wedded to the material organism. Contact with the body, instead of being a tainting of the purity of the soul, is just the condition necessary for developing its nature. Nature is not, as such, evil. It all depends. If the individual rests in his sensuous nature self-satisfied, without directing his vision to God, then nature turns out to be a tempter. If, on the other hand, it is made to become the organ of the higher spirit, nothing can be said against it. By itself nature is a moral. The spirit quickens it. It is the duty of man to transfigure the natural, break its externalism and transitoriness, and make it fully express the spirit for which it is intended.

If we think nature to be separate from God, we are in the world of maya. But if God is immanent in the universe, how can we refuse as dross the material body? The creative love of God is the source of the universe which is destined to reflect in itself the fullness of Divine perfection. The world is not the denial of God. It is His living image and not His enemy. It has to be fashioned into the symbol and instrument of the spirit. The body should be made the sign and utterance of the soul. "The flowers grow out of the dirt, but the foulness of the source is abolished in the flower itself."

The world of nature is neither a delusion of the Creator nor a snare of the devil. It is the playground where we have to build our souls.

Similarly the world of persons and things is not something to be escaped from. It is there to enable the finite individual to reach his goal. "The entire world is given to us, and all our powers have their final meaning in the faith that by their help we are to take possession of our patrimony." Nature and society are but the instruments by which to elicit the infiniteness of the unite being, the material to help the finite to work out its destiny. The whole universe is penetrated and vitalised by the living spirit, and so responds to the call of spirit. Not a fragment of it which is not deeply interesting and divine, if we approach it in the right way. Anything can be made the channel of approach to God, an entrance to immortality. "All paths lead to thee." Nothing in the visible world is too low for the use of spirit. The dull dense world has openings throughout to the white radiance.

Earth is crammed with heaven; all existence is suffused with God. "Why, the whole country is all filled and crammed and packed with the King." As a Greek thinker has it, the earth is bound by a chain of gold to heaven. The smallest details of the world contain prophecies of the unknown. The universe is everywhere a gate through which we can enter our spiritual heritage. Strike it anywhere, lay hold of it anywhere, it opens to the mansion of God. "He comes, comes, ever comes."

Every moment and every age, every day and every night, he comes, comes, ever comes. It is never too late to become a recruit to God's army. "At the end of the day I hasten in fear lest thy gate be shut; but I find that yet there is time." If we miss an opportunity, it is dead and gone, never more to recur. It is no good repenting after the event. At any moment the night may come when no man shall work. We must seize the opportunities as the world presents them, for they do not come at our invitation. We must be ever ready to receive God, for it may well happen that when He comes we are not ready, and when we are ready He does not come. The things of nature and the events of the world will cause trouble and vexation of spirit, if, instead of utilising them for spiritual and unselfish ends, we make use of them for our own sensation and enjoyment.

"Man's abiding happiness is not in getting anything but in giving himself up to what is greater than himself, to ideas which are larger than his individual self, the idea of his country, of humanity, of God." The world gives us opportunities for surrendering our all. There is a touch of the eternal in all such surrenders to unselfish ideals, or dedications to high causes. We then feel the feet of God and forget ourselves. A high and noble ideal releases the self, It delivers us from our selfishness and opens the gateway to immortality. Even the common things of earth's everyday experience, if we wholeheartedly give up ourselves to them, would take us to heaven. In such transactions the characteristic features of religion are present. "Whenever we find a devotion which makes the finite self seem as nothing and some reality to which it attaches itself seem as all, we have the essentially religious attitude."

The transcendent value of the ideal and the utter prostration of the self are complementary aspects of one experience. We should say in the presence of the ideal: "You are all my world. I am lost in you." Look at Arjuna's address to Chitra. "You alone are perfect; you are the wealth of the world, the end of all poverty, the goal of all efforts, the one woman! Others there are who can be but slowly known. While to see you for a moment is to see perfect completeness once and for ever."

Chitra responds to this appeal: "I heard his call, 'Beloved, my most beloved'. And all my forgotten lives united as one and responded to it. I said, "Take me, take all I am'. And I stretched out my arms to him. . . . Heaven and earth, time and space, pleasure and pain, death and life merged together in an unbearable ecstasy." There is nothing more heavenly on earth than the surrender of the soul of a woman to the man she loves. Self-transcendence, the mark of all spiritual experience, is present in the devoted passion for the pursuit of science, art, and morality.

In human love we have such, moments. "Only for a few fragrant hours we two have been made immortal." We then touch the hem of the garment of God, though we do not know it. "Entering my heart unbidden even as one of the common crowd, unknown to me, my King, thou didst press the signet of eternity upon many a fleeting moment of my life."

Religious experience is nothing more than this utter neglect of the self and surrender to God who captures our body, mind, and soul. It is a breaking up of our selfishness and a reaching out towards the whole. The finite ideals we sometimes disinterestedly pursue will sooner or later manifest their inadequacy to satisfy the needs of the soul.

Though perfect human love approximates to this, we soon recognise that it cannot satisfy the infinite craving in us for heavenly perfection. It may open the way to it, but it can never be the end. "If their love has its absolute centre in creatures, whether brute or human, then there win be misery, and they will suffer from disappointments through sickness, death, and separation; but if they have the consciousness of the infinite personality in the centre and background of their personal life, then the power of love will be fully satisfied, and an the gaps will be filled, and their joys and sorrows will join their hands in a harmony of fulfilment which is blessedness."

We long to become one with the perfect ideal. "In that devastation, in the utter nakedness of spirit, let us become one in beauty." No finite object can satisfy this craving. "Alas for my vain desire! Where is this hope for union except in thee, my God?" Finite ideals will have to be transmuted into the infinite before the soul can get perfect satisfaction through them.

8

Tagore's Educational Philosophy

Education in India: Historical Background

Before Rabindranath was born, British power in India had been consolidated and the general foundation of a colonial system of education had been laid. The stated aim of British policy was the promotion of English studies with English language as the medium of instruction and the creation of a class of Indians who had been brought up in an English way. As a result, the traditional system of village, Sanskrit and Islamic schools languished.

National universities had been established at Bombay, Madras and Calcutta, but secondary schools and universities were still the reserve of a small elite. The gulf between the fortunate upper classes and the vast masses of rural poor continued to widen. On the other hand, great socio-economic changes were taking place in the country, and especially in Calcutta and in other towns as they grew in size.

Railways were built; factories sprang up; municipal water supplies arrived. A new class of people came to adopt European dress, manners, attitudes and life styles. Old values and traditions came to be questioned. It was a period of social upheaval and reforms in India.

Towards the end of the nineteenth and in the early-20th centuries the middle class, which had come into being following the establishment of universities in 1857, began to protest against the imposed system of education and its parallel language policy. It is true that in the middle of the nineteenth century, when the British system was being introduced, a powerful group of urban classes expressed their preference for such studies.

But, seeing the consequences and with a growing awareness of the Indian cultural heritage and history, the middle classes had come to resent the education which was being offered. While Tagore preferred the traditional system to the new one, he did not want to bring it back without considerable changes.

This period also saw a rise in Indian nationalism. There was resentment against an imitation of British lifestyles and against British rule, coupled with increased awareness and appreciation of India's cultural traditions. Tagore's educational and other writings of the period reflect this nationalist trend. His concern with educational reform grew in intensity after 1901, and more so after 1905. Dissatisfaction with the existing system of education led to a general concern with reform.

A tragic series of family bereavements probably caused Tagore's withdrawal from the growing national struggle for independence in the country. He retired to his Ashram School to concentrate on its development and on the task of village reconstruction that he had initiated at Seliadah.

Educational Ideas

The difficulty in writing about Tagore's educational ideas lies in the fact that he did not set them down in a connected account. His views are found scattered in a large number of independent essays and journal articles, in speeches to various audiences and in letters to individuals over a number of years. Addresses to foreign audiences about his school at Shantiniketan and on Vishva Bharati are, of course, in English. Only recently have attempts been made to collect and publish these pieces in their original Bengali. There has been a tendency to group these diffuse writings into three broad divisions.

The First Phase (1892-1901)

Tagore considered lack of education to be the main obstacle in the way of India's progress and at the root of all its problems. The prevailing, colonial education system he found unsatisfactory since the only objective it appeared to serve was to produce clerks to man government offices and British businesses in India. The basic objectives of any worthwhile national education system, such as promoting creativity, freedom, joy and an awareness of a country's cultural heritage, were completely ignored.

The education offered was not even modern, since it was unrelated to any developments going on the field of education outside India. Irrespective of the content, the medium of education was English — a foreign language — so that learning this language was an additional burden for young Indian students. Particularly, the educational process failed to develop scientific attitudes and the spirit of enquiry. On the other hand, it divided the Indian people into two classes: those who received this education and those who did not. The second group, comprising nearly everyone living in the countryside, remained almost completely cut off from the affluent, educated, English-speaking class living in cities and towns.

In the pre-colonial system, a common language promoted an unobstructed flow of culture, even if formal education was not available to all. However, there was no place even in informal educational activities for modern subjects, like history, science and geography, and it did not promote objectivity in thinking, nor facilitate desirable social change.

The Second Phase (1901-18)

Tagore's preoccupation during this second phase was with developing an appropriate system of national education for India. Each nation was different and this fact should be reflected, he thought, in its system of education. The Ashram School at Shantiniketan was founded in 1901 on the basis of the ancient Indian forest schools.

In *Tapovan* (The Forest Schools of India) (1909) Tagore asserted that the forest school was typical of the Indian system of education with its emphasis on three basic elements of Indian culture, namely *Advaita* (Non-duality) in the field of knowledge, friendship for all in the field of feeling, and fulfilment of one's duties without concern for the outcomes in the field of action. In his view, the forest school integrated education with *Sadhana* (Disciplining One's Senses and One's Own Life). But Tagore updated this form of school to include science and similar modern subjects.

The second significant essay of this period was *Shikshar Vahana* (The Vehicle of Education) (1915) emphasising the importance of the mother-tongue as the medium of education. The use of English in education hindered assimilation of what was taught, and kept education confined to urban centres and the upper classes. Thus, if the vast rural masses were to benefit, it was absolutely essential to switch over to the use of Bengali in the context of Bengal at all levels of education, including higher education.

The ideal school, according to Tagore, should be established away from the turmoil of human habitation under an open sky and surrounded by vistas of fields, trees and plants. Living in a forest was also associated with austere pursuits and renunciation. The vast background of nature represented a grand perspective against which all objects, all feelings assumed their due proportions. He also referred to the significance of educating feelings as distinct from educating the senses and the intellect. The word 'forest' used in this context, he explained, was not dense jungle, but Tapovana, the forest clearing.

A national system of education in India should try to discover the characteristic truths of its civilization. Those truths are not commercialism, imperialism or nationalism, but rather universalism. The aim was all-round development of the individual personality through harmonious interaction and union of the spirit with the environment.

About the place of religion in education, Rabindranath said: 'Nature and human spirit, wedded together, would constitute our temple and selfless good deeds our worship' (Dharma Sikhsha, 1912).

Tagore himself was a teacher at the Ashram School and also gave thought to educational methods. He taught English language, and in the evenings related stories from Indian history to the children. He wrote plays for the students to perform and entertaining verse for children, as well as simple textbooks in various subjects.

Tagore was against any conspicuous emphasis on materials, buildings, furniture or books that imitated Western educational institutions in India. He thought that this would make education too expensive for the common people. He was against bookish learning:

> Books have come between our mind and life. They deprive us of our natural faculty of getting knowledge directly from nature and life and have generated within us the habit of knowing everything through books. We touch the world not with our mind, but with our books. They dehumanise and make us unsocial.... Let the students gather knowledge and materials from different regions of the country, from direct sources and from their own independent efforts.

The Third Phase (1918-41)

Vishva Bharati, Tagore's conception of a world university, was founded at the end of the First World War with a determination to go beyond aggressive nationalism and to build friendship with all nations.

After 1913, his travels abroad made him increasingly aware of what was going on in other countries. He came also to know a large number of intellectuals in the countries he visited. This in turn led him to emphasise cooperation between East and West, North and South (in today's jargon), in the field of humanistic studies and culture. From children's education and rural development, he increasingly shifted his attention to university education and developing the surrounding villages as one of the university's functions during this third phase. He wanted to devise an alternative form of education:

> In every nation, education is intimately associated with the life of the people. For us, modern education is relevant only to turning out clerks, lawyers, doctors, magistrates and policemen.... This education has not

> reached the farmer, the oil grinder, nor the potter. No other educated society has been struck with such disaster.... If ever a truly Indian university is established it must from the very beginning implement India's own knowledge of economics, agriculture, health, medicine and of all other everyday science from the surrounding villages. Then alone can the school or university become the centre of the country's way of living. This school must practise agriculture, dairying and weaving using the best modern methods.... I have proposed to call this school Vishva Bharati.

Tagore was convinced that no form of education offered in India, be it at school or at university level, would be complete without knowledge of patterns of rural living and without an effort by the universities to rejuvenate rural life. He considered this to be an important aspect of Vishva Bharati's total activity.

Writing about them in 1919 in his paper *Ashantosher Karon* (Cause of Dissatisfaction), he expressed his deep anguish at the contemporary attempts in India to establish new universities in exactly the same mould as existing ones due to a lack of will or a lack of courage to attempt new forms. This had become imperative in view of the fact that the civil service was saturated and, as the student members grew, the majority of graduates failed to get clerical or any other type of white-collar jobs and were good for nothing else. The time had thus come, Tagore urged, to attempt a change in the aims of university education.

How to make education real and our life force? In the addresses he gave and the essays he wrote from 1919 to 1936 he tried to answer this question. In his own words:

> We must try to understand how Indian genius expressed itself [...] Unless we try to put these together and discover the integrating factors behind these diverse streams of thought and make them a subject of study at our universities, we would only be borrowing knowledge from abroad. The natural habitat for knowledge is where it is produced. The

> main task of universities is to produce knowledge, its dissemination is its secondary function. We must invite those intellectuals and scholars to our universities who are engaged in research, invention or creative activity.

While nations sought primarily to give their citizens a means of livelihood through education, Tagore believed that there was a more important aim — that of personal fulfilment and self-improvement. It was important to borrow knowledge and experience from abroad, but not to use them as the foundation for Indian education.

Even so, if there was one European quality which Indian university students must acquire it was 'the desire to know, to find out about the laws of nature and to use them for the betterment of the conditions of human beings'. Science and its applications in the form of technology have led to the power and prosperity of Western countries. Unless India acquired knowledge of science and technology through its universities and schools, poverty and powerlessness would continue. To transform life and make it richer, healthier and more educated, it was imperative to resort to technology and science. But Tagore wanted science to be taught along with India's own philosophical and spiritual knowledge at Indian universities.

However, science without the constraint of self-knowledge, without appreciating that the quest for knowledge is the most important aim of human existence, leads to an endless desire for material goods and well-being, and the meaningless pursuit of the instruments of war and power, which are often the origin of conflict between nations and end, ultimately, in the suppression of the weaker by the stronger. That is why both spiritual and scientific knowledge are considered by Tagore as equally important.

In an address on the functions of the university, Tagore argued that a university is an attempt by a nation to aggregate knowledge at one place, to develop it and to disseminate it to the younger generation.

Long before universities in the West had been established, there existed in India universities, such as Nalanda and Vikramshila, where various branches of knowledge had been pursued by scholars for centuries during the Buddhist period of India's history. Students came to these universities from far and near in Asia to learn about the subjects taught, and to live with the teachers who were respected for their exemplary way of life. When universities came to be founded in Europe, the hold of religion was loosened. New methods of acquiring knowledge led to rapid growth in the fields of social, physical and life sciences.

Modern universities collect existing knowledge in various fields from within a country or abroad, preserve and develop it and make it available to the younger generations. But contemporary Indian universities had not been concerned about collecting and preserving the national heritage, and enriching it by fusing it with knowledge coming from abroad. Neither had they been concerned about improving life in the villages. 'Universities here are like a lighted railway compartment in a train passing through the countryside which is enveloped in darkness.'

Furthermore the use of the English language at universities presents a language barrier confining the flow of knowledge and information. Unless a beginning was made in using the mother-tongue as a medium of instruction in regional universities the flow of knowledge to the countryside would not be restored. Of course, English was needed to build bridges so as to benefit from the growing corpus of knowledge existing abroad in the fields of science, technology and other subjects, but its central importance in India's education process would cease.

In his *Shikhar Suwangeekaran* (Make Education Your Own) (1936), he returned to his recurrent theme of the unnaturalness of the system of education in India, its lack of links with the nation and its management which was in the hands of a foreign government. The working of the government, its courts of law and its education system were conducted in a language completely unintelligible to the majority of Indians. He contrasted the situation in India with what he had seen in the USSR and in Japan, where the governments had been able to educate their people within a very short time. Educating India's entire population and restoring the flow of culture from the educated classes to the rural population would not come about unless the mother-tongue was adopted as the medium of teaching.

The Second Experiment

Shantiniketan developed continuously from 1901 to 1921. The school, called Patha Bhawan, eventually became affiliated to Calcutta University and students could thus take the matriculation examination. For a long time, the funding of the school was entirely assumed by Tagore.

This was possible because teachers' salaries were very low. Most of Tagore's personal income, proceeds from the sale of his property, most of the Nobel Prize money and royalties from his books were the sources of school finance. Only after receiving the Nobel Prize and after being knighted by the British did the Indian Government begin to take an interest in him.

Tagore was convinced that some new form of schooling could be worked out for the village children in India based on life in the countryside. He had purchased an old building and some land at a village called Surul, not far from Shantiniketan. Fortunately for Shantiniketan, Tagore met Leonard Elmhirst in the United States in 1921. Elmhirst was at that time reading agricultural science at Cornell University and was keen on spending some time in India doing rural reconstruction work.

Tagore requested Elmhirst to join him. He told Elmhirst that Shantiniketan was surrounded by a number of villages which, 'for some reason, appeared to be in a state of steady decline'. There was no sign of effort on the part of the villagers: there was no joy, no food, no health, no idea of the importance of their own initiative and no cooperation among them. Tagore wanted Elmhirst first to find out why and then suggest remedial action. The objective was to raise the villagers' income, but the higher aim according to Tagore was to make them happy.

Tagore was somewhat disappointed that Shantiniketan had failed to achieve the ideal of bringing scientific knowledge to bear on life in the countryside. In order to improve the human condition in the villages of Eastern India, the population had to throw off their belief in fate and realise the importance of depending upon their own efforts. This is what Tagore had in mind when he launched the rural reconstruction work at Shantiniketan in a school called Shikshasastra. The objective of the new school was to provide an all-round education for village children, enabling them to earn a decent livelihood but also equipping them to improve rural life in all its aspects.

From the very beginning, the major thrust of the programme at Shantiniketan under Elmhirst came to be increasing the productivity of the land. But Tagore also wanted a total improvement covering agriculture, education, health and social life in the villages. Agricultural research and experiments would be undertaken at Shantiniketan and the fruits of this research were to be carried to the villages. At the same time, medical care and the eradication of malaria were considered equally important. At the centre, specialists in various fields worked together to overcome the difficulties of rural life. In addition, a scout movement was organised to mobilise the children as a starting point for drawing their parents into the village development programme.

A fundamental area of instruction at Shantiniketan was handicrafts; it was compulsory for all students to learn a trade. Another major activity was the launching of some 200 cooperative societies for agricultural credit, irrigation, granaries, etc. Experiments were made on new crops and on new varieties of existing crops that appeared to be suitable for local conditions. A dairy farm gave practical demonstrations of animal husbandry on scientific lines. The villagers were expected to adopt rural industries to supplement their income. The village welfare department initiated public works (repairing and excavating reservoirs), looked after village schools, maintained a mobile library for villages, organised social and cultural activities and ran the scout movement. There was a health section with a central dispensary; and a maternity and child-welfare section was added in 1940.

Shantiniketan aimed at combining work with joy. Picnics, excursions, games, music, theatrical performances and celebrating socio-religious festivals constituted regular features of the calendar. New Year's Day, the Rainy Season festival, the New Rice festival, the Spring festival were-and still are-all regular features. Tagore added *Halkarshan* (ploughing the land festival) and Van Mahotosava (tree planting). Apart from adding joy to dreary village life, some of these festivals brought students and villagers to work together.

For years Tagore tried to convince his countrymen through his speeches, stories, novels, poems and songs to work for rural revival. The call went unheeded until Gandhi came on the Indian political scene. Single handed, the poet had started his work: 'They call you mad. Wait for tomorrow and keep silent' (Poems, 1942).

> Of course, turning out songs is my proper vocation. But those who are unfortunate cannot afford to limit their choice to the works they do. They must also bear the burden of tasks they cannot do. The scale of our enterprise can never be a matter of pride to us, but let us hope that its truth will be. Ideas, if they have the vitality of truth in them, grow and spread in the course of time.

How correct Tagore was in this respect. The entire programme followed at Shantiniketan for rural development was adopted by India's five-year plans as the correct approach to rural community development.

Influences

Apart from the three remarkable Englishmen who were Tagore's collaborators, namely C. F. Andrews, William Pearson and Leonard Elmhirst, numerous other scholars came to Shantiniketan at the poet's invitation to participate in the teaching programmes.

Tagore disowned being influenced by any of the well-known educationists. It was not any new theory of education but the memory of his schooldays that led him to establish his residential schools. 'I established my institution in a beautiful spot away from the town where the children had the greatest freedom possible under the shade of ancient trees.'

Through contact with nature, by making them aware of community relations and with the help of literature, festivals and religious teaching, he tried to develop the souls of his children.

But this turned out to be not quite enough, so he introduced work education as 'a joyous exercise of our inventive and constructive energies that help to build up character.'

In many respects Tagore's ideas relating to the education of children resemble those of Rousseau, Frobel, Dewey, Montessori and others. For instance, Rousseau considered nature as children's teacher, as does Tagore, but unlike Rousseau he retains a significant role for the teacher. Frobel and Tagore both advocate harmony with all that exists to be achieved through education; they are both in favour of play and domestic activities as part of education during infancy and activity in the community as part of the educational process during childhood.

Frobel stops here; but Tagore includes subsequent education under the purview of activity-oriented education. Both are for joy and festivities, and an awareness of the child's dignity as part of the educational environment. The resemblances between Frobel and Tagore's ideas are indeed striking. The same is true to some extent of his approach to children's education compared with some of his contemporaries, such as Dewey, Maria Montessori and Tolstoy.

As Sarkar (1961) points out, Tagore was familiar with many of these views, but all who knew the poet were aware that he was in no way indebted to them. His views were linked with the development of his own mind and spirit, and his profound understanding of India's traditional educational experience and philosophy.

His activity-oriented school for village children appears to have inspired Gandhi's ideas on basic education. Tagore's influence can also be seen in the report of the Kothari Commission on Education in India.

In Tagore's view, the higher aim of education was the same as that of a person's life, that is, to achieve fulfilment and completeness. There was a lesser aim, that of providing the individual with a satisfactory means of livelihood, without which a person would not be able to satisfy his/her basic requirements and thus fail to achieve either of these two aims. Tagore also imagined that the limitless development of man is possible only in an environment free from any kind of bondage. Apart from the scriptures, it would seem that he was influenced by the attitudes that arose in Europe during the Renaissance and the Age of Reason.

In his view, education was not intellectual development alone. It should also develop a student's aesthetic nature and creativity. The quest for knowledge and physical activity in an agreeable environment were integral parts of the process. Freedom and creativity are linked in Tagore's thought, one conditioning the other. The more people go beyond the limitations of their animal nature, the closer they come to humanism, freedom and unity and are then able to develop their creativity. This quest alone gives a meaning to life, and education is an effort to make life meaningful. Here the aims of the individual and those of the community have become almost one.

Tagore did not neglect the lesser aims of life and education. In the colonial system of education that existed at that time the whole focus of education was on employment, to the complete neglect of the higher aims of life. His intention was to correct this wrong emphasis, without ignoring science, technology and agricultural sciences, as well as training in village crafts. Without these, it was not possible to revive the derelict life of rural India. Both categories of aims should thus be considered the objective of education.

It was necessary, Tagore felt, to make the younger generation aware of their national cultural heritage and to grasp its significance for them. At the same time, education should bring children face to face with the cultures of other countries and persuade them to learn from them.

Tagore put great emphasis on the use of a national language as the vehicle of education at all stages of education. He wanted Indian universities to integrate themselves with society and make an effort to educate people living in the countryside. He did not want education to remain confined to the cities and to particular classes of society.

He was very much concerned with women's education. His educational institutions have almost always been co-educational and the number of female students is conspicuously large at Shantiniketan. He wanted women and men to be offered similar theoretical courses with separate practical courses for women, since their roles in life differed from those of men.

Tagore considered teachers to be very important in any scheme of education. He wanted teachers to help young children to grow on their own as a gardener helps the young plants to grow. He wanted to use education as an instrument of change to make Indian young men and women more rational and less subject to meaningless social and individual rituals.

Tagore wanted his students to acquire a scientific temper; in other words, he wanted teachers to stimulate constructive doubt, the love of mental adventure, the courage and longing to conquer the world by enterprise and boldness in thought and in action. These were the virtues cultivation of which had made the West forge ahead.

Tagore was against any form of corporal punishment to impose discipline. He wanted discipline to come from within, from the pursuit of noble and high ambitions in life. Discipline would follow naturally when minor impulses and desires were willingly forgone to pursue grand creative desires.

He wanted his students to think in terms of the whole of mankind. He wanted them to become universal men and women like himself and to overcome feelings of narrow nationalism in order that the world could live and grow in peace and fellowship.

The poet passed away in 1941. The two institutions specific to Tagore's educational ideas and experiments still survive in the form of *Patha Bhawan* (the school section) at Shantiniketan and in the form of Sikshasastra and Shantiniketan-of course, they have been modified a good deal over this long stretch of time. They form the core of the Shantiniketan ideal.

Vishva Bharati survives too; it is now a central university and has changed considerably. The emphasis that Tagore placed on the teaching of the fine arts and crafts, and on music, continues in the form of two separate autonomous institutions under the general supervision of Vishva Bharati. These institutions are: the *Kala Bhawan* (the school of fine arts); and the *Sangeet Bhawan* (the school of music and dance). Emphasis on the teaching of various Indian languages and on the teaching of Asian cultures, and the presence of an international faculty are not very evident. But there is a *Cheena Bhawan* (the school of Chinese language and culture),

Hindi Bhawan, a School of Islamic Studies, and a good number of students from Far Eastern countries, particularly in the Kala Bhawan and the Sangeet Bhawan.

But one can see that Tagore's memory still dominates life on the university campus. The following poem from *Gitanjali* (Song Offerings) brings together the ideals the poet kept before the nation, before mankind, and before his educational institutions.

> Where the mind is without fear, and the heart is held high,
>
> Where the world is not broken up into fragments by narrow domestic walls,
>
> Where the words came out from the depths of truth,
>
> Where tireless striving stretches its arms towards perfection;
>
> Where the clear stream of reason has not lost its way into the dreary desert sand of dead habits,
>
> Where the mind is led forward by thee into everwidening thought and action
>
> Into that heaven of freedom,
>
> My father, let my country awake.

artists. His cousins, who shared the family mansion, were leaders in theatre, science and a new art movement [illegible]

The tremendous excitement and cultural richness of his extended family permitted young Rabindranath to absorb and learn subconsciously at his own pace, giving him a dynamic open model of education, which he later tried to recreate in his school at Shantiniketan. Not surprisingly, he found his outside formal schooling to be inferior and boring and, after a brief exposure to several schools, he refused to attend school. The only degrees he ever received were honorary ones bestowed late in life.

His experience at Jorasanko provided him with a lifelong conviction concerning the importance of freedom in education. He also realized in a profound manner the importance of the arts for developing empathy and sensitivity, and the necessity for an intimate relationship with one's cultural and natural environment. In participating in the cosmopolitan activities of the family, he came to reject narrowness in general, and in particular, any form of narrowness that separated human being from human being. He saw education as a vehicle for appreciating the richest aspects of other cultures, while maintaining one's own cultural specificity. As he wrote:

> I was brought up in an atmosphere of aspiration, aspiration for the expansion of the human spirit. We in our home sought freedom of power in our language, freedom of imagination in our literature, freedom of soul in our religious creeds and that of mind in our social environment. Such an opportunity has given me confidence in the power of education which is one with life and only which can give us real freedom, the highest that is claimed for man, his freedom of moral communion in the human world.... I try to assert in my words and works that education has its only meaning and object in freedom—freedom from ignorance about the laws of the universe, and freedom from passion and prejudice in our communication with the human world. In my institution I have attempted to create an atmosphere of naturalness in

9

Gems of Poetry (Selected Poems)

Rabindranath Tagore became one of the prolific writers in the world, poet, artist, dramatist, musician, novelist, and essayist. He was completely at home both in Bengali and in English, in part because he was educated at University College, London, in 1879-80. He had become the national poet of Bengal by the time of his Golden Jubilee in Calcutta on January 28, 1912, but his international fame only came in November 1913 when he won the Nobel Prize for literature for Gitanjali, a collection of poetry initially brought out in Bengali in 1910 and then translated by the poet and published in English in 1912 with an introduction by W. B. Yeats. He translated so many volumes of his own Bengali poems personally that he can be regarded as an Anglo-Indian poet.

Tagore resided at Shantiniketan and Ashram and founded a school at the former place that turned into Vishva Bharati University in 1918, the present-day holder of the Tagore copyright (which ran out on January 1, 2002). Mrinalini Devi Raichaudhuri and he wed, in an arranged marriage, Dec. 9, 1883, and they had five children: three daughters, Madhurilata, Renuka, and Mira, and two sons, Rabindranath and Samindranath. Tagore obtained honorary degrees from the universities of Calcutta (1913), Dacca (1936), Osmania (1938), and Oxford (1940). He died August 7, 1941, in Calcutta, and was cremated.

Rabindranath Tagore was one of India's greatest poets who was awarded the Nobel Prize for Literature in 1913.

His father Debendranath Tagore was a key figure in the Bengali renaissance which sought to reinvigorate the culture of Bengali by combining elements of Western materialism with traditional Indian culture. Tagore continued this tradition. He led an extremely productive artistic life as well as a poet Tagore was also an artist, writer, and educationalist.

Tagore had his first poetry published at the age of 17. However, the publication of Gitanjali in America and Great Britain sealed his reputation as an international poet. It was for Gitanjali that Tagore was awarded the Nobel Prize for Literature.

Tagore's poetry stems from his love of nature, and commitment to a universalist philosophy which seeks to see God through personal service. Tagore was also influenced by The Upanishads — India's ancient scriptures.

"Love is an endless mystery,

for it has nothing else to explain it"

Moment's Indulgence

I ask for a moment's indulgence to sit by thy side.

The works that I have in hand I will finish afterwards.

Away from the sight of thy face my heart knows no rest nor respite,

and my work becomes an endless toil in a shoreless sea of toil.

Today the summer has come at my window with its sighs and murmurs;

and the bees are plying their minstrelsy at the court of the flowering grove.

Now it is time to sit quite, face to face with thee,

and to sing dedication of life in this silent and overflowing leisure.

Flower

Pluck this little flower and take it, delay not! I fear lest it droop and drop into the dust.

I may not find a place in thy garland, but honour it with a touch of pain from thy hand and pluck it.

I fear lest the day end before I am aware, and the time of offering go by.

Though its colour be not deep and its smell be faint, use this flower in thy service and pluck it while there is time.

Fool

O Fool, try to carry thyself upon thy own shoulders!

O beggar, to come beg at thy own door!

Leave all thy burdens on his hands who can bear all, and never look behind in regret.

Thy desire at once puts out the light from the lamp it touches with its breath.

It is unholy — take not thy gifts through its unclean hands.

Accept only what is offered by sacred love.

Leave This

Leave this chanting and singing and telling of beads!

Whom dost thou worship in this lonely dark corner of a temple with doors all shut?

Open thine eyes and see thy God is not before thee!

He is there where the tiller is tilling the hard ground and where the pathmaker is breaking stones.

He is with them in sun and in shower, and his garment is covered with dust.

Put off thy holy mantle and even like him come down on the dusty soil!

Deliverance?

Where is this deliverance to be found?

Our master himself has joyfully taken upon him the bonds of creation; he is bound with us all for ever.

Come out of thy meditations and leave aside thy flowers and incense!

What harm is there if thy clothes become tattered and stained?

Meet him and stand by him in toil and in sweat of thy brow.

Journey Home

The time that my journey takes is long and the way of it long.

I came out on the chariot of the first gleam of light,

and pursued my voyage through the wildernesses of worlds leaving my track on many a star and planet.

It is the most distant course that comes nearest to thyself,

and that training is the most intricate which leads to the utter simplicity of a tune.

The traveller has to knock at every alien door to come to his own,

and one has to wander through all the outer worlds to reach the innermost shrine at the end.

My eyes strayed far and wide before I shut them and said 'Here art thou!'

The question and the cry 'Oh, where?' melt into tears of a thousand streams and deluge the world with the flood of the assurance 'I am!'

Song Unsung

The song that I came to sing remains unsung to this day.

I have spent my days in stringing and in unstringing my instrument.

The time has not come true, the words have not been rightly set;

only there is the agony of wishing in my heart.

The blossom has not opened; only the wind is sighing by.

I have not seen his face, nor have I listened to his voice;

only I have heard his gentle footsteps from the road before my house.

The livelong day has passed in spreading his seat on the floor;

but the lamp has not been lit and I cannot ask him into my house.

I live in the hope of meeting with him; but this meeting is not yet.

Strong Mercy

My desires are many and my cry is pitiful, but ever didst thou save me by hard refusals;

and this strong mercy has been wrought into my life through and through.

Day by day thou art making me worthy of the simple, great gifts that thou gavest to me unasked — this sky and the light, this body and the life and the mind — saving me from perils of overmuch desire.

There are times when I languidly linger and times when I awaken and hurry in search of my goal; but cruelly thou hidest thyself from before me.

Day by day thou art making me worthy of thy full acceptance by refusing me ever and anon, saving me from perils of weak, uncertain desire.

Mind Without Fear

Where the mind is without fear and the head is held high;

Where knowledge is free;

Where the world has not been broken up into fragments by narrow domestic walls;

Where words come out from the depth of truth;

Where tireless striving stretches its arms towards perfection;

Where the clear stream of reason has not lost its way into the dreary desert sand of dead habit;

Where the mind is led forward by thee into ever-widening thought and action;

Into that heaven of freedom, my Father, let my country awake.

Little Flute

Thou hast made me endless, such is thy pleasure. This frail vessel thou emptiest again and again, and fillest it ever with fresh life.

This little flute of a reed thou hast carried over hills and dales, and hast breathed through it melodies eternally new.

At the immortal touch of thy hands my little heart loses its limits in joy and gives birth to utterance ineffable.

Thy infinite gifts come to me only on these very small hands of mine.

Ages pass, and still thou pourest, and still there is room to fill.

Purity

Life of my life, I shall ever try to keep my body pure, knowing that thy living touch is upon all my limbs.

I shall ever try to keep all untruths out from my thoughts, knowing that thou art that truth which has kindled the light of reason in my mind.

I shall ever try to drive all evils away from my heart and keep my love in flower, knowing that thou hast thy seat in the inmost shrine of my heart.

And it shall be my endeavour to reveal thee in my actions, knowing it is thy power gives me strength to act.

Patience

If thou speakest not I will fill my heart with thy silence and endure it.

I will keep still and wait like the night with starry vigil and its head bent low with patience.

The morning will surely come, the darkness will vanish, and thy voice pour down in golden streams breaking through the sky.

Then thy words will take wing in songs from every one of my birds' nests, and thy melodies will break forth in flowers in all my forest groves.

Free Love

By all means they try to hold me secure who love me in this world.

But it is otherwise with thy love which is greater than theirs, and thou keepest me free.

Lest I forget them they never venture to leave me alone.

But day passes by after day and thou art not seen.

If I call not thee in my prayers, if I keep not thee in my heart, thy love for me still waits for my love.

Little of Me

Let only that little be left of me whereby I may name thee my all.

Let only that little be left of my will whereby I may feel thee on every side, and come to thee in everything, and offer to thee my love every moment.

Let only that little be left of me whereby I may never hide thee.

Let only that little of my fetters be left whereby I am bound with thy will, and thy purpose is carried out in my life — and that is the fetter of thy love.

Give Me Strength

This is my prayer to thee, my lord — strike, strike at the root of penury in my heart.

Give me the strength lightly to bear my joys and sorrows.

Give me the strength to make my love fruitful in service.

Give me the strength never to disown the poor or bend my knees before insolent might.

Give me the strength to raise my mind high above daily trifles.

And give me the strength to surrender my strength to thy will with love.

Closed Path

I thought that my voyage had come to its end at the last limit of my power, — that the path before me was closed,

that provisions were exhausted and the time come to take shelter in a silent obscurity.

But I find that thy will knows no end in me.

And when old words die out on the tongue, new melodies break forth from the heart;

and where the old tracks are lost, new country is revealed with its wonders.

Only Thee

That I want thee, only thee — let my heart repeat without end.

All desires that distract me, day and night, are false and empty to the core.

As the night keeps hidden in its gloom the petition for light, even thus in the depth of my unconsciousness rings the cry — 'I want thee, only thee'.

As the storm still seeks its end in peace when it strikes against peace with all its might, even thus my rebellion strikes against thy love and still its cry is — 'I want thee, only thee'.

Beggarly Heart

When the heart is hard and parched up, come upon me with a shower of mercy.

When grace is lost from life, come with a burst of song.

When tumultuous work raises its din on all sides shutting me out from beyond, come to me, my lord of silence, with thy peace and rest.

When my beggarly heart sits crouched, shut up in a corner, break open the door, my King, and come with the ceremony of a King.

When desire blinds the mind with delusion and dust, O thou holy one, thou wakeful, come with thy light and thy thunder.

Sail Away

Early in the day it was whispered that we should sail in a boat, only thou and I, and never a soul in the world would know of this our pilgrimage to no country and to no end.

In that shoreless ocean, at thy silently listening smile my songs would swell in melodies, free as waves, free from all bondage of words.

Is the time not come yet?

Are there works still to do?

Lo, the evening has come down upon the shore and in the fading light the seabirds come flying to their nests.

Who knows when the chains will be off, and the boat, like the last glimmer of sunset, vanish into the night?

Signet of Eternity

The day was when I did not keep myself in readiness for thee;

and entering my heart unbidden even as one of the common crowd, unknown to me, my King,

thou didst press the signet of eternity upon many a fleeting moment of my life.

And today when by chance I light upon them and see thy signature,

I find they have lain scattered in the dust mixed with the memory of joys and sorrows of my trivial days forgotten.

Thou didst not turn in contempt from my childish play among dust,

and the steps that I heard in my playroom are the same that are echoing from star to star.

Lotus

On the day when the lotus bloomed, alas, my mind was straying, and I knew it not.

My basket was empty and the flower remained unheeded.

Only now and again a sadness fell upon me, and I started up from my dream and felt a sweet trace of a strange fragrance in the south wind.

That vague sweetness made my heart ache with longing and it seemed to me that is was the eager breath of the summer seeking for its completion.

I knew not then that it was so near, tnat it was mine, and that this perfect sweetness had blossomed in the depth of my own heart.

Boat

I must launch out my boat.

The languid hours pass by on the shore — Alas for me!

The spring has done its flowering and taken leave.

And now with the burden of faded futile flowers I wait and linger.

The waves have become clamorous, and upon the bank in the shady lane the yellow leaves flutter and fall.

What emptiness do you gaze upon!

Do you not feel a thrill passing through the air with the notes of the far-away song floating from the other shore?

Friend

Art thou abroad on this stormy night on thy journey of love, my friend?

The sky groans like one in despair.

I have no sleep tonight.

Ever and again I open my door and look out on the darkness, my friend!

I can see nothing before me.

I wonder where lies thy path!

By what dim shore of the ink-black river, by what far edge of the frowning forest,

through what mazy depth of gloom art thou threading thy course to come to me, my friend?

When Day is Done

If the day is done, if birds sing no more, if the wind has flagged tired,

then draw the veil of darkness thick upon me, even as thou hast wrapt the earth with the coverlet of sleep and tenderly closed the petals of the drooping lotus at dusk.

From the traveller, whose sack of provisions is empty before the voyage is ended,

whose garment is torn and dust-laden, whose strength is exhausted, remove shame and poverty, and renew his life like a flower under the cover of thy kindly night.

Sleep

In the night of weariness let me give myself up to sleep without struggle, resting my trust upon thee.

Let me not force my flagging spirit into a poor preparation for thy worship.

It is thou who drawest the veil of night upon the tired eyes of the day to renew its sight in a fresher gladness of awakening.

Lamp of Love

Light, oh where is the light?

Kindle it with the burning fire of desire!

There is the lamp but never a flicker of a flame — is such thy fate, my heart?

Ah, death were better by far for thee!

Misery knocks at thy door, and her message is that thy lord is wakeful, and he calls thee to the love-tryst through the darkness of night.

The sky is overcast with clouds and the rain is ceaseless.

I know not what this is that stirs in me — I know not its meaning.

A moment's flash of lightning drags down a deeper gloom on my sight, and my heart gropes for the path to where the music of the night calls me.

Light, oh where is the light!

Kindle it with the burning fire of desire!

It thunders and the wind rushes screaming through the void.

The night is black as a black stone.

Let not the hours pass by in the dark.

Kindle the lamp of love with thy life.

Dungeon

He whom I enclose with my name is weeping in this dungeon.

I am ever busy building this wall all around;

and as this wall goes up into the sky day by day I lose sight of my true being in its dark shadow.

I take pride in this great wall, and I plaster it with dust and sand lest a least hole should be left in this name;

and for all the care I take I lose sight of my true being.

Who is This?

I came out alone on my way to my tryst.

But who is this that follows me in the silent dark?

I move aside to avoid his presence but I escape him not.

He makes the dust rise from the earth with his swagger; he adds his loud voice to every word that I utter.

He is my own little self, my lord, he knows no shame; but I am ashamed to come to thy door in his company.

Prisoner

'Prisoner, tell me, who was it that bound you?'

'It was my master,' said the prisoner.

'I thought I could outdo everybody in the world in wealth and power,

and I amassed in my own treasure-house the money due to my King.

When sleep overcame me I lay upon the bed that was for my lord,

and on waking up I found I was a prisoner in my own treasure-house.'

'Prisoner, tell me, who was it that wrought this unbreakable chain?'

'It was I,' said the prisoner, 'who forged this chain very carefully.

I thought my invincible power would hold the world captive leaving me in a freedom undisturbed.

Thus, night and day I worked at the chain with huge fires and cruel hard strokes.

When at last the work was done and the links were complete and unbreakable,

I found that it held me in its grip.'

Innermost One

He it is, the innermost one, who awakens my being with his deep hidden touches.

He it is who puts his enchantment upon these eyes and joyfully plays on the chords of my heart in varied cadence of pleasure and pain.

He it is who weaves the web of this maya in evanescent hues of gold and silver, blue and green, and lets peep out through the folds his feet, at whose touch I forget myself.

Days come and ages pass, and it is ever he who moves my heart in many a name, in many a guise, in many a rapture of joy and of sorrow.

Senses

Deliverance is not for me in renunciation.

I feel the embrace of freedom in a thousand bonds of delight.

Thou ever pourest for me the fresh draught of thy wine of various colours and fragrance, filling this earthen vessel to the brim.

My world will light its hundred different lamps with thy flame and place them before the altar of thy temple.

No, I will never shut the doors of my senses.

The delights of sight and hearing and touch will bear thy delight.

Yes, all my illusions will burn into illumination of joy, and all my desires ripen into fruits of love.

Face to Face

Day after day, O lord of my life, shall I stand before thee face to face.

With folded hands, O lord of all worlds, shall I stand before thee face to face.

Under thy great sky in solitude and silence, with humble heart shall I stand before thee face to face.

In this laborious world of thine, tumultuous with toil and with struggle, among hurrying crowds shall I stand before thee face to face.

And when my work shall be done in this world,

O King of Kings, alone and speechless shall I stand before thee face to face.

Lost Star

When the creation was new and all the stars shone in their first splendour,

the gods held their assembly in the sky and sang 'Oh, the picture of perfection! the joy unalloyed!'

But one cried of a sudden

— 'It seems that somewhere there is a break in the chain of light and one of the stars has been lost.'

The golden string of their harp snapped, their song stopped, and they cried in dismay

— 'Yes, that lost star was the best, she was the glory of all heavens!'

From that day the search is unceasing for her, and the cry goes on from one to the other that in her the world has lost its one joy!

Only in the deepest silence of night the stars smile and whisper among themselves

— 'Vain is this seeking! unbroken perfection is over all!'

Let Me Not Forget

If it is not my portion to meet thee in this life then

let me ever feel that I have missed thy sight

— let me not forget for a moment, let me carry the pangs of this sorrow in my dreams and in my wakeful hours.

As my days pass in the crowded market of this world and my hands grow full with the daily profits,

let me ever feel that I have gained nothing

— let me not forget for a moment, let me carry the pangs of this sorrow in my dreams and in my wakeful hours.

When I sit by the roadside, tired and panting, when I spread my bed low in the dust,

let me ever feel that the long journey is still before me

— let me not forget a moment, let me carry the pangs of this sorrow in my dreams and in my wakeful hours.

When my rooms have been decked out and the flutes sound and the laughter there is loud,

let me ever feel that I have not invited thee to my house

— let me not forget for a moment, let me carry the pangs of this sorrow in my dreams and in my wakeful hours.

Roaming Cloud

I am like a remnant of a cloud of autumn uselessly roaming in the sky,

O my sun ever-glorious!

Thy touch has not yet melted my vapour, making me one with thy light, and thus I count months and years separated from thee.

If this be thy wish and if this be thy play, then take this fleeting emptiness of mine,

paint it with colours, gild it with gold, float it on the wanton wind and spread it in varied wonders.

And again when it shall be thy wish to end this play at night, I shall melt and vanish away in the dark,

or it may be in a smile of the white morning, in a coolness of purity transparent.

Where Shadow Chases Light

This is my delight, thus to wait and watch at the wayside where shadow chases light and the rain comes in the wake of the summer.

Messengers, with tidings from unknown skies, greet me and speed along the road.

My heart is glad within, and the breath of the passing breeze is sweet.

From dawn till dusk I sit here before my door, and I know that of a sudden the happy moment will arrive when I shall see.

In the meanwhile I smile and I sing all alone.

In the meanwhile the air is filling with the perfume of promise.

Silent Steps

Have you not heard his silent steps?

He comes, comes, ever comes.

Every moment and every age, every day and every night he comes, comes, ever comes.

Many a song have I sung in many a mood of mind, but all their notes have always proclaimed,

'He comes, comes, ever comes.'

In the fragrant days of sunny April through the forest path he comes, comes, ever comes.

In the rainy gloom of July nights on the thundering chariot of clouds he comes, comes, ever comes.

In sorrow after sorrow it is his steps that press upon my heart,

And it is the golden touch of his feet that makes my joy to shine.

Distant Time

I know not from what distant time thou art ever coming nearer to meet me.

Thy sun and stars can never keep thee hidden from me for aye.

In many a morning and eve thy footsteps have been heard and thy messenger has come within my heart and called me in secret.

I know not only why today my life is all astir, and a feeling of tremulous joy is passing through my heart.

It is as if the time were come to wind up my work, and I feel in the air a faint smell of thy sweet presence.

The Journey

The morning sea of silence broke into ripples of bird songs;

and the flowers were all merry by the roadside;

and the wealth of gold was scattered through the rift of the clouds while we busily went on our way and paid no heed.

We sang no glad songs nor played;

we went not to the village for barter;

we spoke not a word nor smiled;

we lingered not on the way.

We quickened our pace more and more as the time sped by.

The sun rose to the mid sky and doves cooed in the shade.

Withered leaves danced and whirled in the hot air of noon.

The shepherd boy drowsed and dreamed in the shadow of the banyan tree,

and I laid myself down by the water and stretched my tired limbs on the grass.

My companions laughed at me in scorn;

they held their heads high and hurried on;

they never looked back nor rested;

they vanished in the distant blue haze.

They crossed many meadows and hills,

and passed through strange, far-away countries.

All honour to you, heroic host of the interminable path!

Mockery and reproach pricked me to rise,

but found no response in me.

I gave myself up for lost in the depth of a glad humiliation — in the shadow of a dim delight.

The repose of the sun-embroidered green gloom slowly spread over my heart.

I forgot for what I had travelled, and I surrendered my mind without struggle to the maze of shadows and songs.

At last, when I woke from my slumber and opened my eyes,

I saw thee standing by me, flooding my sleep with thy smile.

How I had feared that the path was long and wearisome,

and the struggle to reach thee was hard!

Light

Light, my light, the world-filling light,

the eye-kissing light,

heart-sweetening light!

Ah, the light dances, my darling, at the centre of my life;

the light strikes, my darling, the chords of my love;

the sky opens, the wind runs wild, laughter passes over the earth.

The butterflies spread their sails on the sea of light.

Lilies and jasmines surge up on the crest of the waves of light.

The light is shattered into gold on every cloud, my darling, and it scatters gems in profusion.

Mirth spreads from leaf to leaf, my darling, and gladness without measure.

The heaven's river has drowned its banks and the flood of joy is abroad.

Passing Breeze

Yes, I know, this is nothing but thy love,

O beloved of my heart — this golden light that dances upon the leaves,

these idle clouds sailing across the sky,

this passing breeze leaving its coolness upon my forehead.

The morning light has flooded my eyes — this is thy message to my heart.

Thy face is bent from above, thy eyes look down on my eyes, and my heart has touched thy feet.

Seashore

On the seashore of endless worlds children meet.

The infinite sky is motionless overhead and the restless water is boisterous.

On the seashore of endless worlds the children meet with shouts and dances.

They build their houses with sand and they play with empty shells.

With withered leaves they weave their boats and smilingly float them on the vast deep.

Children have their play on the seashore of worlds.

They know not how to swim, they know not how to cast nets.

Pearl fishers dive for pearls, merchants sail in their ships, while children gather pebbles and scatter them again.

They seek not for hidden treasures, they know not how to cast nets.

The sea surges up with laughter and pale gleams the smile of the sea beach.

Death-dealing waves sing meaningless ballads to the children, even like a mother while rocking her baby's cradle.

The sea plays with children, and pale gleams the smile of the sea beach.

On the seashore of endless worlds children meet.

Tempest roams in the pathless sky, ships get wrecked in the trackless water, death is abroad and children play.

On the seashore of endless worlds is the great meeting of children.

Coloured Toys

When I bring to you coloured toys, my child,

I understand why there is such a play of colours on clouds, on water, and why flowers are painted in tints

— when I give coloured toys to you, my child.

When I sing to make you dance

I truly now why there is music in leaves, and why waves send their chorus of voices to the heart of the listening earth

— when I sing to make you dance.

When I bring sweet things to your greedy hands

I know why there is honey in the cup of the flowers and why fruits are secretly filled with sweet juice

— when I bring sweet things to your greedy hands.

When I kiss your face to make you smile, my darling,

I surely understand what pleasure streams from the sky in morning light, and what delight that is that is which the summer breeze brings to my body

— when I kiss you to make you smile.

Old and New

Thou hast made me known to friends whom I knew not.

Thou hast given me seats in homes not my own.

Thou hast brought the distant near and made a brother of the stranger.

I am uneasy at heart when I have to leave my accustomed shelter;

I forget that there abides the old in the new, and that there also thou abidest.

Through birth and death, in this world or in others, wherever thou leadest me it is thou, the same,

The one companion of my endless life who ever linkest my heart with bonds of joy to the unfamiliar.

When one knows thee, then alien there is none, then no door is shut.

Oh, grant me my prayer that I may never lose the bliss of the touch of the one in the play of many.

She

She who ever had remained in the depth of my being,
in the twilight of gleams and of glimpses;

she who never opened her veils in the morning light,
will be my last gift to thee, my God, folded in my final song.

Words have wooed yet failed to win her; persuasion has stretched to her its eager arms in vain.

I have roamed from country to country keeping her in the core of my heart,

and around her have risen and fallen the growth and decay of my life.

Over my thoughts and actions, my slumbers and dreams, she reigned yet dwelled alone and apart.

Many a man knocked at my door and asked for her and turned away in despair.

There was none in the world who ever saw her face to face, and she remained in her loneliness waiting for thy recognition.

Stream of Life

The same stream of life that runs through my veins night and day runs through the world and dances in rhythmic measures.

It is the same life that shoots in joy through the dust of the earth in numberless blades of grass and breaks into tumultuous waves of leaves and flowers.

It is the same life that is rocked in the ocean-cradle of birth and of death, in ebb and in flow.

I feel my limbs are made glorious by the touch of this world of life.

And my pride is from the life-throb of ages dancing in my blood this moment.

Maya

That I should make much of myself and turn it on all sides, thus casting coloured shadows on thy radiance

— such is thy Maya.

Thou settest a barrier in thine own being and then callest thy severed self in myriad notes.

This thy self-separation has taken body in me.

The poignant song is echoed through all the sky in many-coloured tears

and smiles, alarms and hopes; waves rise up and sink again, dreams break and form.

In me is thy own defeat of self.

This screen that thou hast raised is painted with innumerable figures with the brush of the night and the day.

Behind it thy seat is woven in wondrous mysteries of curves, casting away all barren lines of straightness.

The great pageant of thee and me has overspread the sky.

With the tune of thee and me all the air is vibrant,

and all ages pass with the hiding and seeking of thee and me.

Last Curtain

I know that the day will come when my sight of this earth shall be lost,

and life will take its leave in silence, drawing the last curtain over my eyes.

Yet stars will watch at night, and morning rise as before,

and hours heave like sea waves casting up pleasures and pains.

When I think of this end of my moments, the barrier of the moments breaks

and I see by the light of death thy world with its careless treasures.

Rare is its lowliest seat, rare is its meanest of lives.

Things that I longed for in vain and things that I got

— let them pass.

Let me but truly possess the things that I ever spurned and overlooked.

Farewell

I have got my leave. Bid me farewell, my brothers!

I bow to you all and take my departure.

Here I give back the keys of my door

— and I give up all claims to my house.

I only ask for last kind words from you.

We were neighbours for long,

but I received more than I could give.

Now the day has dawned

and the lamp that lit my dark corner is out.

A summons has come and I am ready for my journey.

Threshold

I was not aware of the moment when I first crossed the threshold of this life.

What was the power that made me open out into this vast mystery like a bud in the forest at midnight!

When in the morning I looked upon the light

I felt in a moment that I was no stranger in this world,

that the inscrutable without name and form had taken me in its arms in the form of my own mother.

Even so, in death the same unknown will appear as ever known to me.

And because I love this life,

I know I shall love death as well.

The child cries out when from the right breast the mother takes it away,

in the very next moment to find in the left one its consolation.

Parting Words

When I go from hence
— let this be my parting word,
that what I have seen is unsurpassable.

I have tasted of the hidden honey of this lotus
that expands on the ocean of light,
and thus am I blessed

— let this be my parting word.

In this playhouse of infinite forms
I have had my play
and here have I caught sight of him that is formless.

My whole body and my limbs
have thrilled with his touch who is beyond touch;
and if the end comes here, let it come

— let this be my parting word.

Still Heart

When I give up the helm.

I know that the time has come for thee to take it.

What there is to do will be instantly done.

Vain is this struggle.

Then take away your hands, and silently put up with your defeat, my heart,

and think it your good fortune to sit perfectly still where you are placed.

These my lamps are blown out at every little puff of wind, and trying to light them I forget all else again and again.

But I shall be wise this time and wait in the dark, spreading my mat on the floor;

and whenever it is thy pleasure, my lord, come silently and take thy seat here.

Ocean of Forms

I dive down into the depth of the ocean of forms,

hoping to gain the perfect pearl of the formless.

No more sailing from harbour to harbour with this my weather-beaten boat.

The days are long passed when my sport was to be tossed on waves.

And now I am eager to die into the deathless.

Into the audience hall by the fathomless abyss where swells up the music of toneless strings.

I shall take this harp of my life.

I shall tune it to the notes of forever,

and when it has sobbed out its last utterance,

lay down my silent harp at the feet of the silent.

Sit Smiling

I boasted among men that I had known you.

They see your pictures in all works of mine.

They come and ask me, 'Who is he?'

I know not how to answer them. I say, 'Indeed, I cannot tell.'

They blame me and they go away in scorn.

And you sit there smiling.

I put my tales of you into lasting songs.

The secret gushes out from my heart.

They come and ask me, 'Tell me all your meanings.'

I know not how to answer them.

I say, 'Ah, who knows what they mean!'

They smile and go away in utter scorn.

And you sit there smiling.

Salutation

In one salutation to thee, my God,

let all my senses spread out and touch this world at thy feet.

Like a rain-cloud of July hung low with its burden of unshed showers

let all my mind bend down at thy door in one salutation to thee.

Let all my songs gather together their diverse strains into a single current and flow to a sea of silence in one salutation to thee.

Like a flock of homesick cranes flying night and day back to their mountain nests

let all my life take its voyage to its eternal home in one salutation to thee.

Lost Time

On many an idle day have I grieved over lost time.

But it is never lost, my lord.

Thou hast taken every moment of my life in thine own hands.

Hidden in the heart of things thou art nourishing seeds into sprouts,

Buds into blossoms, and ripening flowers into fruitfulness.

I was tired and sleeping on my idle bed and imagined all work had ceased.

In the morning I woke up and found my garden full with wonders of flowers.

Endless Time

Time is endless in thy hands, my lord.

There is none to count thy minutes.

Days and nights pass and ages bloom and fade like flowers.

Thou knowest how to wait.

Thy centuries follow each other perfecting a small wild flower.

We have no time to lose, and having no time we must scramble for a chance.

We are too poor to be late.

And thus it is that time goes by while I give it to every querulous man who claims it,

and thine altar is empty of all offerings to the last.

At the end of the day I hasten in fear lest thy gate be shut; but I find that yet there is time.

Chain of Pearls

Mother, I shall weave a chain of pearls for thy neck with my tears of sorrow.

The stars have wrought their anklets of light to deck thy feet, but mine will hang upon thy breast.

Wealth and fame come from thee and it is for thee to give or to withhold them.

But this my sorrow is absolutely mine own, and when I bring it to thee as my offering thou rewardest me with thy grace.

Brink of Eternity

In desperate hope I go and search for her in all the corners of my room;

I find her not.

My house is small and what once has gone from it can never be regained.

But infinite is thy mansion, my lord, and seeking her I have to come to thy door.

I stand under the golden canopy of thine evening sky and I lift my eager eyes to thy face.

I have come to the brink of eternity from which nothing can vanish — no hope, no happiness, no vision of a face seen through tears.

Oh, dip my emptied life into that ocean, plunge it into the deepest fullness.

Let me for once feel that lost sweet touch in the allness of the universe.

Untimely Leave

No more noisy, loud words from me — such is my master's will.

Henceforth I deal in whispers.

The speech of my heart will be carried on in murmurings of a song.

Men hasten to the King's market. All the buyers and sellers are there.

But I have my untimely leave in the middle of the day, in the thick of work.

Let then the flowers come out in my garden, though it is not their time;

and let the midday bees strike up their lazy hum.

Full many an hour have I spent in the strife of the good and the evil,

but now it is the pleasure of my playmate of the empty days to draw my heart on to him;

and I know not why is this sudden call to what useless inconsequence!

Death

O thou the last fulfilment of life,

Death, my death, come and whisper to me!

Day after day I have kept watch for thee; for thee have I borne the joys and pangs of life.

All that I am, that I have, that I hope and all my love have ever flowed towards thee in depth of secrecy.

One final glance from thine eyes and my life will be ever thine own.

The flowers have been woven and the garland is ready for the bridegroom.

After the wedding the bride shall leave her home and meet her lord alone in the solitude of night.

10

Golden Words of Tagore

- Creation is an endless activity of God's freedom; it is an end in itself.
- Freedom is true when it is a revelation of truth.
- India has ever declared that Unity is Truth, and separateness is maya.
- I believe in the true meeting of the East and the West.
- It hurts me deeply when the cry of rejection rings loud against the West in my country with the clamour that the Western education can only injure us.
- That which fails to illuminate the intellect, and only keeps it in the obsession of some delusion, is its greatest obstacle.
- After sixty years of self-experience, I have found that out and out hypocrisy is an almost impossible achievement.
- Our country is the land of rites and ceremonials, so that we have more faith in worshipping the feet of the priest than the Divinity whom he serves.
- The religion of economics is where we should above all try to bring about this union of ours... If this field ceases to be one of warfare, if there we can prove, that not competition but cooperation is the real truth, then indeed

we can reclaim from the hands of the Evil One an immense territory for the reign of peace and goodwill.

- I have no zeal for life. You know the only thing that concerns me? That I have laboured so hard to build Viswabharati, wouldn't it have no value after my exit?... I think i have one reservation regarding death, and that is Vishwa Bharati, nothing else.
- It's difficult to know a person until he turns twenty-five — difficult to say what would happen to him... but it's easy to recognise a twenty seven years old — it can be said he's become what he's supposed to be, and from now on this is how his life would be guided, there's in left anything in his life to get astonished.
- To enjoy something, it's essential to guard it with the fence of leisure.
- The danger inherent in all force grows stronger when it is likely to gain success, for then it becomes temptation.
- Our fight is a spiritual fight, it is for Man.
- I say again and again that I am a poet, that I am not a fighter by nature. I would give everything to be one with my surroundings. I love my fellow beings and I prize their love.

11

Tagore's Life at a Glance

1861: Born on May 7, 1861. Born at the Jorasanko House of the Tagore family. He was the 14th child of Debendranath Tagore, the father, and Sarada Devi, the mother.

1866: Rabindranath started learning basic alphabets along with his brothers.

1868: Was admitted to the Oriental Seminary and subsequently to Normal School.

1869: Rabindranath tried his first attempt to write verse and was profoundly impressed by the Bengali translation of Bernardin de saint-Pierr's Paul et Virginie.

1870: Started learning drawing and music along with other subjects and practiced wrestling and gymnastics

1871: Was admitted to the Bengal Academy, an Anglo-Indian School and began to play truant.

1873: His Upanayan (Brahminical initiation into Gayatri prayers) performed and for the first time visited Shantiniketan; while being there, he wrote a drama Prithviraj Parajaya (manuscript lost) and took an extensive tour of India.

1874: He prepared a verse-rendering of Macbeth and his poem entitled Abhilasha (Desire) was published anonymously, and was admitted to St. Xavier's School, Calcutta

1875: Recited a patriotic poem at a Hindu fair; lost his mother; took part in literary functions, composed a poem and a song and contributed serially his long narrative poem Banaphul (The Wild Flower); and left St. Xavier's School.

1876: Joined the short-lived Secret Society, supposed to have been modelled after Mazzini's Carbonari and his first literary criticism of a book of Bengali poems Bhubanmohini Pratibha appeared in Jnanankur.

1877: Wrote and recited a satirical poem on Delhi Durbar arranged by Lord Lytton on January 1, 1877 to proclaim Queen Victoria, the Empress of India; appeared for the first time on stage in the principal role in a comedy written by Jyotirindranath, privately performed at his house; wrote his first long story Bhikharini (Beggar Maid), and his first unfinished novel, Karuna, and a long poem Kabikahini.

1878: Went to Ahmedabad to study English; composed some lyrics, and contributed a series of articles on English life and letters and also on the romantic love of poets such as Dante, Petrarch and Goethe, to Bharati; embarked on the first foreign tour, September 20, 1878 to February 1880 and went to School at Brighton

1879: Came to London and was admitted to University College; frequently visited The British Museum and contributed a series of letters with laudatory impressions of English society and people published in the Bharati and began to write his first verse-drama Bhagnahriday (The Broken Heart) and wrote one long poem Bhagnatari (The Wrecked Boat).

1880: Returned to India without completing any formal course of study; participated in a privately performed lyrical drama, Manmoyi written by Jyotirindranat

1881: Composed his first set of devotional songs; his first musical play Valmiki - Pratibha with him in a little role, was staged at Jorasanko; two of his books Rudrachanda and Bhagnahriday were published; wrote several articles and delivered his first public lecture on Music and Feeling with vocal demonstration; again sailed for England on April 20, 1881, but returned home from Madras and embarked on several literary undertakings; started writing his first extent novel, Bauthakuranir Hat (The Young Queen's Market), and also began to write his first poems which bear a real individualistic note; these were later published in Sandhya Sangeet (Evening Songs).

1882: Along with Jyotirindranath established Sarasvat Samaj, the precursor of the Academy of Bengali Letters, and had an experience which may be described at the poet's first glimpse of cosmic unity; his first musical play Kalmrigaya (The Fatal Hunt) was performed at Jorasankq; the poem Nirjharer Svapnabhanga (The Awakening of the Fountain) which is the key-poem of his book, Prabhat Sangeet, was written about this time.

1883: Wrote his verse drama Prakritir Pratisodh (Sanyasi); started writing the poems: Chhabi O Gan (Sketches and Songs); contributed several articles in Bharati and married Mriṅalini Devi (born 1873).

1884: Composed the poems: Kadi O Koma (Sharps and Flats); translated some items by Shelley, Elizabeth Barrett Browning, Victor Hugo and others and also began his prose-drama, Nalini originally planned as a cooperative work with other family members; experienced first great sorrow when his sister-in-law, Kadambari Devi died to whom he dedicated three of his books including an anthology called Saisab Sangeet (Songs of Childhood) Was appointed Secretary of the Adi Brahmo Samaj.

1885: Took charge of the Bengali magazine Balak, contributed to it several poems, articles, humorous sketches and essays etc; edited in collaboration with Srish Chandra Majumdar an anthology of Vaishnava lyrics; his first collection of songs was published and so also a first collection of his series of essays.

1886: Was entangled in controversies over social and socio-religious subjects; composed and sang the inaugural song for the second session of the Indian National Congress; first daughter was born, and received from his father a handsome cheque, his first literary price, for composing devotional songs.

1887: Started composing the Manasi group of poems, having a distinct note of originality and vigour both in theme and technique; under a pseudo name published a series of imaginary letters between an old fashioned grandfather and his modernised grandson; began writing his musical play Mayar Khela (Play of Illusion).

1888: Published Samalochana, the first collection of essays on literary criticism; continued to write the Manasi poems; tries to render into English one of his own poems; Devendranath, his father, executed the Trust Deed of the Shantiniketan Trust on March 8, 1888.

1889: Wrote his first five-act drama, Raja 0 Rani (The King and the Queen); appeared in the role of the King in a play and wrote his famous play Visarjan (Sacrifice) which was staged in 1890.

1890: Severely attacked the anti-Indian Policy of Lord Cross; took charge of the management of the Tagore Estate; tried to read Goethe's Faust in the original, and sailed for England; also visited Italy and France and maintained a travel diary published in 1891; returned home on November 4, 1890.

1891: Wrote first six short stories, especially Post Master, and the first of Chitrangada; also with his nephew started a Bengali magazine Sadhana contributing numerous short stories, poems and articles, etc.; attended the festival connected with the consecration of the prayer hall at Shantiniketan on December 22.

1892: Spent the summer at Shantiniketan; frequently toured North Bengal; wrote his first criticism on English education system; off and on practised the art of drawing; started to write poems of Sonar Tari (The Golden Barge) which punctuates a landmark in his poetry; and was associated with Sangeet Samaj.

1893: Visited Orissa; commenced writing the diary; Panchabhuter (Diary of the Five Elements), a series of brilliant dialogues on life, literature and art; visited Bihar, Shimla hills and went to Shantiniketan; read out two papers and wrote his dramatic poem Viday Abhisap (Curse of Farewell).

1894: Wrote poems, read papers and collected folk-rhymes and nursery songs to draw public attention towards this neglected area; was elected Vice-President of Academy of Bengali Letters and became the editor of the magazine Sadhana; also wrote the story: Megh O Raudra (The Cloud and the Sun).

1895: Wrote remarkable short stories beginning with Kshudita Pashan (Hungry Stones); read a paper on the future of Bengali literature and attended the anniversary at Shantiniketan; Sadhana, the magazine ceased its publication.

1896: Wrote the poems, Nadi (The River) and Jivandevata (The Muse of Life) and wrote in collaboration with Hemchandra Bhattacharya, Sanskrita Siksha (Sanskrit Primer) in two parts; the first collected edition of his poetical works, Kavyagranthavali was published; and composed and sang a song for the 12th session of the Indian National Congress; also composed Malini, a lyrical drama.

1897: Wrote his comedy Baikunther Khata (The Manuscript of Baikuntha) and performed the role of Kedar in its stage presentation; and wrote the dramatic poems, Sati.

1898: Became the editor of Bharati and contributed during the course of the year a number of poems, short stories and essays; strongly opposed the reactionary policies of British Government; and Balendranath drew up plans for setting up a School at Shantiniketan for imparting religious education, the autobiography of his father was published.

1899: Family moved temporarily to Shantiniketan; assisted Sister Nivedita (Margaret Noble) to organise relief for plague victims in Calcutta, and was involved in family financial matters; delivered his first sermon in the Mandir at Shantiniketan at its anniversary.

1900: Published Katha (Lays and Ballads) and Kahini (Story-poems) and a first collection of his short stories, Galpaguchchha was also brought out; performed his play Visarjan, himself appearing in the role of Raghupati.

1901: Started editing Bangadarsan and contributed serially his first psychological novel Chokher Bali (English translation Binodini) and composed the poems of Naivedya (Offerings); deplored a blind imitation of the West; contributed to Bharati, a humorous play Chirakumar Sabha (The Bachelors' Club): established with his father's consent and blessings a School at Shantiniketan on December 22, following the model of ancient forest schools (Tapovana) of India and he himself taught sharing students' life.

1902: Faced severe financial handicaps for running the school at Shantiniketan for which he sold personal property including the part of his personal library and his wife's ornaments; wife died on November 23 and composed Smaran (In Memoriam), a series of moving poems in memory of his wife; wrote an article Bharatvarsher Itihas, a thought provoking article giving a new interpretation to the history of India; while reviewing Lowes Dickinson's Letters of John Chinaman, wrote about the unity of life and thought of Asia.

1903: Mostly remained in Shantiniketan to attend to the school's, business, continuously interrupting literary and editorial activities; composed the poems of Sisu (some of these were published later in English translation: The Crescent Moon); and regularly contributed instalments of his novel Naukadubi (The 'Wreck) to Bangadarsan.

1904: Wrote important essays culminating with Swadeshi Samaj (Indigenous Society) in which the need of rural constructions based on mutual aid was emphasised; along with J .C. Bose and Sister Nivedita visited Bodh Gaya, the seat of Buddha's enlightenment; sold for a small sum to Hitabadi publishing House, the right of limited edition of his works in order to raise funds for the school in Shantiniketan; wrote for the book Bangabhashar Lekhar, his first autobiographical article interpreting his life as a poet, which raised a considerable controversy.

1905: His father Debendranath Tagore died at the age of 88; translated from the original Pali into Bengali verse, the first four chapters of the Buddhist scripture Dhammapada; started editing a new Bengali Magazine Bhandar; appealed to the rulers of Indian states to patronise indigenous arts and crafts and took keen interest in the founding of Indian Arts Society, Calcutta; advocated a policy of constructive non-cooperation against the British and immediately after a public speech raised Rs. 5000/- on the spot for a National Fund: took active part in formulating proposals for the establishment of National Council of Education.

1906: Was invited to preside over the first session of Bangiya Sahitya Sammilani (Bengali Literary Conference) which could not be held due to magisterial interference; wrote a series of articles on problems of education and spoke at a literary conference in Calcutta, which was held simultaneously with the Congress Exhibition (December).

1907: Withdrew from active politics due to growing differences between Hindus and Muslims and agitational excesses of Swadeshi Movement; wrote an article Byadhi O Pratikar (The Disease and its Cure); these drew severe criticism from his close friends; for the first time the seasonal festivals-a feature of the community life-were organised at Shantiniketan; published an edition of his prose works, the proceeds of which were given to Shantiniketan School; and relinquished the editorship of Bangadarsan; began one of the richest and most significant phases of his creative life; his major novel Gora started appearing in Pravasi serially; presided over the adjourned first session of Bangiya Sahitya Sammilani; due to the death of his youngest son went into a solitary retirement, leaving the Shantiniketan School in the charge of a colleague.

1908: Presided over the Annual Bengal Provincial Conference; exhorted Bengali youths to dedicate themselves for constructive work and initiated organised village uplift work in one of the regions of Tagore estates; read a paper Path O Patheya (The Way and the Means) describing revolutionary activities as a reaction against the repressive policies of the Government; Parjanya Utsav (Rains Festival) to be followed by performance of seasonal plays and Sarodotsav (Autumn Festival) were organised at Shantiniketan; wrote his drama Prayaschitta (Atonement); on December 2, started delivering a series of sermons at Shantiniketan Temple day after day for about 6 months, later published in a series of booklets entitled Shantiniketan (Some portion translated into English in Thought Relics); presided over the opening of a new premises of Bangiya Sahitya Parishad, Calcutta.

1909: Delivered a sermon entitled. Navajuger Utsav (Festival of the New Age) on the occasion of the anniversary of Brahmo Samaj), upholding the ideal of universal religion and synthesis of cultures; his essays on Bengali philology and semantics were collected and published in a book Sabdatatva; continued monthly contribution from his novel Gora to the Pravasi magazine; the publication of Chayanika, first anthology of his selected poems with illustrations by Nandalal Bose appeared; completed his play

Prayaschitta; composed a number of songs later incorporated in Gitanjali; read a paper Tapoban (The Forest School) emphasising that India should achieve unity in the midst of diversity; The Modern Review published the first English translation of his short stories (Samasyapuran or The Riddle Solved); he also translated into Bengali some of his favourite Vedic hymns and addressed the congregation on the ideal of Asrama schools of ancient India.

1910: Delivered a sermon on Vishvabodh (Realisation of the Infinite in Sadhna) at the anniversary of Brahmo Samaj; The Modern Review published the English translation of his short story. Hungry Stones (Kshudita Pashan); attended and addressed a literary conference at Bhagalpur; the students of the Ashrama at Shantiniketan celebrated his birthday and performed his play Prayaschitta; the magazine Sahitya published a series of scurrilous articles severely attacking his literary writings; appeared in the role of the mendicant hero in the repeat performance of Prayaschitta; wrote his well-known allegorical play Raja (The King of the Dark Chamber) and for the first time Christmas day was observed in Shantiniketan.

1911: Met William Rothenstein, the English portrait painter and Count Harmann Keyserling, the German Philosopher, in Jorasanko; delivered the sermon entitled Karmayog at the anniversary of Brahmo Samaj; Ananda Kumaraswamy who visited him at Shantiniketan, translated into English some of his poems with the help of the poet and one of the teachers; The Modern Review published first of these translations (Janmakatha from Sisu); Shantiniketan celebrated his 50th birthday staging his play Raja in which he played the role of Thakurda; accepted the editorship of Tattvabodhini Patrika: wrote the play Achalyatan (The Citadel of Immobility); faced acute financial problems; Pravasi serialised his reminiscences under the Title Jivansmriti, played the role of Sanyasi at the performance of Sarodotsav at Shantiniketan; wrote the play Dakghar (The Post Office) and contributed several short stories to Bharati and Pravasi and composed his famous song Jana-ganamana-adhinayaka, sung at the 26th session of the Indian National Congress, Calcutta, which became the National song after India's independence.

1912: 191 Bengal's intelligentsia felicitated him on his jubilee; described by The Modern Review as 'an unparalleled ovation the first time that such an honour has been done to a literary man in India; read a paper: Atmaparichay (Introducing Myself) in the Sadharan Brahmo Samaj; Shantiniketan was described, as 'altogether unsuitable for the education of the sons of Government servants by the Government of East Bengal and Assam; Myron H. Phelps, an American lawyer visited Shantiniketan and wrote a glowing account of the human values inculcated through the type of education obtained at Shantiniketan; delivered a lecture, its English translation: My Interpretation on Indian History, by Jadunath Sarkar appeared in The Modern Review; his friends urged him to visit England and passage was booked; however, the trip was cancelled as he fell ill; started translating some of his lyrics into English; while departing for England wrote a message Yatrar Purvapatra (On the Eve of My departure) describing that the object of his visit was to acquaint the West with his education work at Shantiniketan, while on board; translated some of his poems into English; while in London met Rothenstein and gave him the notebook containing English translation who sent its typed copies to William Butler Yeats, Stopford Brooke and Andrew Bradley - all of them deeply impressed; visited Cambridge where he met Bertrand Russell; Rothenstein arranged reading of Tagore's poems largely attended and admired by several literary luminaries; one of his short stories Dalia, under the title, The Maharani of Arakan was dramatised by George Calderon and the play was performed at the Royal Albert Hall; met Bernard Shaw, H. G. Wells and others; his plays Raja and Dak Ghar were translated into English; sailed to USA, October 28, and went to Urbana (Illinois) and delivered a series of discourses on metaphysical topics at the Unity Club (later published in the book Sadhana, Realisation of Life). The India Society of London published a limited edition of Gitanjali or Song Offerings with an introduction by Yeats; it was hailed by the English Literary public as the greatest literary event of the day; the journal Poetry (Chicago) published six poems from Gitanjali; C. F. Andrews returned to India and wrote about Tagore in Civil and Military Gazette of Lahore.

1913: Reached Chicago and lectured at the University on the Ideals of Ancient Civilization of India and on The Problem of Evil at the Unitarian Hall of Chicago; attended the Congress of religious Liberals and spoke on Race Conflict at Rochester; visited Boston and delivered a course of lectures at the Emerson Hall of Harvard University; visited New York; The Macmillan & Co, London, published a popular edition of Gitanjali followed by The Gardner, The Crescent Moon and Chitra; reached London on April 14; his play The Post Office was performed at the Irish Theatre; delivered a series of lectures at Caxton Hall; returned to Shantiniketan in November; University of Calcutta resolved to confer on him the Honorary Degree of D.Litt. on November 13, news reached Shantiniketan about the award of the Nobel Prize for Literature to the Poet; University of Calcutta awarded him D.Litt. Degree on December 26.

1914: At the special reception in Calcutta, received Nobel Prize Diploma and Medal on behalf of the Swedish Academy; dedicated his book of poems Utsarga to C. F. Andrews; accorded an impressive ceremonial welcome to Nandalal Bose who for the first time visited Shantiniketan; the Literary monthly, Sabujpatra (Green Leaves) started its publication on May 8, the poet's birth date and the same day Achalayatan (The Citadel of Immobility) was staged with the poet in the role of a Guru; regularly contributed essays, stories and poems to Sabujaptra; his poems took on a new sense of dark foreboding character both in form and content; his literary work- were translated in principal European languages and some also into Arabic; composed the poems Chhabi and Shahjahan while at Allahabad; his premonition about a global disaster came true with a declaration of war in Europe; delivered an enlightened sermon Ma Ma Rimsi (Thou shalt not hate) at Shantiniketan; composed 108, songs for Gitali, visited Bodh Gaya and welcomed a group of students and teachers of Phoenix Settlement, (started by Mahatma Gandhi in Natal South Africa) known for their austere living and hard manual labour; started writing a cycle of four stories, later published under the title Chaturanga (Eng. tr. Broken Ties) and addressed the congregation at Shantiniketan.

1915: Delivered inaugural address at the Bengal Social Service League on Karmayajna (The Worship by Labour): this talk presaged the-theme of his play Phalguni; Mahatma Gandhi visited Shantiniketan to meet the members of the Phoenix party; by the time Tagore reached Shantiniketan, Mahatma Gandhi had to go to Poona, however, on March 6, the two met at Shantiniketan; started writing Phalguni (The Cycle of Spring); wrote songs and poems and one of his major novels Ghare Bahire (The Home and The World); the play Phalguni was staged at Shantiniketan with the poet as a blind Baul; composed several poems of the Balaka series while at Kashmir, contributed a sonnet on the English poet in Bengali to the Shakespeare Tercentenary Commemoration Volume at the request of the Shakespeare Society, England; delivered a lecture on Sikshar Bahan (Medium of Education) emphasising the adoption of mother tongue along with English as a medium of instruction; the Indian Press, Allahabad published his collected works in Bengali in ten volumes.

1916: Phalguni was staged at Jorasanko House, the poet appearing in the dual role of the young Kabisekhar and the old blind Baul; organised a service camp against Cholera epidemic; advised village workers for systematic tea planting and cautioned against the growing estrangement between the English and Indians and wrote an article Chatra-Sasan (Student Discipline). Sailed for USA on a lecture tour accompanied by Mukul Dey, the painter, along with others, stopping at Rangoon, Penang, Singapore, Hong Kong and Kobe; delivered his first lecture in Japan at the Imperial University, Tokyo; his two lectures The Nation and The Spirit of Japan in which he condemned Japan's imperialist policy towards China, roused a considerable resentment; did not accept the invitation to visit Canada as a protest against Canada's discriminating immigration laws; in the USA he visited Seattle, Portland, San Francisco, Santa Barbara, Los Angeles, Pasadena, San Diego, Salt Lake City, Chicago, Iowa, Milwaukee, Detroit, Cleveland, New York, Philadelphia and Boston, etc.; delivered numerous lectures to the extent that he terminated the contract to lecture any further, being fully exhausted; his lecture on Nationalism delivered at Detroit was bitterly criticised.

1917: Reached Calcutta via Honolulu and Japan; Vichitra School of Art and Craft at the J orasanko house was fully organised under the guidance of Abanindranath and Gaganendranath

Tagore; as an adjunct to it, a literary and cultural organisation Vichitra was set up by his son Rabindranath in which the poet took keen interest; encouraged attempts to popularise spoken Bengali as a vehicle of literary expression and himself wrote stories in colloquial Bengali; Sadharan Brahmo Samaj felicitated him; read his famous political paper Kartar Ichchay Karma (As the Master Wills) in Calcutta to be followed by the singing of one of his national songs; supported the candidature of Anne Besant for the Presidentship of the Indian National Congress session in Calcutta; his play Dak Ghar (The Post Office) was staged at the Vichitra Hall, the poet himself appearing as Thakurda; returned to Shantiniketan and received Sir Michael Sadler and other members of Calcutta University Commission; attended the Calcutta Congress Session on the opening day; received great ovation and read the poem India's Prayer.

1918: Acknowledged Hindi as the only possible national language; started writing a series of story-poems, later published as Palataka (The Flitting One); contributed his paper on Samavya (Cooperation); during the autumn he conceived the idea of Inter Cultural Centre at Shantiniketan and became acquainted with South Indian Music particularly Veena during his trip to South India; formulated his idea about creating an institution which could be a true centre for the different cultures of the East; the formal foundation stone of Vishva Bharati was laid.

1919: Supported Patel's Inter-Caste Marriage Bill in an open letter; lectured on The Message of the Forest at Bangalore and received a purse from students of Mysore for Vishva Bharati; visited and lectured at various cities in South India; started a new monthly Shantiniketan Patra after returning from South and was busy writing prose sketches of Lipika; cautioned Mahatma Gandhi against the use of 'passive resistance' as a political weapon without first preparing the minds of the masses; in protest of Jalianwala Bagh renounced his Knighthood and at the request of Romain Rolland he signed La declaration pout I' Independence de I' esprit on June 26; the nucleus of Vishva Bharati was formed on July 3 when a new department (Vidya Bhavan) was opened; Mahatma Gandhi invited him to attend the Gujarati Literary Conference at Ahmedabad. Nandalal Bose joined Shantiniketan and in collaboration with Asit Kumar Haldar and Surendranath Kar started a department of fine arts under the name of Kala Bhavan; took up residence in a mud cottage in the Uttaryan area.

1920: After spending .early part of the year at Shantiniketan, took a tour of Western India; Presided over the Gujarati Literary Conference, Ahmedabad; spent the night at Gandhi's Sabarmati Ashram and visited Bhavnagar, Limbdi and Nadiad; sent a message at the request of Muhammad Ali Jinnah for the anniversary of Jalianwala Bagh. Left for England on a lecture tour to raise funds for Vishva Bharati; discussed Sufism with Agha Khan while on ship; translated during the voyage some of his Shantiniketan sermons later published as Thought Relics; although made several new friends in England, was somewhat surprised due to the aloofness of several English friends who resented his outspoken criticism of British rule and renunciation of his Knighthood; the Union of East and West Society gave reception at Caxton Hall in his honour, visited France and stayed at the guest house of Albert Kahn; met Le Brun, Sylvain Levi, Bergson and other French Scholars; was accorded reception at Musee Guimet and witnessed the performance of Goethe's Faust; visited Rotterdam, the Hague, Leiden, Utrecht, Brussels, Antwerp and back to Paris; returned to London and reached New York on October 28, and lectured at Brooklyn on November 10, on the topic The Meeting of the East and the West; lectured at the Bryn Bawr College and the American League of Political Educationist, on the topic The Poet's Religion; conveyed in his letter to Andrews his feeling of disappointment towards the cold reception received in England and America.

1921: Visited Helen Keller on January 4 at her home; lectured at Harvard University; at a farewell meeting organised by the Poetry Society of New York, he expressed his feeling of frustration and went to Chicago; on his way he also stopped at Paris, met Romain Rolland and Fatrick Geddes and lectured at Musee Guimet; received the valuable library collection for Shantiniketan from Sridhar Rana, an Indian settled in Paris; witnessed the performance of Wagner's Opera Valkyrie; went to Strassbourg and lectured on The Message of the Forest; from there he went to Geneva; on the occasion of his 61st birthday, a German Committee presented a magnificent collection of the classics of German literature for Vishva Bharati; visited several cities in Germany, Denmark and Sweden and addressed the Members of the Swedish Academy at Stockholm under the terms of the Nobel Awards; visited and lectured at Berlin, Munich, Darmstadt and Frankfurt; later he went to Vienna and Prague; returned to Shantiniketan in July; wrote the poems of Sisu Bholanath series and received Professor Sylvain Levi who organised the Tibetan and Chinese studies; on December 23, Vishva Bharati was formally inaugurated.

1922: Completed his drama Muktadhara (The Waterfall); disapproved the spirit of violence as contrary to the Non-cooperation Movement; the Rural Reconstruction Institute at Shantiniketan was formally inaugurated; Vishva Bharati Society started a local Committee at Calcutta; his play Barsha-Mangal (The Rain Festival) was performed for the first time in Calcutta and the play Sarodotsav was performed, the poet in the role of Sanyasi, in aid of Vishva Bharati; visited Poona and again went for tour in South India and Ceylon; later delivered a series of lectures at Colombo and Galle; Moritz Winternitz joined Vishva Bharati as visiting professor along with other visiting scholars; V. Lesny, Stella Kramrisch, Shlomit Flaum, Fernand Benoit, Mark Collins, L. Bogdanov, Arthur Geddes and Stanley Jones.

1923: Rabindranath visited Shantiniketan and was given a formal reception; the Governor of Bengal also visited Shantiniketan; he dedicated his musical drama Basanta to Qazi Nazrul Islam which was staged in Calcutta; presided over the first session of Pravasi Banga Sahitya Sammelan, Benaras; visited several parts of India including Sindh; foundation stone of Ratan Kuthi was laid and the journal Vishva Bharati Quarterly started publication under his editorship; wrote the first draft of his drama Raktakaravi (Red Oleanders); showed interest in the newly formed Swaraj Party and took interest in strengthening Hindu Muslim relations; his drama Visarjan was staged in Calcutta and he appeared in the role of young Jayasinha; issued an appeal to raise funds for a hospital in memory of Pearson at Shantiniketan; during his tour to Western India raised funds for the Kala-Bhavan.

1924: Lived in a cottage perched on a tree, designed by a Japanese Craftsman, Kasahara; delivered a course of three lectures at the University of Calcutta, later incorporated in Sahityer Pathe; visited China accompanied by Kshitimohan Sen, Nandalal Bose, Elmhirst and Kalidas Nag at the invitation of Liang-Chi Chao, trip financed by G. D. Birla; visited Rangoon, Penang, Kualalampur, Singapore and Hong Kong, reaching Shanghai on April 12; addressed several meetings and also the meeting of the Japanese community deprecating Japan's imperialist tendency; lectured at Nanking and Shantung and was accorded a reception by the Tagore Reception Committee in Beijing, his outspoken address on East-West Relations provoked a bitter criticism from the leftist press; he was received by Ex-Emperor at the Imperial Palace; and on the occasion of his birthday was given a Chinese name Chu-Chen-Tan (Thundering Morn of India); on May 30, he left China for Japan and visited several cities; he met Rashbehary Bose, a well-known Indian revolutionary in exile; the culmination of his far-eastern tour resulted in the organisation of an Asiatic Association at Shanghai; after returning to Calcutta took part in Tableaux performance of Arupratan; visited Peru to attend the centenary celebrations of her independence, on board the ship he started writing his diary Yatri and also the poem of Puravi, could not proceed beyond Buenos Aires due to his illness and became the guest of Madam Victoria Ocampo; continued composing poems of Puravi, dedicated to his hostess whom he called Vijaya when the book was published in 1925; met the President of the Argentine Republic on the eve of his departure on December 30.

1925: On way to India visited Geneva and Milan where he gave a discourse on music in a public meeting, presided over by the Duke of Milan; visited Venice and reached India on February 17; Mahatma Gandhi visited him to discuss the ethics of Khadi; wrote a paper on the Ideals of Indian Marriage for the book by Count Keyserling; his play Chirakumar Sabha (The Bachelors' Club) was performed in Calcutta and also dramatised two of his stories in order to make them suitable for stage; Carlo Formichi arrived at Shantiniketan as a Visiting Professor with a gift of valuable Italian books from Mussolini, to be followed by Giuseppe Tucci; presided over the first Indian Philosophical Congress in Calcutta speaking on deeper truths of folk culture and folk religions of India.

1926: Attended the All India Music Conference at Lucknow; accepted the invitation of the University of Dacca, lectured there and addressed several public meetings; visited several towns of East Bengal; representative men of different nations offered him felicitations on his 65th Birthday; Maharaja of Porbunder sent a handsome donation for Kala Bhavan; Natir Puja (Worship of the Dancing Girl) was also staged at this occasion; visited Naples where he was welcomed by city officials bearing a message from Mussolini whom he met in Rome and delivered a lecture on The Meaning of Art attended by Mussolini and others; attended the performance of his play Chitra in Italian and was also received by the King Benedetto Croce, who was virtually home-interned was brought to Rome so that Tagore could meet him; visited Florence and read a paper, My School at the University; visited Turin and was invited by Romain Rolland to visit Switzerland; reached Villeneuve via Montreaux and stayed at Hotel Byrone, occupying the same room in which Victor Hugo lived a long time; Romain Rolland visited him often and showed him his statements appeared in the Italian press, quoted out of the context which upset him deeply; delivered a lecture; recited poem and became acquainted with the Fascist high-handedness which made him write a letter in the Manchester Guardian against Fascism; after being in Vienna he passed through Paris and reached London to give a sitting to Jacob Epstein for a head study; addressed the Oriental Academy, Oslo; lectured at the University hall and visited the studio of Gustav Vigeland; visited Stockholm; met the members of Swedish Academy; delivered a lecture on September 10 in Hamburg on Culture and Progress and in Berlin on Indian Philosophies; met Albert Einstein; visited Munich, Nurenburg, Stuttgart, Cologne, Dusseldorf and Dresdon where he lectured and recited his poems and plays; visited Prague where he saw the Czech version of his play The Post Office; visited Budapest, Sofia and Bukharest where he lectured and received great honours; in Athens, the Greek Government decorated him with the "Order of the Redeemer", visited Egypt and on board the ship started writing a series of letters to Nirmal-Kumari Mahalanobis later published as Pathe O Pather Prane; reached Shantiniketan on December 19.

1927: His play Natir Puja was performed in Calcutta in which he played the role of Upali, a Buddhist monk; a song and dance sequence entitled Natraja Rituranġasala was produced at Shantiniketan; contributed the poem of the same name to the inaugural issue of the magazine Vichitra; went to Bharatpur to preside over the Hindi Literary Conference; started writing his novel Tin Purush (Three Generations, later named Yogayog); went on a South-East Asian tour visiting Singapore, Malacca, Kuala Lampur, Ipoh, Taiping and Penang where he lectured and appealed for financial support for Vishva Bharati; he also visited Java, Bali where the Balinese dance and drama were of much interest to him; went to Djakarta where he visited a school modelled after Shantiniketan; visited Borobudur, stayed at Bandung and reached Bangkok where he lectured on Education; returned to Calcutta where he recasted his play Natraja, produced under the title of Rituranga.

1928: Delegates of the Indian Science Congress visited Vishva Bharati; tried to reconcile the differences between two sections of Bengali literary men over the issue of ultra modernism in literature; received invitation from Oxford to deliver Hibbert lectures which he could not do so due to illness; visited Sri Aurobindo in Pondicherry and reached Colombo; however, as he was not well, he returned to the main land, stayed in Bangalore and started writing the novel Sesher Kavita (English translation Farewell, My Friend) and continued contributing to the Yogayog; at Shantiniketan he introduced two seasonal festivals: Vriksharopana (Tree-Planting) and Halakarshana (Ploughing); was the guest of Mukul Dey in Calcutta and on September 10 onward assumed full administrative responsibility for all institutions at Shantiniketan; devoted much time to the new medium of creative self-expression, painting.

1929: A song sequence, Sundar (The Beautiful) at Jorasanko; presided over the Conference of the International Religions and also the Cooperative Conference of the Burdwan Division, delivering a forceful speech on the "Principles of Cooperation". Participated in the Triennial Conference, Canada, travelling by way of Singapore, Hong Kong, Shanghai, Kobe and Tokyo; delivered a lecture on The Philosophy of Leisure at Victoria, and The Principles of Literature at Vancouver; was invited by the University of California, USA; visited Detroit, Harvard, Columbia and Washington, terminating his tour at Los Angeles as a protest against the derogatory remark by the Passport Officer. After returning to Shantiniketan recasted his play Raja O Rani as Tapati; delivered two lectures Sahityer Svarup (Nature of Literature) and Sahityer Vichar (Judgement of Literature) at Calcutta; Tapati staged in Calcutta in which he played the role of young King Vikram.

1930: About this time painting was pursued very seriously devoting much time; delivered a lecture, Man the Artist at Baroda and discussed the problem of Education at the Teachers Training College; Shantiniketan received three-year grant from the Government which attracted public criticism. Visited Oxford University to deliver the Hibbert Lecture; arrived it Marseilles via Colombo and finally to Paris to exhibit his paintings at Gallery Pigalle; after the Hibbert Lecture, he also gave a lecture at the Chapel of Manchester College; broadcast a talk in Berlin and also met Einstein; visited Dresden and Munich where he visited Deutsches Museum; completed the only one original English poem; The Child; visited Frankfurt, Marburg and Coblenz and went to Denmark; visited Geneva and went to Moscow via Warsaw; at Moscow he met leading writers and artists; visited Central Ethnographic State Museum and the Museum of Handicrafts, etc.; from Soviet Union he went to Germany and later to USA; he was greatly honoured and met Will Durant.

1931: Was in London where he had a long talk with Bernard Shaw; reached Calcutta on January 31; wrote a review on Will Durant's book: The Case for India; his letters from Russia were collected and published as a Russiar Chithi on his 70th Birthday; citizens of Calcutta celebrated his birthday by way of a week long festival during Christmas; Sisutirtha, the Bengali adaptation of The Child was presented at Calcutta; The Sanskrit College, Calcutta conferred on him the title of Kavi-Sarvabhauma (The Poet Paramount); celebrated the 50th birthday anniversary of Nandalal Bose on October 25 at Shantiniketan and visited Calcutta to attend the Rabindra Jayanti Celebrations, during which an exhibition of his drawings and paintings was also arranged for the first time in India; The Golden Book of Tagore was presented to him by its editor Ramananda Chatterji.

1932: Wrote a number of poems illustrating some of them and others by the well-known artists of the Bengal School. (These poems were later collected in the book Vichitrita dedicated to Nandlal Bose). Visited Persia on an invitation from the King; went to Shiraz passed through Persepolis (Herzfeld received him and showed selected specimens of Iranian art and archaeology); reached Ispahan and Tehran receiving much honour and affection; on his way visited Baghdad and spent a day at Bedouin; accepted the Calcutta University Chair of Bengali and also the invitation to deliver the Kamala Lectures; was involved in several conciliatory political activities.

1933: Presided over the inaugural meeting of the Rammohan Centenary and delivered a lecture on Rammohan Roy; also gave a second University lecture on Sikshar Bikiran (Diffusion of Education); his dance drama Sapmochan (Redemption) was staged in Calcutta; organised the work for compiling a glossary of technical terms in Bengali; received Uday Shankar at Shantiniketan who gave a performance of dance before the poet; his play Taser Des (The Kingdom of Cards) and Chandalika (The Untouchable Maid) were staged with poet on the stage in Calcutta; Bombay celebrated a Tagore week with performance of his plays by students of Shantiniketan, exhibition of his paintings and those of other artists of Kala Bhavan; lectured at Bombay, Hyderabad, Secunderabad and finally delivered his address on the death anniversary of Raja Rammohan Roy in Calcutta.

1934: Strongly protested against anti-Gandhi agitation and fulfilled one of his lecture engagements as University Professor at Calcutta; started writing the poem of Bithika series and spoke at the International Relations Club; went to Ceylon and delivered lecture on Vishva Bharati at Colombo; an exhibition of his own paintings and those of other artists of Kala Bhavan was held and also performance of Sapmochan; laid the foundation stone at Horana, of an Institution modelled after Shantiniketan which he called *Sripalli;* witnessed Kandyan dance and mask dances; while in Kandy completed his novel Char Adhayay (Four Chapters); also visited Anuradhapur; made some administrative changes at Shantiniketan and offered the hospitality of Vishva Bharati for the establishment of Headquarters of Sino-Indian Cultural Society; on October 24, an exhibition of his painting and the paintings of Shantiniketan School was held at Madras and he lectured on Myself and Bengal Renaissance; visited Banaras, later returned to

Calcutta where he inaugurated the session of a Pravasi Banga Sahitya Sammilani and also that of All Bengal Music Conference.

1935: The Banaras Hindu University conferred on him the Degree of D.Litt. (Honoris Causa); the journal Vishva Bharati Quarterly which had ceased publication after 1931, reappeared in its new series; Sarodotsav was staged at Shantiniketan with the poet as a role of Sanyasi. Japanese poet, Yone Neguchi visited Shantiniketan; his play Arupratan was staged at Calcutta with the poet in the role of Thakurda; in a letter to Mukul Dey he outlined his scheme for the establishment of National Gallery of Art.

1936: Delivered lectures in Calcutta on Ideals of Education, Place of Music in Education and Education Naturalised; was engaged in preparing a new version of Chitrangada as a dance-drama produced in Calcutta in aid of Vishva Bharati; this play was also performed in Patna, Allahabad, Lahore and Delhi; the University of Dacca conferred on him the Degree of D.Litt.; dramatised his poem Parisodh (Retribution) and set it to music; a new dance-drama Syama was staged at Calcutta, the poet being present on stage.

1937: Delivered the Convocation address in Bengali in Calcutta University and addressed Ramkrishna Centenary Parliament of Religions in Calcutta on the subject: Religion of the Spirit and Sectarianism; China Bhavan was opened in Vishva Bharati on April 14; was busy in writing Vishvaparichay at Almorah and received the title of Kavi Samrat (Prince of Poets) from the Bharati-tirtha of Andhra; while preparing to go to Gwalior, fell ill, was shifted to Calcutta and received intensive medical treatment; the text of his address Pralayer Srishti (Creation of Chaos) to the congregation at the Prayer Hall, Vishva Bharati, reflected his agony at Japan's aggression in China; wrote a number of poems with an undertone of mystic realisation, later published as Praritik (Borderland).

1938: C. F. Andrews laid the foundation of Hindi Bhavan at Vishva Bharati; Osmania University conferred a Degree of D.Litt. on him; attended the performance of his dance-drama Chandalika at Calcutta; Expressed great dismay towards Japanese and Nazi's aggression; Lord Zetland opened an exhibition of his paintings at the Calmann Gallery, London on November 18; he inaugurated the Havell Hall at Kala Bhavan, Vishva Bharati on December 19.

1939: Inaugurated Vishva Bharati Sammilani at Calcutta as a literary and cultural centre after the example of Vichitra Club; attended the performances of his plays Syama, Chandalika and Taser Des; Vallatholi, the leading poet of Kerala visited Shantiniketan and gave a performance of Kathakali; the Raja of Puri honoured him with the title of 'Paramaguru' (The Great Preceptor); laid the foundation stone of Mahajati Sadan at Calcutta; the first Volume of the Vishva Bharati edition of his complete work (Rabindra Rachanavali) appeared in September; on the Christmas Day wrote a song on the martyrdom of Jesus Christ; Ju Peon, the well-known Chinese artist came to Shantiniketan as a Visiting Professor of Fine Art.

1940: Condemned Soviet Russia's aggression in Finland; spoke on village service on the anniversary of Shantiniketan; visited Bankura to inaugurate the Bankura Exhibition; inaugurated Gitali, an organisation for propagation of music in Calcutta on June 29; on August 7, the Oxford University held a special convocation at Shantiniketan to confer on him the Degree of D.Litt.; was taken seriously ill on September 26; was shifted to Calcutta and returned to Shantiniketan on November 18; dictated an address entitled Arogya (Recovery) dealing with the theme of sick world slowly returning to wholeness.

1941: His last address on Rammohan Roy was read on January 24; his message Sabhyatar Samkat (Crisis in Civilization) was read on the occasion of his birthday' anniversary; the Maharaja of Tripura conferred on him the title of Bharat-Bhashkar; on July 30, he dictated his last poem which contained the following lines:

> "... the last reward he carries to his treasure-house...
>
> the unwasting right to peace"

— Died on August 7, 1941

Bibliography

Achalayatan: *The Petrified Place: Rabindranath Tagore,* Translated by Bandana Sanyal, Rupa, 2006.

Ananda Lal: *Rabindranath Tagore,* Three Plays, OUP, 2001.

Andrews, C. F.: *Rabindranath Tagore,* Selected Stories, Srishti, 2004.

Anna Nikolaev and Nikolay Nikolaev: *Rabindranath Tagore and The Bulgarian Connection: Facts and Documents,* Visva-Bharati, 2009.

Aparna Chaudhuri: *He (Shey): Rabindranath Tagore,* Penguin Books, 2007.

Aparna Mukherjee: *The Social Philosophy of Rabindranath Tagore,* Classical, 2004.

Asit Kumar Datta: *Aesthetics and the Poetic Image of Rabindranath Tagore,* Abhijeet Pub, 2007.

Athmesh Kansangara, M.: *Critical Perspectives on Rabindranath Tagore's "Gora" and The Wreck,* Sarup, 2009.

Aurobindo Bose: *Later Poems of Rabindranath Tagore,* Rupa & Co, 2002.

Basanta Koomar: *Rabindranath Tagore: The Man and His Poetry,* New York, 1915.

Bela Duttgupta: *Rabindranath Tagore and His World Windows,* A Symphony in Poems, The Asiatic Society, 2005.

Bihari Nayak: *Sustainable Development: An Alternative Approach in Rabindranath Tagore's Vision,* Kunja - Serials Pub, 2008.

Biswajit Sinha, Raj: *Rabindranath Tagore (2 Parts-Set):* Encyclopaedia of Indian Theatre, 2003.

Chaudhuri, A.: *The Vintage Book of Modern Indian Literature,* Vintage, 2004.

Chinmoy Howlader: *Influence of Kalidasa on Rabindranath Tagore,* Bharatiya Kala Prakashan, 2003.

Das Gupta, S. P.: *Rabindranath Tagore: Thought Relics,* New Expanded Version, Sadesh, 2007.

Datta, P. K.: *Rabindranath Tagore's the Home and the World,* A Critical Companion, Permanent Black, 2008.

Debabrata Mukhopadhyay: *Rabindranath Tagore: The Post Office,* Wisdom Tree, 2002.

Deutsch, A. and Robinson, A.: *Selected Letters of Rabindranath Tagore,* Cambridge University Press, Cambridge, 1997.

———: *The Art of Rabindranath Tagore,* Monthly Review Press, 1989.

Dipali Ghosh: *Bengali Works of Rabindranath Tagore into English,* Sanjoy Academy, 2007.

Dominic, K. V.: *Pathos in the Short Stories of Rabindranath Tagore,* Sarup Book Pub, 2009.

Dutta, Krishna and Andrew Robinson: *Rabindranath Tagore: The Myriad-Minded Man,* Bloomsbury, London, 1995.

Dyson, Ketaki Kushari: *In Your Blossoming Flower-Garden: Rabindranath Tagore and Victoria Ocampo,* Sahitya Akademi, New Delhi, 1988.

Ernest Rhys: *Rabindranath Tagore: A Biography,* Shubhi Publications, 2004.

Gaurav Pradhan: *Rabindranath Tagore,* Literary Concepts, APH, 2002.

Ghare Baire: *Rabindranath Tagore,* Bengali by Sreejata Guha, Penguin, 2005.

Ghose, Sisirkumar: *The Later Poems of Tagore,* London, 1961.

Jadu Saha: *Rabindranath Tagore: Selected Writings for Children,* Shipra Publications, 2004.

Jose Chunkapura: *The God of Rabindranath Tagore: A Study of the Evolution of His Understanding of God,* Visva-Bharati, 2002.

Joyasree Mukerji: *She: A Collection of Short Stories of Rabindranath Tagore,* UBSPD, 2004.

Kalpana Bardhan: *Of Love, Nature and Devotion: Selected Songs of Rabindranath Tagore,* Oxford University Press, Oxford, 2008.

Kedar Nath Mukherjee: *Rabindranath Tagore's Concepts of State,* Nation and Nationalism, Punthi Pustak, 2003.

Kripalani, Krishna: *Rabindranath Tagore,* Visva-Bharati, Calcutta, 1980.

Krishna Dutta and Andrew Robinson: *Selected Letters of Rabindranath Tagore,* 1997.

Mohit Chakrabarti: *Rabindranath Tagore: A Miscellany,* Kanishka Pub, 2003.

———: *Rabindranath Tagore: Selected Songs of Joy,* Indian Pub, 2003.

———: *Rabindranath Tagore: Songs of Awakening,* Kanishka Pub, 2007.

———: *Rabindranath Tagore: Songs of Prayer,* New Age Books, 2006.

Mohit Ray, K. and Rama Kundu: *Rabindranath Tagore's Gora,* Atlantic, 2008.

Mohit Ray, K.: *Studies on Rabindranath Tagore (2 Vols-Set),* Atlantic, 2004.

———: *The English Writings of Rabindranath Tagore,* Atlantic, 2007.

Munshiram Manoharlal: *Rabindranath Tagore,* Pabitrakumar Roy, The Builders of Indian Philosophy Series, 2002.

Nityapriya Ghosh: *The English Writings of Rabindranath Tagore,* A Miscellany, Sahitya Akademi, 2007.

O'Connell, Kathleen: *Rabindranath Tagore: The Poet as Educator,* Visva-Bharati, Calcutta, 2002.

Paul, S. K. and Amar Nath Prasad: *Recritiquing Rabindranath Tagore,* Sarup, 2006.

Paul, S. K.: *The Complete Poems of Rabindranath Tagore's Gitanjali,* Texts and Critical Evaluation, Sarup, 2006.

Pulinbihari Sen and Kshitis Roy: *Rabindranath Tagore: A Tribute,* Hope India Publications, 2006.

Purabi: *The East in Its Feminine Gender (With CD),* Rabindranath Tagore, Seagull Books, 2007.

Rabindranath Tagore and Okakura Tenshin: *Another Asia: Rustom Bharucha,* Oxford University Press, Oxford, 2006.

Rabindranath Tagore: *A Tagore Reader: Edited by Amiya Chakravarty,* Beacon Press, Boston, 1966.

————: *Collected Stories,* Wisdom Tree, 2004.

————: *Creative Unity,* Macmillan & Co., London, 1922.

————: *Gitanjali: Song Offerings,* UBSPD, 2003.

————: *Ideals of Education,* The Visva-Bharati Quarterly, 1929.

————: *Letters from a Sojourner in Europe,* Visva-Bharati, 2008.

————: *Our Universe: Translated by Indu Dutt,* Jaico Publishing House, Bombay, 1980.

————: *Personality,* Macmillan & Co., London, 1917.

————: *Poems and Plays,* Abhishek Pub, 2008.

————: *Rabindranath Tagore: Selected Poems,* Penguin Books, Middlesex, 1985.

————: Selected Writings on Literature and Language: Edited by Sisir Kumar Das and Sukanta Chaudhuri, Oxford University Press, 2001.

————: *The Home and the World,* Wisdom Tree, 2004.

————: *The Religion of Man,* Beacon Press, Boston, 1961.

————: *Towards Universal Man,* The Macmillan Company, New York, 1961.

Radhakrishnan, Sarvapalli: *The Philosophy of Rabindranath Tagore,* Macmillan, London, 1918.

Raj Kumar Singh: *Encyclopaedia of Rabindranath Tagore Literature,* Anmol Pub, 2009.

Ramananda Chatterjee: *Calcutta The Golden Book of Tagore: A Homage to Rabindranath Tagore, From India and the World,* Golde Book Committee, 1931.

Rimli Bhattacharya: *Rabindranath Tagore: Four Chapters: Char Adhyay,* Srishti, 2002.

Rita Sil, D.: *Profile of Rabindranath Tagore in World Literature,* Khama, 2002.

Rothenstein: *William, Six Portraits of Rabindranath Tagore,* London, 1915.

Sadhana: *The Realisation of Life: Rabindranath Tagore,* Abhishek Pub, 2008.

Sankha Ghosh and Sukanta Chaudhuri: *Rabindranath Tagore: Relationships Jogajog,* Translated by Supriya Chaudhuri, Oxford University Press, 2006.

————: *Rabindranath Tagore: Selected Poems,* Oxford University Press, 2004.

Saswati Sengupta, Shampa Roy and Sharmila Purkayastha: *Towards Freedom: Critical Essays on Rabindranath Tagore's Ghare Baire,* The Home and the World, Orient Longman, 2007.

Saumyendranath Tagore: *Rabindranath Tagore: Philosophy of Life and Aesthetics,* Aparna Book, 2006.

Sharma T. R.: *Ghaziabad Essays on Rabindranath Tagore,* Vimal Prakashan, 1987.

Sharma, S. R.: *Life and Works of Rabindranath Tagore,* Book Enclave, 2003.

Sinha, Sasadhar: *Social thinking of Rabindranath Tagore,* London, 1962.

Sinjita Gupta: *Mystic Moods: Short Stories of Rabindranath Tagore,* UBS Pub, 2005.

Sisir Kumar Das: *The English Writings of Rabindranath Tagore,* Sahitya Akademi, 2002.

————: *The English Writings of Rabindranath Tagore,* Sahitya Akademi, 1996.

Som, R.: *Rabindranath Tagore: The Singer and His Song*, Viking, 2009.

Sreejata Guha: *A Grain of Sand: Chokher Bali*, Rabindranath Tagore, Penguin, 2003.

Subrata Dasgupta: *The Bengal Renaissance: Identity and Creativity from Rammohun Roy to Rabindranath Tagore*, Permanent Black, 2007.

Sukanta Chaudhuri: *Rabindranath Tagore: Selected Short Stories*, OUP, 2002.

————: *Rabindranath Tagore: Selected Short Stories*, OUP, 2000.

————: *Rabindranath Tagore: Selected Writings for Children*, OUP, 2002.

Suren Deb Barman: *Rabindranath Tagore and Tripura*, Minerva, 2006.

Tapati Das Gupta: *Social Thought of Rabindranath Tagore a Historical Analysis*, Abhinav, 1997.

Thompson, Edward John: *Rabindranath Tagore: Poet and Dramatist*, Oxford University Press, London, 1948.

Uma Das Gupta: *Difficult Friendship: Letters of Edward Thompson and Rabindranath Tagore 1913-1940*, Oxford University Press, 2003.

Uma Das Gupta: *Rabindranath Tagore: A Biography*, Oxford University Press, 2004.

Verma, Rajendra: *Rabindranath Tagore: Prophet Against Totalitarianism*, London, 1964.

William Radice: *The Post Office (Dakghar, 1912); Card Country (Taser Desh, 1939), Vols. I and II: Rabindranath Tagore*, Visva-Bharati Publishing Department, 2008.

Yeats, W. B.: *Rabindranath Tagore: Gitanjali: Song Offerings: A Collection of Prose Translations Made by the Author from the Original Bengali*, Wisdom Tree, 2003.

Index

M

N

O

P

Q

R

S

❑❑❑